CCH®

COST ESTIMATING AND CONTRACT PRICING

Tools, Techniques and Best Practices

D1538607

GREGORY A. GARRETT

Wolters Kluwer
Law & Business

ACQUISITION
SOLUTIONS®

Editorial Director: Aaron M. Broaddus
Cover Design: Heather Buchanan
Interior Design and Layout: Craig L. Arritola

Copyright Notice

Notice of Trademarks

Product No.: 0-4975-400

ISBN: 978-0-8080-1819-3

CONTENTS

Foreword v

Dedications vii

Acknowledgements ix

About the Authors...xi

Introduction xv

Key Acronyms List..xvii

Chapter 1: Cost Estimating: Methods, Processes, and
Sources of Risk (Gregory A. Garrett) 1

Chapter 2: Cost Estimating Fundamentals
(Gregory A. Garrett) 19

Chapter 3: Cost Accounting Standards
(Gregory A. Garrett) 43

Chapter 4: Cost Analysis: Tools and Techniques
(Dr. Rene G. Rendon)..63

Chapter 5: Profit Analysis: Tools and Techniques
(Juanita Rendon) 79

Chapter 6: Contract Pricing Strategies, Methods,
and Best Practices (Gregory A. Garrett)..............103

Chapter 7: Fixed-Price and Cost-Reimbursement
Pricing Arrangements (Gregory A. Garrett).......121

Chapter 8: Time-and-Materials and Labor-Hour Pricing
Arrangements (Catherine Poole, Paul Cataldo,
Shaw Cohe)..153

Chapter 9: Price Analysis: Tools, Techniques,
and Best Practices (Gregory A. Garrett)..............185

Chapter 10: Total Ownership Cost in the Department
of Defense (Michael Boudreau, Brad Naegle) 199

Chapter 11: A Guide to Earned Value Management Systems
(Gregory A. Garrett)..213

Bibliography **241**

Glossary of Key Terms..**247**

Index **281**

FOREWORD

Once again, Gregory A. Garrett and a team of cost and pricing experts have created a highly practical, informative, and fact-filled book. This time the topic is cost estimating and contract pricing. Simply stated, this book is a must-read for anyone involved in developing cost estimates, analyzing cost, evaluating profit/fees, and/or determining the right contract pricing arrangement. What makes this book such a valuable asset is the highly pragmatic approach that Gregory A. Garrett and a team of seven contributing authors use to address each topic with a wealth of tools, techniques, and best practices.

This book is a tremendous resource for both buyers and sellers, ranging from beginners to experienced business professionals. I highly recommend this book to all cost/price analysts, accountants, contract managers, financial managers, and project managers, in both government and industry, to help them better understand, develop, and analyze cost estimates and determine the right contract pricing.

Sincerely,

Dr. William C. Pursch, CPCM
Villanova University–Contract Management Faculty
and
Past National President, National Contract Management Association

DEDICATION

Personal

To my lovely and talented wife, Carolyn Garrett, for her patience, support, and the three greatest gifts: our children, Christopher, Scott, and Jennifer.

In memory of

W. Gregor Macfarlan, scholar, teacher, and a gentleman, a true leader in the education and training of contract management professionals worldwide.

ACKNOWLEDGMENTS

I would like to recognize and thank the following people for their support, advice, and valued contributions to this book.

Michael Boudreau

Paul Cataldo

Shaw Cohe

Brad Naegle

Catherine Poole

Dr. William C. Pursch, CPCM

Juanita Rendon, CPA

Dr. Rene G. Rendon, CPCM, C.P.M., PMP

Charles Wilkins, CPA

Plus, a special thank you to Mrs. Barbara Hanson for her outstanding administrative support of this book project.

ABOUT THE AUTHOR

Gregory A. Garrett, is a best-selling and award-winning author, a dynamic speaker, an international educator, and a practicing industry leader. He currently serves as the Chief Operating Officer (COO) for Acquisition Solutions, Inc. He leads a team of more than 200 consultants providing a wide range of acquisition professional support services and business solutions to more than 30 U.S. federal government agencies, including the U.S. Departments of Defense, Homeland Security, State, Justice, Treasury, Agriculture, Interior, Education, Commerce, Energy, Veterans' Affairs, Small Business Administration, NASA, and foreign governments. He has successfully led more than $30 billion of high-technology contracts and projects during the past 25 years. He has taught, consulted, and led contract and project teams in more than 40 countries. He has served as a lecturer for The George Washington University Law School and the School of Business and Public Management. He has taught and/or consulted with more than 25,000 people worldwide.

Prior to joining Acquisition Solutions, Inc., Mr. Garrett served as an executive at Lucent Technologies in a number of capacities, including: Chief Compliance Officer, U.S. Federal Government Programs; Vice President, Program Management, North America, Wireless; Chairman, Lucent Technologies Project Management Leadership Council (representing more than 2,000 Lucent project managers globally); and as Lucent Technologies' first Director, Global Program Management, at the company headquarters.

At ESI International, Mr. Garrett served as Executive Director of Global Business, where he led the sales, marketing, negotiation, and implementation of bid/proposal management, project management, commercial contracting, and government contract management training and consulting programs for numerous Fortune 100 multinational corporations, government agencies, and small businesses worldwide, including: ABB, AT&T, BellSouth, Boeing, Dell, IBM, Inter-America Development Bank, Israel Aircraft Industries, Lucent Technologies, Motorola, NCR, NTT, the Panama Canal Commission, the United States Trade Development Agency, the United Nations, the United States Department of Energy, and the United States Department of Defense.

Formerly, Mr. Garrett served as a highly decorated military officer for the United States Air Force and was awarded more than 17 medals, badges, and citations. He completed his active-duty career as the youngest Acquisition Action Officer in the Colonel's Group Headquarters USAF, the Pentagon. He was the youngest Division Chief and Professor of Contracting Management at the Air Force Institute of Technology, where he taught advanced courses in contract administration and program management to more than 5,000 people from the Department of Defense and NASA.

Previously, he was the youngest Procurement Contracting Officer for the USAF Aeronautical Systems Center, where he led more than 50 multi-million dollar negotiations and managed the contract administration of over $15 billion in contracts for major weapon systems. He served as a Program Manager at the Space Systems Center, where he managed a $300 million space communications project.

Mr. Garrett is a Certified Purchasing Manager (CPM) of the Institute for Supply Management (ISM). He is a Certified Project Management Professional (PMP) of the Project Management Institute (PMI) and has received the prestigious PMI Eric Jenett Project Management Excellence Award and the David I. Cleland Project Management Literature Award. He is a Certified Professional Contracts Manager (CPCM), a Fellow, and member of the Board of Advisors of the National Contract Management Association (NCMA). He has received the NCMA National Achievement Award, NCMA National Educational Award, the Charles J. Delaney Memorial Award for Contract Management literature, and the Blanche Witte Memorial Award for outstanding service to the contract management profession.

A prolific writer, Mr. Garrett has authored 12 books, including: *Managing Contracts for Peak Performance* (NCMA, 1990), *World-Class Contracting* (4th ed., CCH, 2006), *Managing Complex Outsourced Projects* (CCH, 2004), *Contract Negotiations* (CCH, 2005), *The Capture Management Life-Cycle* (CCH, 2003), *Contract Management Organizational Tools* (NCMA, 2005), *Performance-Based Acquisition: Pathways to Excellence* (NCMA, 2006), *Leadership: Building High-Performance Buying and Selling Teams* (NCMA, 2007), *U.S. Military Program Management: Lessons Learned and Best Practices* (Management Concepts, 2007), *Solicitations, Bids, Proposals, and Source Selection*

(CCH, 2007), and *Getting Results: The Six Disciplines of Performance Based Project Management,* (CCH, 2008), and he has served as principal author and series editor for the new *Federal Acquisition ActionPack Series* (Management Concepts, 2007). In addition, he has authored more than 70 published articles on bid/proposal management, supply chain management, contracting, project management, and leadership.

Mr. Garrett resides in Oakton, Virginia, with his wife Carolyn and three children– Christopher, Scott, and Jennifer.

INTRODUCTION

In this electronically enhanced, digital, virtual world of high-speed communications and growing customer expectations, business in both the public and private sectors is full of change, uncertainty, and risk. Thus, cost estimating and contract pricing are indeed challenging for both buyers and sellers. The process of estimating the cost for the development and delivery of a product, service, or solution can range from simple to highly complex based upon multiple factors, including: technology maturity, urgency, geographic location, quantity, quality, availability of skilled resources, hardware, software, systems integration, historical cost information, availability of parametric cost analysis tools, and cost/price analysts' skills.

This book provides a comprehensive discussion of cost estimating and contract pricing with extensive use of tools, techniques, and best practices from both the public and private sectors. The book begins (Chapter 1) with an overview of the basic characteristics of credible cost estimates, provides a brief discussion of the primary cost estimating methods, introduces a 12-step cost estimating process, and concludes with a review of the major sources of risk that must be factored into all cost estimates and contract pricing. Chapter 2 contains a detailed discussion of the fundamentals of cost estimating using a simple and practical question-and-answer format. Chapter 3 provides a solid discussion of U.S. Cost Accounting Standards (CAS).

Chapters 4 and 5 provide a wealth of tools, techniques, and best practices for conducting cost analysis, profit analysis, and properly assessing risk vs. reward to determine the appropriate profit or fee. Further, Chapters 6, 7, and 8 contain an abundance of strategies, methods, tools, techniques, and best practices for developing the appropriate contract pricing arrangement. Chapter 9 discusses how to effectively conduct price analysis. Chapter 10 provides a practical and informative discussion of the concept of total ownership cost (TOC). Finally, Chapter 11 reviews the key elements of effective earned value management systems (EVMS).

In addition, the book contains a simple yet proven effective opportunity and risk assessment tool to aid sellers in bid/no bid decision making, a glossary of more than 200 key terms, a reference list to support further research, and a user-friendly index to help the reader find key items quickly.

We hope you will find this book an excellent resource for many years to come!

Sincerely,

Gregory A. Garrett, CPCM, CPM, PMP

KEY ACRONYMS LIST

ACO	Administrative Contracting Officer
ACWP	Actual Cost of Work Performed
BCWP	Budgeted Cost of Work Performed
BCWS	Budgeted Cost of Work Scheduled
B&P	Bid and Proposal
BOE	Basis of Estimate
BOM	Bill of Material
BU	Business Unit
CAM	Cost Account Manager
CAP	Contractor Acquired Property
CAS	Cost Accounting Standards
CASB	Cost Accounting Standards Board
CDRL	Contract Data Requirements List
CE&P	Cost Estimating and Pricing
CER	Cost Estimating Relationship
CFO	Chief Financial Officer
CLIN	Contract Line Item Number
COM	Cost of Money
COTR	Contracting Officer's Technical Representative
CR	Cost Reimbursement
CPAF	Cost-Plus-Award-Fee
CPFF	Cost-Plus-Fixed-Fee
CPIF	Cost-Plus-Incentive-Fee
C/SCSC	Cost/Schedule Control System Criteria
DCAA	Defense Contract Audit Agency
DCMC	Defense Contract Management Command
DFARS	Department of Defense FAR Supplement
DID	Data Item Description
DLS	Detail Level Schedules
DoD	Department of Defense
DTA	Designated Travel Agency
EAC	Estimate at Completion
EOQ	Economic Order Quantity
EPA	Economic Price Adjustment
ETC	Estimate to Complete
EVMS	Earned Value Management System
FAR	Federal Acquisition Regulation
FCCM	Facilities Capital Cost of Money
FE&O	Facilities Engineering and Operations
FICA	Federal Insurance Contributions Act
FFP	Firm-Fixed-Price
FPI	Fixed-Price Incentive
FPR	Forward Pricing Rate

FPRA	Forward Pricing Rate Agreement
G&A	General and Administrative Expense
GEF	General Engineering Forecast
GFP	Government Furnished Property
GP	Government Property
HMO	Health Maintenance Organization
HR	Human Resources
ID	Identification
IR&D	Independent Research and Development
MPS	Master Program Schedule
MRL	Master Rate Listing
NPV	Net Present Value
OBS	Organizational Breakdown Structure
ODC	Other Direct Cost
ORB	Opportunity Review Board
PBR	Provisional Billing Rate
PCO	Procuring Contracting Officer
PDP	Proposal Development Plan
PDP	Proposal Development Process
P&L	Profit and Loss Statement
PR	Public Relations
QA	Quality Assurance
RAM	Responsibility Assignment Matrix
RF	Realization Factor
RFP	Request for Proposal
RFQ	Request for Quotation
ROM	Rough Order of Magnitude
SB	Small Business
SBU	Sub-Business Unit/Strategic Business Unit
SCN	Supply Chain Network
SLIN	Subcontract Line Item Number
SOA	Schedule of Authorizations
SOW	Statement of Work
SSP	Source Selection Plan
STBI	State Tax Base on Income
T&L	Travel and Living
TOC	Total Ownership Cost
TINA	Truth in Negotiations Act
TPNW	Time Paid Not Worked
TPW	Time Paid Worked
WBS	Work Breakdown Structure
WPN	Work Package Number

CHAPTER 1

COST ESTIMATING: METHODS, PROCESSES, AND SOURCES OF RISK

Introduction

What should a product, service, or integrated business solution cost? How much is it worth to the buyer? What is the appropriate rate of return or profitability for a product or service? What constitutes a fair and reasonable price? How can buyers ensure they are not paying too much? How can sellers maximize both sales revenue and profitability in a consistent manner? The answers to the above-stated questions range from simple to complex and are the focus of this book.

In this world of outsourcing, customer requirements are increasingly demanding, and nearly everything is expected to be rapidly delivered, easy to use, transportable, highly reliable, and reasonably priced, based upon the global competitive marketplace. Worldwide, buyers are challenged to conduct appropriate market research to identify the right sources of products, services, and solutions. Likewise, sellers are challenged to efficiently and effectively develop, deliver, and price their respective products, services, and solutions.

For buyers and sellers in both the public and private sectors, most basic commodities or commercial-off-the-shelf (COTS) products and standard services are fairly priced based upon competition in the marketplace and price comparison. However, with the continual growth of global outsourcing, more new products, services, and integrated solutions are being developed and delivered, requiring new contract pricing to be established. Simply stated, creating a price for a product, service, or solution is not usually difficult. However, creating a fair and reasonable price for buyers that also motivates a high volume of sales and provides a healthy rate of return or profitability for the seller—considering all of the potential risk factors—can be extremely challenging. In this chapter, we will discuss the basic characteristics of credible cost estimates, the primary cost estimating methods, the 12 steps of a high-quality cost estimating process, and the major sources of risk involved in cost estimating and contract pricing.

Basic Characteristics of Credible Cost Estimates

The Government Accountability Office (GAO) has studied the basic characteristics of effective cost estimating for over 40 years. The GAO has developed a list of nine basic characteristics that have proven over time to affect the accuracy and reliability of cost estimates developed by both U.S. government agencies and industry (see Table 1-1).

Table 1-1 The GAO's Basic Characteristics of Credible Cost Estimates	
Characteristics	**Description**
Clear identification of task	Estimator must be provided with the system description, ground rules and assumptions, and technical and performance characteristics.
	The estimate's constraints and conditions must be clearly identified to ensure the preparation of a well-documented estimate.
Broad participation in preparing estimates	All players should be involved in deciding mission need and requirements and in defining parameters and other system characteristics.
	Data should be independently verified for accuracy, completeness, and reliability.
Availability of valid data	Numerous sources of suitable, relevant, and available data should be used.
	Relevant historical data should be used from similar systems to project costs of new systems. The historical data should be directly related to the system's performance characteristics.
Standardized structure for the estimate	A standard work breakdown structure (WBS), as detailed as possible, should be used, refining it as the cost estimate matures and the system becomes more defined. A major automated information system (MAIS) program may have only a cost estimate structure.
	The WBS ensures that no portions of the estimate are omitted and makes it easier to make comparisons to similar systems and programs.
Provision for program uncertainties	Uncertainties should be identified and allowance developed to cover the cost effect.
	Known costs should be included and unknown costs should be allowed for.
Recognition of inflation	The estimator should ensure that economic changes, such as inflation, are properly and realistically reflected in the life-cycle cost estimate.
Recognition of excluded costs	All costs associated with a system should be included; if any cost has been excluded, it should be disclosed and given a rationale.
Independent review of estimates	Conducting an independent review of an estimate is crucial to establishing confidence in the estimate. The independent reviewer should verify, modify, and correct an estimate to ensure realism, completeness, and consistency.
Revision of estimates for significant program changes	Estimates should be updated to reflect changes in a system's design requirements. Large changes that affect costs can significantly influence program decisions.

Source: Government Accountability Office, *Cost Assessment Guide: Best Practices for Estimating and Managing Program Costs,* GAO-07-1134SP. (Washington, DC: July 2007).

PRIMARY COST ESTIMATING METHODS

There are five primary methods for preparing cost estimates used by both buyers and sellers in the public and private sectors. They are summarized below.

Analogy Method

The analogy method is a cost estimating approach that is based upon historical data for products or services similar to those for which the estimate is being prepared. The cost estimator describes how the estimate is similar to previous programs, cites assumptions used to project from factual data to estimated costs, and provides copies of charge number accounting cost summaries with each estimate as appropriate or available.

An analogy takes into consideration that no new program, no matter how technologically state of the art it may be, represents a totally new system. Most new programs evolve from programs already fielded that have had new features added on or that simply represent a new combination of existing components. The analogy method uses this concept for estimating new components, subsystems, or total programs. That is, an analogy uses actual costs from a similar program with adjustments to account for differences between the requirements of the existing and new systems. A cost estimator typically uses this method early in a program's life cycle, when insufficient actual cost data are available but the technical and program definition is good enough to make the necessary adjustments.[1]

Table 1-2 An Example of the Analogy Cost Estimating Method			
Parameter	**Existing System**	**New System**	**Cost of New System (assuming linear relationship)**
Engine	F-100	F-200	
Thrust	12,000 lbs	16,000 lbs	
Cost	$5.2 million	X	(16,000/12,000) × $5.2 million = $6.9 million
Source: Society of Cost Estimating and Analysis, Cost Programmed Review of Fundamentals (CostPROF): Costing Techniques—The Basic Types of Cost Estimates. (Vienna, VA: Society of Cost Estimating and Analysis, 2003).			

The equation in Table 1-2 implicitly assumes a linear relationship between engine cost and amount of thrust. However, there should be a compelling scientific or engineering reason why an engine's cost is directly proportionally to its thrust. Without more data (or an expert on engine costs), it is hard to know what parameters are the true drivers of cost. Therefore, when using the analogy method, it is important that the estimator research and discuss with program experts the reasonableness of technical program drivers to determine whether they are significant cost drivers.

The analogy method has several advantages:
- It can be used before detailed program requirements are known.
- If the analogy is strong, the estimate will be defensible.
- An analogy can be developed quickly and at minimal cost.
- The tie to historical data is simple enough to be readily understood.

Using analogies also has some disadvantages:
- An analogy relies on a single data point.
- It is often difficult to find the detailed cost, technical, and program data required for analogies.
- There is a tendency to be too subjective about the technical parameter adjustment factors.

Parametric Analysis Method

The parametric analysis method uses parametric models to derive cost data from key cost driver factors such as product weight, complexity, inputs/outputs, software code types, historical data, etc. The cost estimator cites the model and factors used and any assumptions, and it provides copies of the model outputs with each estimate. In the parametric method, a statistical relationship is developed between historical costs and program, physical, and performance characteristics. The method is sometimes referred to as a "top-down" approach. Some types of physical characteristics used for parametric estimating are weight, power, and lines of code. Other program and performance characteristics include site deployment plans for information technology installations, maintenance plans, test and evaluation schedules, technical performance measures, and crew size. These are just some examples of what can be cost drivers for a particular program.

The goal of parametric estimating is to create a statistically valid cost estimating relationship (CER) using historical data. The parametric CER can then be used to estimate the cost of the new program by entering its specific characteristics into the parametric model. CERs established early in a program's life cycle should be continually revisited to make sure they are current and the input range still applies to the new program. In addition, parametric CERs should be well documented, because serious estimating errors could occur if the CER is improperly used. Parametric techniques can be used in a wide variety of situations, ranging from early planning estimates to detailed contract negotiations. It is always essential to have an adequate number of relevant data points, and care must be taken to normalize the dataset so that it is consistent and complete. In software, the development environment (i.e., the extent to which the requirements are understood, along with the programmers' skill and experience) is usually the major cost driver. Because parametric relationships are often used early in a program, when the design is not well defined, they can easily be reflected in the estimate as the design changes simply by adjusting the values of the input parameters.

It is important to make sure that the program attributes being estimated fall within (or at least not far outside) the CER dataset. For example, if a new software program was expected to contain 1 million software lines of code, and the data points for a software CER were based on programs with lines of code ranging from 10,000 to 250,000, it would be inappropriate to use the CER to estimate the new program.

To develop a parametric CER, cost estimators must determine the cost drivers that most influence cost. After studying the technical baseline and analyzing the data through scatter charts and other methods, the cost estimator should verify the selected cost drivers by discussing them with engineers. The CER can then be developed with a mathematical expression, which can range from a simple rule of thumb (for example, dollars per pound) to a complex regression equation.

The more simplified CERs include rates, factors, and ratios. A rate uses a parameter to predict cost, using a multiplicative relationship. Since rate is defined to be cost as a function of a parameter, the units for rate are always dollars per something. The rate most commonly used in cost estimating is the labor rate, expressed in dollars per hour.

Table 1-3 An Example of the Parametric Analysis Cost Estimating Method	
Program Attribute	**Calculation**
A cost estimating relationship (CER) for site activation (SA) is a function of the number of workstations (NW)	SA = $82,800 + ($26,500 × NW)
Data range for the CER	7–47 workstations based on 11 data points
Cost to site activate a program with 40 workstations	$82,800 + ($26,500 × 40) = $1,142,800
Source: Society of Cost Estimating and Analysis, Cost Programmed Review of Fundamentals (CostPROF): Costing Techniques—The Basic Types of Cost Estimates. (Vienna, VA: Society of Cost Estimating and Analyis, 2003).	

In Table 1-3, the number of workstations is the cost driver. The equation is linear but has both a fixed component (i.e., $82,800) and a variable component (i.e., $26,500 × NW).

In addition, the range of the data is from 7 to 47 workstations, so it would be inappropriate to use this CER for estimating the activation cost of a site with as few as 2 or as many as 200 workstations.

In fact, at one extreme, the CER estimates a cost of $82,800 for no workstation installations, which is not logical. Although we do not show any CER statistics for this example, the CERs should always be presented with their statistics. The reason for this is to enable the cost estimator to understand the level of variation within the data and model its effect with uncertainty analysis.

CERs should be developed using regression techniques, so that statistical inferences may be drawn. To perform a regression analysis, the first step is to determine what relationship exists between cost (dependent variable) and its various drivers (independent variables). This relationship is determined by developing a scatter chart of the data. If the data are linear, they can be fit by a linear regression. If they are not linear and transformation of the data does not produce a linear fit, nonlinear regression can be used. The independent variables should have a high correlation with cost and should be logical.[2]

Weighted Average Method

The weighted average method involves evaluation of three or more similar products and/or services to derive a weighted average in support of estimated costs. The cost estimator cites historical resource expenditures on at least three programs and produces a weighted average calculation, including weighting criteria and rationale as to why and how the programs are similar to the current product or service. The advantages to the weighted average method are that it is simple and easy to use, while the disadvantages are that it is only as accurate as the historical data and the weightings assigned.

Technical Consensus Method

Group consensus for estimated resources involves using experienced, qualified personnel to prepare resource estimates and considerations/assumptions. The cost estimator cites specific personnel involved, their qualifications, estimating assumptions, data, and the median response to support each estimate. Technical consensus is used when no structured resource estimating model can be applied.

Engineering Build-up Method

The engineering build-up method is a step-by-step, bottoms-up description of task requirements and estimated resources for labor, material, and other direct costs (ODCs), with descriptive rationale as to why resources are required and the considerations used by the engineer to develop the estimate.

An engineering build-up estimate is done at the lowest level of detail and consists of labor and materials costs that have overhead and fees added to them. In addition to labor hours, a detailed parts list is required. Once in hand, the material parts are allocated to the lowest WBS level, based on how the work will be accomplished. In addition, quantity and schedule have to be considered in order to capture the effects of learning. Typically, cost estimators work with engineers to develop the detailed estimates. The cost estimator's focus is to get detailed information from the engineer in a way that is reasonable, complete, and consistent with the program's ground rules and assumptions. The cost estimator must find additional data to validate the engineer's estimates. See Table 1-4 for an example of this method.

Table 1-4 An Example of the Engineering Build-up Cost Estimating Method			
Problem	**Similar Aircraft**	**Solution**	**Result**
Estimate sheet metal cost of the inlet nacelle for a new aircraft.	F/A-18 inlet nacelle	Apply historical F/A-18 variance for touch labor effort and	
Apply support labor factor to adjust estimated touch labor hours.	2,000 hours × 1.2 = 2,400 touch labor hours and		
2,400 labor hours × 1.48 = 3,522 labor hours (touch labor plus support labor) estimate for new aircraft.			
Standard hours to produce a new nacelle are estimated at 2,000 for touch labor; adjust to reflect experience of similar aircraft and support labor effort.	F/A-18 inlet nacelle experienced a 20% variance in touch labor effort above the industrial engineering standard. In addition, F/A-18 support labor was equal to 48% of the touch labor hours		Average labor rates would then be used to convert these total labor hours into costs.

Source: Society of Cost Estimating and Analysis, Cost Programmed Review of Fundamentals (CostPROF): Costing Techniques—The Basic Types of Cost Estimates. (Vienna, VA: Society of Cost Estimating and Analysis, 2003).

The several advantages to the engineering build-up method include:

- The estimator is able to determine exactly what the estimate includes and whether anything was overlooked.
- It can be uniquely applied to the specific program and manufacturer.
- It gives good insight into major cost contributors.
- It allows easy transfer of results to other programs.

Some disadvantages of the engineering build-up method include:

- It can be expensive to implement and it is time consuming.
- It is not flexible enough to answer what-if questions.
- New estimates must be built for each alternative.
- The product specification must be well known and stable.
- All product and process changes must be reflected in the estimate.[3]

Table 1-5 provides a list of factors and considerations used for selecting the estimating methodology required for preparing typical cost estimates including labor, material, travel and living, ODCs, and subcontractors.

Table 1-5 Summary of Cost Estimating Methods and Selection Criteria		
Resource Category	**Factors/Considerations in Method Selection**	**Suggested Estimating Methods**
Labor	• Task complexity • Skill mix requirements • Resource availability • Delivery schedule • Specifications/quality requirements	Analogy, parametric, weighted average, technical consensus, and engineering estimate methods should be considered.
Material	• Bill of material preparation • Delivery schedule • Specification review • Customer drawing review • Make-vs.-buy analysis	Analogy, parametric, weighted average and engineering estimate methods should be considered.
Other direct costs	• Resource availability • Delivery schedule • Task complexity • Period of performance	Analogy, parametric, weighted average, and engineering estimate methods should be considered.
Subcontractors	• Resource availability • Delivery schedule • Task complexity • Period of performance • Make-vs.-buy/source selection plan	Subcontractor quotations secured through supplier management.
Travel and living	• Required labor resources and their availability for travel to meetings, training or other program support • Delivery schedule • Task complexity • Period of performance	Analogy, weighted average, and vendor quotes

THE 12 STEPS OF A HIGH-QUALITY COST ESTIMATING PROCESS

The Government Accountability Office (GAO) in its new *Cost Assessment Guide* (July 2007) offers a relatively simple, logical, and practical process approach to developing high-quality cost estimates. The proposed cost estimating process, contained in Figure 1-1, is based upon proven-effective best practices from government and industry.

Figure 1-1 The Cost Estimating Process

Initiation and Research	Assessment	Analysis	Presentation
Your audience, what you are estimating, and why you are estimating it are of the utmost importance.	Cost assessment steps are iterative and can be accomplished in varying order or concurrently.	The confidence in the point or range of the estimate is crucial to the decision maker.	Documentation and presentation make or break a cost estimating decision outcome.

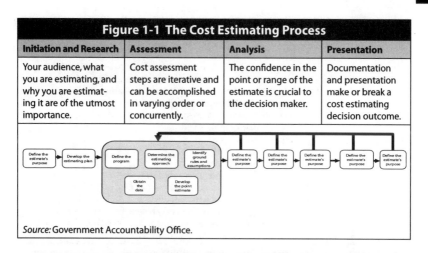

Source: Government Accountability Office.

Table 1-6 The 12 Steps of a High-Quality Cost Estimating Process

Step	Description	Associated Task
1.	Define the estimate's purpose.	• Determine: • The estimate's purpose • The level of detail required • Who will receive the estimate • The overall scope of the estimate
2.	Develop an estimating plan.	• Determine the cost estimating team. • Outline the cost estimating approach • Develop the estimate timeline • Determine who will do the independent cost estimate. • Develop the team's master schedule
3.	Define the program characteristics.	• Identify in a technical baseline description document: • The program's purpose • Its system and performance characteristics • Any technology implications • All system configurations • Program acquisition schedule • Acquisition strategy • Relationship to other existing systems • Support (manpower, training, etc.) and security needs • Risk items • System quantities for development, testing, and production • Deployment and maintenance plans • Predecessor or similar legacy systems
4.	Determine an estimating approach.	• Define work breakdown structure (WBS) and describe each element in a WBS dictionary; a major automated information system may have only a cost element structure. • Choose the estimating method best suited for each WBS element. • Identify potential cross-checks for likely cost and schedule drivers. • Develop a cost estimating checklist.

Table 1-6 The 12 Steps of a High-Quality Cost Estimating Process

Step	Description	Associated Task
5.	Identify ground rules and assumptions.	• Clearly define what is included and excluded from the estimate. Identify global and program-specific assumptions such as: • The estimate's base year, including time-phasing and life cycle • Program schedule information by phase • Program acquisition strategy • Any schedule or budget constraints • Inflation assumptions • Travel costs • Equipment the government is to furnish • Prime contractor and major subcontractors • Use of existing facilities or new modification or development • Technology refresh cycles • Technology assumptions and new technology to be developed • Commonality with legacy systems and assumed heritage savings • Effects of new ways of doing business
6.	Obtain data.	• Create a data collection plan with emphasis on collecting current and relevant technical, programmatic, cost, and risk data. • Investigate possible data sources. • Collect data and normalize them for cost accounting, inflation, learning, and quantity adjustment. • Analyze the data to look for cost drivers, trends, and outliers; compare results against rules of thumb and standard factors derived from historical data. • Interview data sources and document all pertinent information, including an assessment of data reliability and accuracy. • Store data for future estimates
7.	Develop point estimates.	• Develop the cost model by estimating each WBS element using the best methodology from the data collected. • Include all estimating assumptions in the cost model. • Express costs in constant year dollars. • Time-phase the results by spreading costs in the years they are expected to occur, based on the program schedule. • Sum the WBS elements to develop the overall point estimate. • Validate the estimate by looking for errors like double counting and omitting costs. • Compare the estimate against the independent cost estimate and examine where and why there are differences. • Perform cross-checks on cost drivers to see if results are similar. • Update the model as more data become available or as changes occur; compare results against previous estimates.
8.	Conduct sensitivity analysis.	• Test the sensitivity of cost elements to changes in estimating input values and key assumptions. • Identify effects of changing the program schedule or quantities on the overall estimate. • On the basis of this analysis, determine which assumptions are key cost drivers and which cost elements are affected most by changes.

Step	Description	Associated Task
colspan:3 **Table 1-6 The 12 Steps of a High-Quality Cost Estimating Process**
9.	Conduct risk and uncertainty analysis.	• Determine the level of cost, schedule, and technical risk associated with each WBS element and discuss with technical experts. • Analyze each risk for its severity and probability of occurrence. • Develop minimum, most likely, and maximum ranges for each element risk. • Use an acceptable statistical analysis methodology (e.g., Monte Carlo simulation) to develop a confidence interval around the point estimate. • Determine type of risk distributions and reason for their use. • Identify the confidence level of the point estimate. • Identify the amount of contingency funding and add this to the point estimate to determine the risk-adjusted cost estimate. • Recommend that the project or program office develop a risk management plan to track and mitigate risks.
10.	Document the estimate.	• Document all steps used to develop the estimate so that it can be recreated quickly by a cost analyst unfamiliar with the program and produce the same result. • Document the purpose of the estimate, the team that prepared it, and who approved the estimate and on what date. • Describe the program, including the schedule and technical baseline used to create the estimate. • Present the time-phased life-cycle cost of the program. • Discuss all ground rules and assumptions. • Include auditable and traceable data sources for each cost element. • Document for all data sources how the data were normalized. • Describe in detail the estimating methodology and rationale used to derive each WBS element's cost (more detail rather than too little is preferred). • Describe the results of the risk, uncertainty, and sensitivity analyses and whether any contingency funds were identified. • Document how the estimate compares to the funding profile. • Track how this estimate compares to previous estimates, if applicable.
11.	Present the estimate to management for approval.	• Develop a briefing that presents the documented life-cycle cost estimate (LCCE) for management approval, including: • an explanation of the technical and programmatic baseline and any uncertainties; • a comparison to an independent cost estimate (ICE) with explanations of any differences; • a comparison of the LCCE or independent cost estimate to the budget; and • enough detail so the presenter can easily defend the estimate by showing how it is accurate, complete, and high in quality. • Focus the briefing, in a logical manner, on the largest cost elements and drivers of cost. • Make the content crisp and complete so that those who are unfamiliar with it can easily comprehend the competence that underlies the estimate results. • Make backup slides available for more probing questions • Act on and document feedback from management. • The cost estimating team should request acceptance of the estimate.

Table 1-6 The 12 Steps of a High-Quality Cost Estimating Process		
Step	**Description**	**Associated Task**
12.	Update the estimate to reflect actual costs and changes.	• Update the estimate to: • reflect any changes in technical or program assumptions; or • keep it current as the program passes through new phases or milestones. • Replace estimates with earned value management (EVM) estimate at completion (EAC) and independent EAC from the integrated EVM system. • Report progress on meeting cost and schedule estimates. • Perform a post mortem and document lessons learned for elements whose actual costs or schedules differ from the estimate.
Document all changes to the program and how they affect the cost estimate.		

Source: Government Accountability Office, *Cost Assessment Guide: Best Practices for Estimating and Managing Program Costs,* GAO-07-1134SP (Washington, DC: July 2007).

Each of these 12 steps is important to ensure that high-quality cost estimates are developed and delivered in time to support important decisions.

Sources of Major Risk

Uncertainty and risk in cost estimating and contract pricing arise from six main sources:

- Lack of buyer understanding of its requirements
- Shortcomings of human language and differing interpretations
- Behavior of the parties
- Haste
- Deception
- Poor cost estimating and pricing practices

Lack of Buyer Understanding of Its Requirements

If the buyer does not have a clear understanding of its requirements or cannot express that understanding effectively in terms of specific deliverables or level of effort, an agreement cannot be reached with another party to fulfill those requirements. Many buyers have only a vague notion of their requirements, as revealed in the language of their specifications, statements of work, or statement of objectives. Broad, ambiguous expressions that obligate a seller to do something "as required" or "as necessary" are often used because the buyer does not know its requirements or needs but wants to put the seller in the position of having to do whatever is needed whenever the buyer finds out what that is. How can the seller estimate the cost of meeting such obligations?

Ironically, some buyers overcompensate by specifying their needs down to the smallest detail. If these details have been well researched, the specification may indeed reflect the buyer's needs. But such detailed requirements are often specified by people who are not familiar with the technology available, or soon to become available, in the marketplace or with industry methods or market practices. As a result, the statement of work may describe processes discarded by the industry or product features not yet available, no longer available, or not available in combination with other specified features.

These difficulties arise because many, if not most, buyers are uninformed about goods and services they must purchase from an industry other than their own. Rare is the buyer who knows as much about a product or service as the companies that design, produce, and market that product or service for a living. This fact is the source of much difficulty in writing and interpreting requirements and of performance crises for the project manager who must fulfill contractually specified requirements.

Shortcomings of Human Language and Differing Interpretations

A party to a contract may mean one thing but say another. An inability to express ideas clearly may result in a contract document that does not accurately reflect the intended agreement. Meaning may be clear in the language of one country but become obscured during translation. Unfortunately, these scenarios are all too common in the world of contracting.

Behavior of the Parties

The actions of one or both of the parties after the contract is signed may give meaning to the words of the contract that the parties did not originally intend. For example, the seller may choose not to enforce a late payment penalty clause when an important buyer consistently pays late. Thus, the seller establishes a precedence of performance, or lack thereof, which is inconsistent with the language of the contract.

Haste

In business, haste causes many problems. Because of impatience with the bureaucratic contracting process, government project managers and industry sales managers often promote haste in contract formation. In the rush to "get on contract," many ideas are not fully developed or discussed by the parties. As a result, the expectations of both parties may never be fully understood, by themselves or by each other. Unrealistic expectations go unchallenged. Realistic expectations go uncommunicated. These expectations do not disappear, however, and will rise to haunt buyers and sellers, both contract managers and project managers, after the project is under way.

Deception

Deception, with both ill and benign intent, is a reality of the business world; hence the warning "caveat emptor," or "let the buyer beware." Deception is a deliberate defect in the communication process. As discussed previously, buyers often do not fully understand the nature of the goods and services they buy, the methods of the industry producing them, or the practices of the market selling them. Buyers may have only a vague idea of the results they hope to obtain from those goods and services, an idea limited to the expectation that "things will be better."

In trying to give expression to their vague ideas and unrealistic expectations, buyers may develop faulty requirements. In these circumstances, sales representatives and proposal writers may find acceding to such requirements more convenient than educating the buyer. They adopt the strategy of winning the contract first and educating the buyer after contract award.

Although the strategy may involve outright fraud, it is probably more commonly based on the belief (or hope) that "once they have it, they'll be satisfied" or "if they really knew what they wanted, they would want what we plan to give them." A remarkable degree of self-deception can exist on the parts of both buyer and seller involved in such a strategy. Even when the intention is ultimately to make the buyer happy, the method is deceptive and often leads to trouble.[4]

Poor Cost Estimating and Pricing Practices

According to both research and experience there are several well-documented, recurring, and significant cost estimating challenges or frequent poor practices including:

- Known costs had been excluded without adequate or valid justification.
- Historical cost data used as a basis for computing estimates were sometimes invalid, unreliable, and unrepresentative.
- Inflation was not always included or uniformly treated when it was included.
- There was a lack of parametric estimating tools available.
- The people developing cost estimates and pricing arrangements lacked formal education or training.

Confronting the Challenges of Risk in Cost Estimating and Contract Pricing

Although intended to reduce uncertainties and risks associated with business transactions, contract pricing can introduce new risk. For example, the agreement may prove to be incomplete (essential aspects of the relationship left unaddressed or unresolved and subject to dispute), or the parties to a contract may dispute the precise interpretation of the contract document. Either circumstance will cause problems for both parties.

Furthermore, one party may be unwilling or unable to keep its promise (the threat of litigation notwithstanding) but will be able to prevent or evade enforcement or will be unable to comply with a court order for compensation or restitution. One party may also inadvertently breach the contract (fail to comply with the contract without a legal excuse), exposing itself to sanctions or allowing the other party to avoid its obligations. Unfortunately, a foolproof, loophole-free contract has never been written and will never be written as long as human beings are involved in the process. Merely having a signed contract does not ensure that the parties have a fully formed agreement, and it is certainly no guarantee against trouble.

Part of managing a contract is working out the relationship on a day-to-day, issue-by-issue basis. Differences between the contracting parties will arise and must be resolved in a businesslike manner, professionally and without rancor. If the parties discover that their agreement did not anticipate all contingencies, ad hoc settlements must be negotiated. Such circumstances do not mean that the contract terms and pricing should be ignored; they simply indicate that a signed contract is just the beginning of the contract manager's and project manager's work.

Having a contract with an agreed-upon pricing arrangement does not eliminate business risk; at best, it exchanges one set of risks for another. The contracting parties must make an effort to form and administer the contract properly to minimize these and other risks that may arise.

SUMMARY

The bottom line is this: Cost estimating is full of risk! Cost estimating and contract pricing can be very challenging to properly conduct, and nearly everything contained in a contract directly or indirectly affects the price. In this chapter, we have provided a brief review of the basic characteristics of credible cost estimates, the primary cost estimating methods, the 12 steps of a high-quality cost estimating process, and the major sources of risk in cost estimating and contract pricing. The remaining chapters of this book will expand upon the topics of cost estimating, cost accounting standards, cost analysis, profit analysis, price analysis, pricing arrangements, total ownership cost, and earned value management systems. In Chapter 2, we will discuss the cost estimating fundamentals in much more detail.

QUESTIONS TO CONSIDER

1. Does your organization have an efficient and effective cost estimating process?

2. Which cost estimating method(s) does your organization use most frequently?

3. How accurate are your organization's cost estimates?

4. What major sources of risk does your organization typically encounter when developing cost estimates and negotiating a contract price?

ENDNOTES

[1] Government Accountability Office, Cost Assessment Guide: Best Practices for Estimating and Managing Program Costs, GAO-07-1134SP (Washington, DC: July 2007).

[2] Ibid.

[3] Ibid.

[4] Gregory A. Garrett, World-Class Contracting, 4th ed. (Chicago: CCH, 2007).

CHAPTER

COST
ESTIMATING
FUNDAMENTALS

INTRODUCTION

The key question in business is often, "How much does it cost?" Cost estimating is defined as the predicting or forecasting, within a defined scope, of all costs required to construct and equip a facility or furnish products, services, or solutions. Estimates are prepared by functional organizations such as engineering, program/project management, and other technical support in response to formal or informal customer requirements for buyers and requests for proposals or quotations for sellers. Estimates take the form of proposals, budgetary estimates, and rough order of magnitude (ROM) estimates. Cost estimates utilize experience, historical costs, quotes, calculations, and forecasts of future costs for materials, resources, methods, and management within a scheduled time frame, using methods to project from factual data to future requirements. This chapter provides an overview of cost estimating fundamentals and best practices using a simple yet highly effective question-and-answer approach.

WHAT IS THE DIFFERENCE BETWEEN COST ESTIMATING AND COST ANALYSIS?

According to the Government Accountability Office's *Cost Assessment Guide*:

> Although "cost estimating" and "cost analysis" are often used interchangeably, cost estimating is a specific activity within cost analysis. Cost analysis is a powerful tool, because it requires a rigorous and systematic analysis that results in a better understanding of the program being acquired. This understanding, in turn, leads to improved program management in applying resources and mitigating program risks.[1]

Cost analysis, used to develop cost estimates for such things as hardware systems, automated information systems, civil projects, manpower, and training, can be defined as:

- the effort to develop, analyze, and document cost estimates with analytical approaches and techniques;
- the process of analyzing and estimating the incremental and total resources required to support past, present, and future systems—an integral step in selecting alternatives; and

■ a tool for evaluating resource requirements at key milestones and decision points in the acquisition process.

Cost estimating involves collecting and analyzing historical data and applying quantitative models, techniques, tools, and databases to predict a program's future cost. More simply, cost estimating combines science and art to predict the future cost of something based on known historical data that are adjusted to reflect new materials, technology, software languages, and development teams.

Because cost estimating is complex, sophisticated cost analysts should combine concepts from such disciplines as accounting, budgeting, computer science, economics, engineering, mathematics, and statistics and should even employ concepts from marketing and public affairs. And because cost estimating requires such a wide range of disciplines, it is important that the cost analyst either be familiar with these disciplines or have access to an expert in these fields.

WHAT ARE THE TYPES OF COST ESTIMATES?

See Table 2-1, "Types of Cost Estimates," for a listing of the various types of cost estimates.

Table 2-1 Types of Cost Estimates		
Estimate Type	Level of Effort	Description
Life-Cycle Cost Estimate (LCCE)		
Independent cost estimate (ICE)	Requires a large team, may take many months to accomplish, and addresses the full LCCE.	An ICE, conducted by an organization independent of the acquisition chain of command, is based on the same detailed technical and procurement information used to make the baseline estimate— usually the program or project LCCE. ICEs are developed to support new programs or conversion, activation, modernization, or service life extensions and to support Department of Defense (DoD) milestone decisions for major defense acquisition programs. An estimate might cover a program's entire life cycle, one program phase, or one high-value, highly visible, or high-interest item within a phase. ICEs are used primarily to validate program or project LCCEs and are typically reconciled with them. Because the team performing the ICE is independent, it provides an unbiased test of whether the program office cost estimate is reasonable. It is also used to identify risks related to budget shortfalls or excesses.

Table 2-1 Types of Cost Estimates

Estimate Type	Level of Effort	Description
Total owner-ship cost estimate	Requires a large team, may take many months to accomplish, and addresses the full LCCE.	Related to LCCE but broader in scope, a total ownership cost estimate consists of the elements of life-cycle cost plus some infrastructure and business process costs not necessarily attributable to a program. Infrastructure includes acquisition and central logistics activities; nonunit central training; personnel administration and benefits; medical care; and installation, communications, and information infrastructure to support military bases. It is normally found in U.S. Army and some U.S. Navy ship programs.
Business Case Analysis		
Analysis of alternatives (AOA) and cost effective-ness analysis (CEA)	Requires a large team, may take many months to accomplish, and addresses the full LCCE.	AOA compares the operational effectiveness, suitability, and LCCE of alternatives that appear to satisfy established capability needs. Its major components are a CEA and cost analysis. AOAs try to identify the most promising of several conceptual alternatives; analysis and conclusions are typically used to justify initiating an acquisition program. An AOA also looks at mission threat and dependencies on other programs. When an AOA cannot quantify benefits, a CEA is more appropriate. A CEA is conducted whenever it is unnecessary or impractical to consider the dollar value of benefits, as when various alternatives have the same annual monetary benefits. Both the AOA and CEA should address each alternative's advantages, disadvantages, associated risks, and uncertainties and how they might influence the comparison.
Economic analysis (EA) and cost ben-efit analysis	Requires a large team, may take many months to accomplish, and addresses the full LCCE.	EA is a conceptual framework for systematically investigating problems of choice. Posing various alternatives for reaching an objective, it analyzes the LCCE and benefits of each one, usually with a return on investment analysis. Present value is also an important concept: Since this type of analysis does not consider the time value of money, it is necessary to determine when expenditures for alternatives will be made. EA expands cost analysis by examining the effects of the time value of money on investment decisions. After cost estimates have been generated, they must be time-phased to allow for alternative expenditure patterns. Assuming equal benefits, the alternative with the least present value cost is the most desirable: It implies a more efficient allocation of resources.
Other		
Rough order of magnitude (ROM)	May be done by a small group or one person; can be done in hours, days, or weeks; and covers only a portion of LCCE.	Developed when a quick estimate is needed and few details are available. Usually based on historical ratio information, it is typically developed to support what-if analyses and can be developed for a particular phase or portion of an estimate to the entire cost estimate, depending on available data. It is helpful for examining differences in high-level alternatives to see which are the most feasible. Because it is developed from limited data and in a short time, an ROM analysis should never be considered a budget-quality cost estimate.

Table 2-1 Types of Cost Estimates		
Estimate Type	**Level of Effort**	**Description**
Independent cost assessment (ICA)	Requires a small group; may take months to accomplish, depending on how much of the LCCE is being reviewed.	An ICA is an outside, nonadvocate's evaluation of a cost estimate's quality and accuracy, looking specifically at a program's technical approach, risk, and acquisition strategy to ensure that the program's cost estimate captures all requirements. Typically requested by a program manager or outside source, it may be used to determine whether the cost estimate reflects the program of record. It is not as formal as and ICE and does not have to be performed by an organization independent of the acquisition chain of command, although it usually is. An ICA usually does not address a program's entire life cycle.
Independent government cost estimate (IGCE)	Requires a small group, may take months to accomplish, and covers only the LCCE phase under contract.	An IGCE is conducted to check the reasonableness of a contractor's cost proposal and to make sure that the offered prices are within the budget range for a particular program. It is submitted by the program managers as a part of a request for contract funding. It documents the government's assessment of the program's most probable cost and ensures that enough funds are available to execute it. It is also helpful in assessing the feasibility of individual tasks to determine if the associated costs are reasonable.
Estimate at completion (EAC)	Requires nominal effort once all earned value management (EVM) data are on hand and have been determined reliable; covers only the LCCE phase under contract.	An EAC is an independent assessment of the cost to complete authorized work based on a contractor's historical EVM performance. It uses various EVM metrics to forecast the expected final cost: EAC = actual costs incurred + (budgeted cost for work remaining/EVM performance factor). The performance factor can be based on many different EVM metrics that capture cost and schedule status to date.

What Are the Key Elements of a Cost Estimate?

As applicable, cost estimates should be completed following the development and analysis of the program requirements, the program schedule, work breakdown structure (WBS), and key performance requirements associated with a customer need. A completed cost estimate should include the following key elements:

Direct Costs

- **Labor:** Supported by a basis of estimate (BOE) for each WBS cost account. Time-phased labor requirements are summarized at the task and total program level within the cost proposal.
- **Material**: Supported by vendor quotations or other methods. Time-phased material requirements are summarized by task and vendor in a consolidated bill of material (BOM).

- **Other direct costs (ODCs):** Supported by a BOE or other descriptive data for each cost account, to include description of the ODC resource required, rationale, and time-phased resource requirements for each task. Included under ODC are subcontractors, travel and living, and miscellaneous costs.
  - *Subcontractors:* Supported by subcontractor quotations, with technical evaluations and cost/price analyses prepared by the program/project management, engineering, and supplier management organizations.
  - *Travel and living:* Supported by BOE for each WBS cost account.
  - *Miscellaneous costs:* Supported by BOE for each WBS cost account. May include computer time, reproduction, technical publications, photography, etc.

Indirect Costs (Overhead)

Indirect costs are components of the overhead pools used in developing the business unit overhead and labor overhead rates. These indirect costs include, but are not limited to:

- **Expense salaries:** Includes indirect employee salaries associated with the time spent performing expense-related activities that are not specifically required for performance on contracts. Individual managers may estimate the amount of time employees in their individual organizations will be charging expenses as opposed to direct labor based on historical data, the general forecast of business volume, known future requirements that are not specific to contracts, or a combination of the preceding factors. This time estimate is then converted to an equivalent expense headcount estimate, by level. The equivalent expense headcount estimate, by level, is then loaded into an organizational forecasting model and multiplied by the appropriate salary amount to determine expense salaries. An alternative approach would be to use the previous year's direct-to-expense employee headcount ratios if headcount and work activities within the given organization are expected to remain constant.
- **General and administrative (G&A) costs**
- **Fringe expenses**

WHAT ARE SOME OF THE TYPICAL CONTRACT-RELATED EXPENSE ITEMS?

The examples of expense items listed below may be forecasted based on historical data, known future requirements that are not specific to contracts, affordability, or a combination of the preceding factors. Note that the overhead rate includes only the indirect expense portion of the following:

- **Travel, living, meals:** Includes forecasted costs for items such as meals, lodging, car rentals, and other miscellaneous incidentals incurred while on business travel (per diem applies).
- **Employee transfer/relocation:** Includes forecasted costs for relocating/transferring employees (e.g., lump sums, house-hunting costs, costs associated with purchase/sale of home). Only applicable/allowable expense is included.
- **Training and tuition refund:** Includes forecasted tuition reimbursement, costs of attending training courses, and other training-related costs.
- **Repro/office supplies:** Includes forecasted costs for supplies, stationery, books, and publications.
- **Communications:** Includes forecasted costs for telephone services, data services, and other information movement and management charges.
- **Purchased materials/services:** Includes forecasted costs for items such as outside-vendor-purchased materials/services, purchased software, and associated transportation costs.
- **Miscellaneous:** Includes forecasted costs for items such as employee recognition awards, professional licenses, permits, overnight express mail, and passports.
- **Unallowables:** Includes forecasted costs for items such as alcoholic beverages, per diem excesses, advertising, and trade shows (when unallowable).
- **Charges from others:** Includes transfers from other company business units or corporate centers.
- **Charges to others:** Includes transfers for specific services rendered to other company business units or corporate centers.

Some organization cost elements are managed centrally by the accounting and finance organization and therefore are not forecasted by the individual organizations. These cost elements typically include, but are not limited to, landlord services, IT services, depreciation, and benefits.

What are some of the major cost estimating challenges?

According to the GAO's *Cost Assessment Guide*:

> Developing a good cost estimate requires stable pro-
> gram requirements, access to detailed documentation
> and historical data, well-trained and experienced cost
> analysts, a risk and uncertainty analysis, the identifi-
> cation of a range of confidence levels, and adequate
> contingency and management reserves. Cost estimat-
> ing is nonetheless difficult in the best circumstances.
> It requires both science and judgment. And, since
> answers are seldom—if ever—precise, the goal is to find
> a "reasonable" answer. However, the cost estimator
> typically faces many challenges in doing so.[2]

How should purchased materials and services cost estimates be handled?

- **Outside purchases:** Materials and services as well as leases or
  rentals may be deemed a direct cost or indirect cost depending
  upon their application. The costs are based on purchase orders
  or outside vendor quotes acquired through the purchasing or
  supplier management group. These quotes are developed
  through competitive sourcing or based on historical data. Valid
  historical data include:
  - Recent purchase orders (i.e., less than one year old)
  - Purchasing or supplier management trend data (i.e., over
    a period of time with significant purchases)
  - Parametric analysis of cost accounting summaries (i.e.,
    factor developed as a percentage of total material cost)
- Interdivisional transfers
  - Company material and services are transferred as an ODC
    to the government-facing business segment and are sup-
    ported with a quote or documentation.
  - Company commercial material and services are supported
    via information other than cost or pricing data.

What is time-phasing of material cost estimates?

Material is quoted on a "point-of-receipt" basis, typically at or near
the time when it will actually be consumed. That is generally assumed to be the month the material will be utilized. Cost Account-

ing Standards (CAS) require that effort be quoted the same way it is to be incurred. Since material is paid for when it is received, not when it is ordered, that is the way it is reflected in proposals.

WHAT ARE THE TYPICAL ROLES AND RESPONSIBILITIES OF A COST ESTIMATING AND PRICING TEAM?

A typical cost estimating and pricing team is organized and staffed appropriately to meet specific proposal requirements. The team supports all planning, estimating, proposal development, and supporting functions, and ensures complete coverage of all customer requirements and compliance with cost estimating system guidelines set forth in this manual. Members of the team are selected based upon customer proposal requirements such as bid complexity, number and types of participating organizations, proposal response schedule, experience with customer/program, program size, and reporting requirements. Depending on the complexity and breadth of the proposal, a team member may serve in more than one capacity for a given proposal.

The team is staffed by the respective functional organizations based upon the factors listed above; however, we recommend that the designated cost estimating and pricing manager should be selected by the capture manager or program manager who has overall responsibility for meeting all customer requirements. Cost estimating and pricing managers are selected based upon their knowledge of proposal development, estimating system guidelines, and customer reporting requirements.

We suggest either the program manager or the capture manager be responsible for the overall leadership of the cost estimating and pricing team. The pricing specialist(s) assist in preparing the proposal. The project controls manager, subcontracts manager, and contracts manager should play supporting roles in proposal preparation, if required. The roles and responsibilities of each of these individuals are identified in Table 2-2. In some cases, proposal staff will be required to perform multiple functions to support proposal efforts.

Table 2-2 Typical Roles and Responsibilities of a Cost Estimating and Pricing Team

Team Member	Roles/Responsibilities
Program manager/ project manager (PM)	• Has overall program responsibility for program profit/loss and operating income objectives. • Discusses and reviews the overall work effort, what resources will be needed, how long it will take, and determines the milestones that identify stages of completion. • Coordinates the WBS. • Coordinates resource estimates prepared by the respective organizations. • Coordinates cost estimates and proposals. • Coordinates final negotiated fee, terms, and conditions prior to contract signature. • Has overall program/project responsibility. • Monitors compliance with customer requests. • Coordinates with capture manager. • Coordinates with contracts manager.
Project controls manager	• Interfaces with PM in support of preparing the WBS/WBS dictionary/organizational breakdown structure (OBS)/responsibility assignment matrix (RAM) and program/proposal schedules and documentation to support cost estimating activities as required. • Prepares contract line item number (CLIN)/WBS/statement of work (SOW)/contract data requirements list (CDRL)/cross-reference tables to support cost estimating activities. • Participates in program management cost/price reviews and executive cost/price reviews. • Reviews and verifies all BOEs submitted by the PM to ensure compliance with estimating procedures. • Reviews and submits BOE package to the pricing specialist for cost proposal generation. • Prepares and obtains approval on business case, as required.
Cost estimating and cost analysis	• Has overall cost/price proposal responsibilities. • Single point of contact to the pricing organization. • Analyzes cost/price inputs from participating organizations for accuracy and completeness. • Analyzes customer request focusing on pricing instructions, pricing strategy, etc. • Monitors proposal schedule, compliance, reviews, and approvals.
Technical lead	• Overall technical point of contact. • Coordinates the WBS, SOW, OBS, and RAM with the PM. • Defines the specific work effort, what resources will be needed, how long it will take, and milestones that identify stages of completion. • Develops the BOE documentation. • Interfaces with purchasing related to outside purchased material and subcontracted work and services. • Submits BOE package to the project controls manager for review.

Table 2-2 Typical Roles and Responsibilities of a Cost Estimating and Pricing Team

Team Member	Roles/Responsibilities
Pricing specialist	• Analyzes customer request focusing on proposal pricing requirements, including CAS/Federal Acquisition Regulation (FAR) requirements, financial clauses, etc. • Ensures proper techniques and policies are applied to the cost/price proposal. • Ensures compliance with cost estimating system requirements. • Ensures current rates are utilized. • Interfaces with program/project manager to interpret WBS, resource data, obtain audit support documentation, etc. • Utilizes resource information for generating cost/price proposals. • Coordinates the business case process, prepares the financial data, and analyzes the data to determine if proposal price incorporates full cost recovery and normal profit margins. • Provides updated cost and pricing information to Contracts prior to and during negotiations, including revised proposals, as required. • Assists Contracts in fact-finding and negotiations with government contracting officers and auditors (Defense Contract Audit Agency [DCAA]/Defense Contract Management Agency [DCMA], etc.). • Coordinates the internal sweep to obtain internal certification for current, accurate, and complete data from cost proposal participants, when required. • Develops final contract pricing data for project accounting and permanent files.
Subcontracts manager	• Ensures current FAR policies and practices are applied to the cost proposal as it relates to outside purchased material and subcontracted work and services. • Works with the technical lead to ensure proper documentation and support of the outside vendor bill of materials and services and subcontractor summary by obtaining quotes for equipment, materials, and services specified in the BOE, seeking competition when available. • Performs small disadvantaged business analysis of outside purchased material and subcontracted work and services. • Maintains supporting documentation for outside purchased material and subcontracted work and services. • Performs vendor/subcontractor price or cost analysis, as required.
Contracts manager	• Serves as the authorized contractual representative. • Analyzes the request for proposal (RFP) and identifies any risk areas that may impact the cost estimating and pricing process (i.e., terms and conditions, CLIN structure, etc.) and generates responsive terms and conditions mitigating risks. • Participates in the cost/pricing review meetings in order to review the proposal for compliance with the RFP requirements and to become familiar with the proposal. • Assists in the pricing strategy through evaluation of weighted guidelines relative to profit objectives, as appropriate to the specific procurement. • Addresses specific pricing or other proposal issues. • Negotiates the contract or, for larger procurements, leads the fact-finding and negotiation team. • Executes final contract agreement and commits organization to contractual obligations.

These are intended to be brief descriptions of the functions that may be required to support bid/proposal development. Specific roles and responsibilities may vary dependent on the scope and scale of the project.

WHAT IS THE VALUE OF A WORK BREAKDOWN STRUCTURE?

The work breakdown structure (WBS) provides a framework for defining work functions, tasks, and product/service requirements to ensure complete planning for all cost elements. The WBS is the basic cost/management tool used to organize the elements and activities required to perform the specifications of the customer's request; it later becomes the tool for accumulating and recording incurred costs. The WBS resembles a family tree in which the top level represents the total project. Each lower element of the WBS defines the task to be accomplished (i.e., program/project management, hardware, software, etc.) in more detail. This detailing process continues until a level is reached in which the tasks to be performed become manageable under each WBS element, along with the appropriate statement of objective (SOO), performance work statement (PWS) or statement of work (SOW) paragraphs, participants, CLIN, and CDRL.

The WBS is usually prepared by the project manager and technical team members to meet customer requirements for presentation of work effort and cost/price proposal responses. The WBS is developed in conjunction with the master program schedule and other detailed schedules to define all work requirements to support product and service deliveries. Typically, the WBS follows MIL-STD 881B for government proposal requirements; however, individual customer requirements and preferences will prevail.

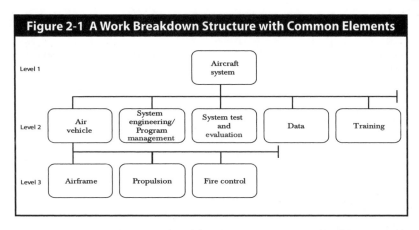

Figure 2-1 A Work Breakdown Structure with Common Elements

Source: Neil F. Albert, *Developing a Work Breakdown Structure* (McLean, VA.: MCR LLC, June 16, 2005).

The top-level WBS in Figure 2-1 encompasses the program as a whole. This WBS is typically developed by the program office. For a given piece of hardware, however, the contractor must also develop a WBS called a *contract WBS*. It defines the lower-level components of what is to be developed and procured and includes all the elements (hardware, software, data) that a contractor defines as its responsibility. The contract WBS forms the framework for the contractor's EVM control system.

HOW DO YOU BREAK DOWN AND TRACK CONTRACT COSTS?

To support the development of cost estimates and provide adequate visibility and coverage of pricing data, depending on the size of the contract, the customer request may need to be further segmented into the following basic elements:

- Statement of work (SOW) or performance work statement (PWS)
- Work breakdown structure (WBS)
- Contract line item number (CLIN)
- Contract data requirements list (CDRL)

This contract segmentation and identification will ensure, as necessary, that cost reporting data is traceable to the customer requirements and that pricing reports can be generated for internal management and customer review and for proposal evaluations (see Table 2-3).

Table 2-3 Sample PWS or SOW/WBS/CLIN/CDRL Matrix

Performance Work Statement (PWS) or Statement of Work (SOW)	Work Breakdown Structure (WBS)		Contract Line Item Number (CLIN)	Contract Data Requirement List (CDRL)
Task Description	WBS Level	WBS Description	Title/Description	Title DD1423 Form
	1	1.0 Develop a Spatial Optical Scanning System		
Develop and Deliver a Spatial Optical Scanning System (SOW Paragraph 3.0)	2	1.1 Design a Spatial Optical Scanning System		
	3	1.1.1 Conduct a Preliminary Design	CLIN 0001AA Conduct a Preliminary Design Review (PDR)	Deliver a Preliminary Design Review Report
	4	1.1.1.1 Develop a Preliminary Design		

WHAT ARE DESIGN-TO-COST/TARGET ALLOCATIONS?

Prior to preparation of detailed estimates, cost targets are established at the total program level, major functional level, and to the extent possible, at the WBS task level. Factors and considerations that will support the preparation of cost targets are as follows:

- Analysis of historical cost performance data on programs with similar products and services requirements
- Complexity of program specifications and requirements
- Schedule requirements
- Learning/staffing curves
- Programmatic and technical judgment

Cost targets should be established through a combined effort of technical managers, program/project management, cost estimating and pricing, contracts management, and other organizations as needed to provide a yardstick to support pricing strategy development and effective cost estimating efforts.

WHAT ARE SOME OF THE KEY ACQUISITIONS-RELATED PLANS THAT IMPACT COST ESTIMATES?

Cost estimating and proposal development efforts require various support plans for successful execution, including:

- Outsourcing make-or-buy plans
- Subcontractor source selection plan
- Small business subcontracting plan

OUTSOURCING MAKE-OR-BUY PLANS—KEY ITEMS

1. **Introduction/requirements:** Make-or-buy plans are generated by the program/project manager as required by FAR and are intended to provide a decision method to analyze the most cost effective manner in which to provide major item products and/or services to the customer. Make-or-buy plans may be required, per FAR 15.407-2, for negotiated acquisitions of $10,000,000 or more, except for research and development (R&D) contracts with no anticipated significant follow-on production. Make-or-buy plans may be required for negotiated acquisitions under $10,000,000 if the contracting officer determines the information is necessary.

2. **Reference documents:** FAR Subpart 15.407-2–Make-or-Buy Programs.

3. **Major item description:** Major items are classified as those that require management review, due to their complexity, cost, high quantity, or need for additional facilities. They do not normally include items of value less than 15 percent of anticipated contract value, raw materials, commercial products, or off-the-shelf items. Items of value less than $500,000, of an experimental nature, or not for sale to the customer do not require make-or-buy decisions.

4. **Must-make items:** Must-make items are defined as those that are regularly manufactured or provided by the contractor and are not available from any other firm at a similar or lower price.

5. **Must-buy items:** Must-buy items are those that are not regularly made by the contractor or are available from other firms at a lower price.

6. **Can-make-or-buy items:** All other major items or work can be either "make" or "buy" items.

7. **Make recommendations:** Items will normally be "make" items if they are:
   - The contractor's designed and manufactured product

- The contractor's proprietary design
- New technical or manufacturing art
- Prototype manufacture of the contractor's design
- Items for which outside suppliers cannot meet specialized specification or performance requirements

8. **Buy recommendations:** Items will normally be "buy" items if they are:
   - Non-contractor's design
   - Not normally manufactured by the contractor
   - An adaptation of a commercial product
   - Outside supplier proprietary design
   - Items for which the contractor cannot meet specialized requirements

9. **Justification and documentation for each major item:** The outsourcing make- or-buy plan provides justification and requires documentation for the make-or-buy decision for each major item. This justification includes the following topics:
   - Nature of the item
   - New facilities required (government or contractor)
   - Make/buy history for similar items
   - Potential subcontractors
   - Opportunities for small, small disadvantaged, and woman-owned small businesses
   - Future requirements
   - Tooling/startup costs
   - Technical superiority
   - Availability of personnel and materials
   - Basis of estimate

Subcontract Source Selection Plan—Key Items

The subcontract manager, working with the capture team, uses the customer's request for proposal (RFP), along with the approved make-or-buy plan, to determine source selection. This allows the contractor to plan, manage, and control the selection process to determine potential sources for materials and services. The function of the subcontract source selection is to minimize misunderstandings regarding selection criteria and nonresponsive bids. It contains the following elements:

- List of deliverables and due dates
  - Hardware
  - Software
  - Data
  - Services
- List of qualified bidders, as determined by:
  - Previous subcontractors
  - Subcontractor surveys
  - Requests for information
  - Supplier management files
  - On-site audits
- Statement of contract type and award/incentive provisions
  - Source selection organization
  - Source selection schedule
  - Ground rules for conduct during evaluation
  - Evaluation and scoring criteria

SMALL BUSINESS SUBCONTRACTING PLAN

All government contractors are required to give maximum consideration to small business concerns, veteran-owned small business concerns, service-disabled veteran-owned small business concerns, HUBZone small business concerns, small disadvantaged business concerns, and woman-owned small business concerns. The Small Business Subcontracting Plan addresses goals for allocations of planned purchases to these business concerns. Goals for subcontracting plans are developed by the capture team in conjunction with the supplier management group and provides to contracts management for incorporation into the proposal or contract, as appropriate and as required.

Who is responsible for preparing the key support plans?

- **Program/project management:** Prepare make-or-buy plan with input from supporting organizations and identify major items. Prepare source selection plans and support supplier management in source selection.
- **Project controls management:** Develop goals, with input from supplier management group, for the Small Business Subcontracting Plan and provide to contracts management.
- **Supplier management group:** Provide information relating to potential and actual "buy" items for use in make-or-buy decisions. Implement source selections. Evaluate bills of material to identify opportunities for subcontracting with small business concerns, veteran-owned small business concerns, service-disabled veteran-owned small business concerns, HUBZone small business concerns, small disadvantaged business concerns, and woman-owned small business concerns. Provide input to the project controls manager for preparation of the Small Business Subcontracting Plan submission.
- **Cost estimating and pricing:** Verify that all "buy" items are identified as such in the bill of material, and verify that all "make" items are identified as such in the bill of material.
- **Contract management:** Determine RFP and contractual requirements regarding preparation of the Small Business Subcontracting Plan and advise project controls management.

What is the value of industry conducting a cost/price proposal kickoff meeting?

When applicable, the purpose of the cost/price proposal kickoff meeting is to present pre-proposal planning information to cost proposal development and management personnel and to initiate resource-estimating activities performed by all functional organizations. This meeting is normally held in conjunction with (or directly following) a proposal kickoff (for technical and management proposals), with the objective of establishing an understanding of the customer request, basic approach, proposal responsibilities, and schedule.

The cost/price proposal manager, supported by the cost/price proposal team, has the lead responsibility for initiating the cost/price proposal kickoff meeting. Basis of estimate review is normally provided at this meeting. Participants typically include cost/price proposal management, project/program management, cost estimating and pricing, finance, contract management, and supplier management, as appropriate. Other presentation data, which will initiate resource-estimating activities, are prepared prior to the meeting. Understanding of functional responsibilities and schedule for proposal responses, reviews, and approvals for all participants are generated from this meeting.

WHAT ARE SOME OF THE U.S. GOVERNMENT AUDITOR'S CRITERIA FOR COST ESTIMATING?

Government auditors use criteria as benchmarks for how well a program is performing. Criteria provide auditors with a context for what is required, what the program's state should be, or what it was expected to accomplish. Criteria are the laws, regulations, policies, procedures, standards, measures, expert opinions, or expectations that define what should exist. When auditors conduct an audit, they should base their selection of criteria on whether they are reasonable, attainable, and relevant to the program's objectives. Criteria include the:

- purpose or goals prescribed by law or regulations or set by the audited entity's officials;
- policies and procedures established by the audited entity's officials;
- technically developed norms or standards;
- expert opinions;
- earlier performance;
- performance in the private sector; and
- best practices of leading organizations.

HOW DO AUDITORS DETERMINE COST DATA RELIABILITY?

For cost estimates, auditors must confirm that at a minimum, internal quality control checks show that the data are reliable and valid. To do this, they must have source data and must estimate the rationale for each cost element to verify that:

- the parameters (or input data) used to create the estimate are valid and applicable;
- labor costs include a time-phased breakdown of labor hours and rates;
- the calculations for each cost element are correct and the results make sense;

- the program cost estimate is an accurate total of subelement costs; and
- escalation was properly applied to account for differences in the prices of goods and services over time.

WHAT ARE SOME COMMON SOURCES OF DATA?

Since all cost estimating methods are data-driven, analysts must know the best data sources. Table 2-4 lists some basic sources. Analysts should use primary data sources whenever possible. Primary data are obtained from the original source, can usually be traced to an audited document, are considered the best in quality, and are ultimately the most useful. Secondary data are derived rather than obtained directly from a primary source. Because they are derived, and thus changed, from the original data, their overall quality is lower and less useful. In many cases, secondary data are actual data that have been "sanitized" to obscure their proprietary nature. Without knowing the details, such data will be of little use.

Table 2-4 Basic Primary and Secondary Data Sources		
Data Type	Primary	Secondary
Basic accounting records	X	
Data collection input forms	X	
Cost reports	X	X
Historical databases	X	X
Interviews	X	X
Program briefs	X	X
Subject matter experts	X	X
Other organizations	X	X
Technical databases	X	X
Contracts or contractor estimates		X
Cost proposals		X
Cost studies		X
Focus groups		X
Research papers		X
Surveys		X

Source: Government Accountability Office, *Cost Assessment Guide: Best Practices for Estimating and Managing Program Costs*, GAO-07-1134SP. (Washington, DC: July 2007).

WHAT ARE SOME OF THE COMMON SOFTWARE RISKS THAT AFFECT COST AND SCHEDULE?

Table 2-5 Common Software Risks That Affect Cost and Schedule	
Risk	**Typical Cost and Schedule Elements**
Sizing and technology	• Overly optimistic software engineers tending to underestimate the amount of code needed • Poor assumptions on the use of reused code (which requires no modifications) or adapted code (which requires some redesign, recoding, and retesting) • Vague or incomplete requirements, leading to uncertain size counts • Not planning for additional effort associated with commercial off-the-shelf software (e.g., systems engineering, performance testing, developing glue code)
Complexity	• Programming language: the amount of design, coding, and testing (e.g., object-oriented languages require more up-front design but result in less coding and testing) • Applications: software purpose and reliability (e.g., criticality of failure, loss of life) • Hardware limitations with respect to the need for more efficient code • Number of modules affecting integration effort • Amount of new code to be developed • Higher quality requiring more development and testing but resulting in less and easier-to-perform maintenance
Capability	• A developer with better skill, resulting in more effective software with fewer defects, allowing for faster software delivery • Optimistic assumption that a new development tool will increase productivity • Optimistic assumption about a developer's productivity, leading to cost growth, even if sizing is accurate • Geographically dispersed development locations, making communication and coordination more difficult
Management and executive oversight	• Management's dictation of an unrealistic schedule • A decision to concurrently develop hardware and software, increasing risk • Incorporating a new method, language, tool, or process for the first time • Incomplete or inaccurate definition of system requirements • Not handling creeping requirements proactively • Inadequate quality control, causing delays in fixing unexpected defects • Unanticipated risks associated with commercial off-the-shelf software upgrades and lack of support
Source: Government Accountability Office, *Cost Assessment Guide: Best Practices for Estimating and Managing Program Costs*, GAO-07-1134SP. (Washington, DC: July 2007).	

WHAT QUESTIONS SHOULD YOU ASK FOR CHECKING THE ACCURACY OF COST ESTIMATING METHODS?

Table 2-6 Questions for Checking the Accuracy of Cost Estimating Methods	
Cost Estimating Methods	**Questions**
Analogy	• What heritage programs and scaling factors were used to create the analogy? • Are the analogous data from reliable sources? • Did technical experts validate the scaling factor? • Can any usual requirements invalidate the analogy? • Are the parameters used to develop an analogous factor similar to the program being estimated? • How were adjustments made to account for differences between existing and new systems? Were the adjustments logical, credible, and acceptable?
Engineering build-up	• Was each WBS cost element defined in enough detail to use this method correctly? • Are data adequate to accurately estimate the cost of each WBS element? • Were experienced experts relied on to determine a reasonable cost estimate? • Was the estimate based on specific quantities that would be ordered at one time, allowing for quantity discounts? • Did the estimate account for contractor material handling overhead? • Is there a definitive understanding of each WBS cost element's composition? • Were labor rates based on auditable sources? Did they include all applicable overhead, general and administrative costs, and fees? Were they consistent with industry standards? • Is a detailed and accurate materials and parts list available?
Technical consensus	• Do quantitative historical data back up the expert opinion? • How did the estimate account for the possibility that bias influenced the results?
Weighted average	• Were cost reports used for extrapolation validated as accurate? • Was the cost element at least 25% complete before using its data as an extrapolation? • Were functional experts consulted to validate the reported percentage as complete? • Were contractors interviewed to ensure the cost data's validity? • Were recurring and nonrecurring costs separated to avoid double counting? • How were first unit costs of the learning curve determined? What historical data were used to determine the learning curve slope? • Were recurring and nonrecurring costs separated when the learning curve was developed? • How were partial units treated in the learning curve equation? • Were production rate effects considered? • How were production break effects determined?
Parametric analysis	• Was a valid statistical relationship, or CER, between historical costs and programs, physical, and performance characteristics established? • How logical is the relationship between key cost drivers and cost? • Was the CER used to develop the estimate validated and accepted? • How old are the data in the CER database? Are they still relevant for the program being estimated? • Do the independent variables for the program fall within the CER data range? • What is the level of variation in the CER? How well does the CER explain the variation, and how much of the variation does the model not explain? • Do any outliers affect the overall fit? • How significant is the relationship between cost and its independent variables? • How well does the CER predict costs?

Source: Government Accountability Office, *Cost Assessment Guide: Best Practices for Estimating and Managing Program Costs*, GAO-07-1134SP. (Washington, DC: July 2007).

WHAT DOES A SAMPLE COST ANALYSIS FORM LOOK LIKE?

Figure 2-2 Sample Cost Analysis Form

Cost Analysis for
(Company Name) / (Program Description)

	Proposed			Technical		Auditor Recommended			Negotiated			Notes
	Hours	Rate	Value	Hours	Value	Hours	Rate	Value	Hours	Rate	Value	
Material												1
Direct Labor												2
Factory												3
Engineering Labor												4
Engineering Lead												5
ODC												6
G&A Total Cost												7
Profit												8
Cost of Money												9
Total Price												10

Signature _____ Date _____

HOW DO THE THREE MOST COMMONLY USED COST ESTIMATING METHODS COMPARE TO EACH OTHER?

Table 2-7 Three Most Commonly Used Cost Estimating Methods Compared

Method	Strength	Weakness	Application
Analogy	• Requires few data • Based on actual data • Reasonably quick • Good audit trail	• Subjective adjustments • Accuracy depends on similarity of items • Difficult to assess effect of design change • Blind to cost drivers	• When few data are available • Rough order of magnitude estimate • Cross-check
Engineering build-up	• Easily audited • Sensitive to labor rates • Tracks vendor quotes • Time-honored	• Requires detailed design • Slow and laborious • Cumbersome	• Production estimating • Software development • Negotiations
Parametric	• Reasonably quick • Encourages discipline • Good audit trail • Objective, little bias • Cost driver visibility • Incorporates real-world effects (funding, technical, risk)	• Lacks detail • Model investment • Cultural barriers • Need to understand model's behavior	• Budgetary estimates • Design-to-cost trade studies • Cross-check • Baseline estimate • Cost goal allocations

Source: Government Accountability Office, *Cost Assessment Guide: Best Practices for Estimating and Managing Program Costs,* GAO-07-1134SP. (Washington, DC: July 2007).

SUMMARY

In retrospect, this chapter included a comprehensive discussion of the fundamentals of cost estimating using a practical question-and-answer approach. In the next chapter, we will provide you a detailed understanding of the U.S. government's Cost Accounting Standards: what they are, when they apply, and how they work.

QUESTIONS TO CONSIDER

1. How well trained/educated are you in cost estimating?

2. How well does your organization develop cost estimating skills or competencies within their employees?

3. On a scale of 1 to 10 (1 = low/poor performance; 10 = high/ outstanding performance), how would you rate your organization's capability of developing timely and accurate cost estimates?

4. What do you believe are your organization's key strengths and challenges in cost estimating?

ENDNOTES

[1] Government Accountability Office, *Cost Assessment Guide: Best Practices for Estimating and Managing Program Costs*, GAO-07-1134SP (Washington, DC: July 2007), 27.

[2] Ibid., 15.

CHAPTER 3

COST ACCOUNTING STANDARDS

INTRODUCTION

When the U.S. government decides (1) a contract contains a great deal of risk, (2) the requirements are very difficult to adequately determine prior to the start of the work, and (3) a typical fixed-price type pricing arrangement is not suitable, then it may agree to a cost-reimbursement type of contract. The basic government obligation under a cost-reimbursement contract is to reimburse the contractor for certain specified costs it incurs in the performance of the work. Simply stated, costs that are reimbursed are deemed "allowable" costs, and costs that are not reimbursed by the government are deemed "unallowable" costs.

The primary contractual provisions describing allowable and unallowable costs are portions of procurement regulations incorporated by reference into government contracts. Those regulations are most commonly referred to as *cost principles*. The cost principles are sometimes supplemented by *advance agreements* specifically tailored for certain contracts.[1] For contracts that are subject to the Cost Accounting Standards (CAS), contractors must adhere to certain accounting methods. Thus, for many U.S. government contracts, whether or not a contractor's costs will be reimbursed depends on how effectively the contractor has followed and implemented the required CAS accounting methods. This chapter discusses the applicability of CAS to federal government prime contractors, both large and small businesses, and subcontractors; reviews the standard format of the CAS; and then reviews the title, purpose, and requirements of each cost accounting standard.

Public Law 100-679 (41 U.S.C. 422) requires certain contractors and subcontractors to comply with CAS. Contracts and subcontracts that are exempt from CAS include:

- Sealed bid contracts
- Negotiated contracts and subcontracts not in excess of $550,000 (an order from one business segment to another business segment is considered a subcontract)
- Contracts and subcontracts with small businesses
- Contracts and subcontracts with foreign governments or their agents or instrumentalities
- Contracts and subcontracts in which the price is set by law or regulation

- Contracts and subcontracts in which the price is based on established catalog or market prices of commercial items sold in substantial quantities to the general public
- Subcontractors under the NATO PHM Ship program performed outside the United States
- Contracts and subcontracts to be executed and performed entirely outside the United States, its territories, and possessions
- Firm-fixed-price contracts and subcontracts awarded without submission of any cost data

While small businesses are exempt from all provisions of CAS, government representatives often try to incorporate the provisions of CAS into contracts with small business contractors. Understand what triggers modified or full CAS and take steps to assure compliance when these thresholds are reached.

Generally, all other contracts and subcontracts are either fully or partially subject to CAS.

Full coverage requires a contractor to comply with all 19 of the cost accounting standards that are in effect on the date of the contract award, and with any CAS that become applicable because of later award of a CAS-covered contract. Full CAS applies when:

- a contractor receives a single CAS-covered contract award of $50 million or more; or
- a contractor receives $50 million or more in net CAS-covered awards during its preceding cost accounting period.

Modified coverage requires a contractor to comply with CAS 401, Consistency in Estimating, Accumulating, and Reporting Costs; CAS 402, Consistency in Allocating Costs Incurred for the Same Purpose; CAS 405, Accounting for Unallowable Costs; and CAS 406, Cost Accounting Period. Modified CAS applies:

- to a covered contract of less than $50 million awarded to a business unit that received less than $50 million in net CAS-covered awards in the immediately preceding cost accounting period; and
- if any one contract is awarded with modified CAS coverage, all CAS-covered contracts awarded to that business unit during that cost accounting period must also have modified coverage; however, if the business unit receives a single CAS contract

award of $50 million or more, that contract must be subject to full CAS coverage, and any covered contract awarded in the same cost accounting period must also be subject to full CAS coverage.

Companies that are eligible for modified coverage should elect (i.e., check the solicitation response at FAR 52.230-1 entitled Cost Accounting Standards–Eligibility for Modified Contract Coverage) modified coverage in response to contract solicitations. In the absence of such a response the contract may be covered by all standards.

The cost accounting standards all follow a standard format and may be grouped into five categories:
1. Consistency in cost accounting, 401 and 402;
2. Allocation concepts, 403, 406, 410, 418, and 420;
3. Fixed asset accounting, 404, 409, 414, and 417;
4. Compensation of personnel, 408, 412, 413, and 415; and
5. Other, 405, 407, 411, and 416.

Contractors should implement an internal system of tracking all contracts that contain the CAS clause, FAR 52.230-2, Cost Accounting Standards. Such tracking should include the contract number, award date, contract value, and type of contract. Contractors should routinely monitor themselves against the CAS criteria previously discussed.

STANDARD FORMAT OF THE CAS

Purpose–Consistency and comparability of accounting information

Definitions—All contained in 48 CFR 9903.301

A. Prominent terms in fundamental requirement
B. Terms unique to particular standards
C. All terms in subpart 9903.301 apply to every standard

THREE

Fundamental Requirements

A. Broad principles or practices
B. Concepts of the standards

Techniques for Application

A. Criteria for selecting among alternatives
B. Narrow options
C. Special circumstances for applying fundamental requirements
D. Not structured consistently from standard to standard

Illustrations

A. Use only one issue
B. Constructed to give a narrative, a statement it does or does not comply, and what must be done to comply

Exemptions and Effective Date

A. Exemptions, if any
B. Effective date (all standards are now effective)
C. Conditions that trigger applicability

Supplement–Preambles (also called Prefatory Comments). Not enforceable as part of standard.

Rationale for What CASB Did or Did Not Do

A. Factors leading to a specific provision
B. Provides informal interpretations of meaning[2]

CAS 401 applies to the entire cost accounting system, meaning that every portion of the cost accounting system should be consistently applied.

CAS 401		
Title	**Purpose**	**Requirement**
Consistency in Estimating, Accumulating, and Reporting Costs	To ensure that the contractor's practices used in estimating costs for a proposal are consistent with cost accounting practices used to accumulate and report costs. Consistency will: • increase the likelihood that comparable transactions are treated alike; and • facilitate preparation of reliable cost estimates and their comparison with the costs of performance. Comparison, in turn, will: • provide a basis for financial control over costs; • aid in establishing accountability; and • provide a basis for evaluating estimating capabilities.	The contractor's practices used in estimating costs in pricing a proposal shall be consistent with its cost accounting practices used in accumulating and reporting costs. Cost accounting practices must be consistent in regard to the following areas: • classification of elements or functions of costs as direct or indirect; • the indirect cost pools to which each element or function of costs charged or proposed to be charged; and • methods of allocating indirect costs to the contract.
Comment: Applies under modified and full coverage. 48 CFR 9904.401		

CAS 402 is a total system standard. Throughout the cost accounting system, like costs in like circumstances should be treated the same.

CAS 402		
Title	**Purpose**	**Requirement**
Consistency in Allocating Costs Incurred for the Same Purpose	Requires that each type of cost be allocated only once and on only one basis to any contract or other cost objective. Criteria for determining the allocation of costs to a product, contract, or other cost objective should be the same for all similar objectives. The standard helps prevent overcharging and double-counting.	No final cost objective shall have any cost allocated as an indirect cost, if other costs incurred for the same purpose, in like circumstances, have been included as a direct cost of that or any other final cost objective, and vice versa. Equally applicable to estimates of costs to be incurred as used in contract proposals.
Comment: Applies under modified and full coverage. 48 CFR 9904.402		

CAS 403 applies to home office costs that typically flow into the general and administrative (G&A) indirect cost pool.

CAS 403		
Title	**Purpose**	**Requirement**
Allocation of Home Office Expenses to Segments	To establish criteria for allocation of the expenses of a home office to the segments based on the beneficial or causal relationship between such expenses and the receiving segments through: • identification of expenses for direct allocation of segments to the maximum extent practical; • accumulation of significant non-directly allocated expenses into logical and relatively homogeneous pools to be allocated on bases reflecting the relationship of the expenses to the segments; and • allocation of any remaining office expenses to all segments.	Home office expense shall be allocated on the basis of the beneficial or causal relationship between supporting and receiving activities. 　Centralized service functions, if not directly allocable, shall be allocated to segments on the basis of service furnished to or received by each segment. (For example, centralized purchasing could be allocated by the number or value of orders for each segment). 　Staff or line management, if not directly allocable, shall be allocated using bases representative of total activity being managed (e.g., manufacturing costs for manufacturing management). 　Central payment or accruals such as pension expenses, if not directly allocable, shall be allocated using an allocation base representative of the factors on which the total payment is based, such as payroll. 　Staff management such as the chief financial officer shall be allocated on a base representative of the segment's total activity.
Comment: Applies under full coverage only. 48 CFR 9904.403		

CAS 404 and 409 deal with the capitalization of fixed asset costs and the resulting depreciation. These assets are retained, utilized, and charged to operations through the indirect cost pools, including G&A. Accordingly, we identify CAS 404 and 409 with the cost pools.

CAS 404		
Title	**Purpose**	**Requirement**

Capitalization of Tangible Assets	To facilitate the measurement of costs associated with tangible assets consistently over time.	Contractor must establish a reasonable and consistently followed policy. The policy shall designate economic and physical characteristics for capitalization of tangible assets. Policy must come within the following guidelines:
		• Term:
		  • Minimum service life, which shall not exceed 2 years, but may be a shorter period.
		  • Minimum acquisition cost criterion which shall not exceed $5,000 but which may be a smaller amount.
		• Contractor may designate other specific characteristics pertinent to capitalization policy.
		• Contractor's policy shall provide for identification of assets to the maximum extent practical.
		
		Costs incurred which result in extending the life or increasing the productivity of an asset and meet the criteria of the capitalization policy shall be capitalized. (Repair and maintenance are period costs.)

Comment: Applies under full coverage only. 48 CFR 9904.404		

CAS 409		
Title	**Purpose**	**Requirement**
Depreciation of Tangible Capital Assets	To provide a systematic and rational flow of the costs of tangible assets to benefited cost objectives over the expected service lives of the assets.	Depreciable cost shall be assigned to cost accounting periods. • The depreciable cost shall be its capitalized costs less estimated residual value; • Estimated service life shall be used to determine the accounting periods to which the depreciation cost will be assigned; • The method of depreciation shall reflect the pattern of consumption of services over the life of the asset; and • The gain or loss recognized upon disposition shall be assigned to the period in which disposition occurs. Annual depreciation cost shall be allocated to cost objectives. • Cost may be charged directly to the cost objective if charges are made on the basis of usage and only if costs of all like assets used for similar purposes are charged in the same manner; • Where tangible capital assets function as an organizational unit whose costs are charged to other cost objectives based on measurement of the services provided by the organizational unit; • If not allocated in #1 or #2, costs should be included in an appropriate indirect cost pool; and • Gain or loss shall be allocated in the same manner as depreciation cost.

Comment: Applies under full coverage only. 48 CFR 9904.409

CAS 405 relates to identifying and segregating unallowable costs.

CAS 405		
Title	**Purpose**	**Requirement**

Accounting for Unallowable Costs	To facilitate the negotiation, audit, administration, and settlement of contracts by establishing guidelines covering:
	• identification of costs specifically described as unallowable, and
	• the cost accounting treatment to be accorded such identified unallowable costs.
	Note: Unallowable costs are determined by contracts and applicable procurement regulations and statutes, including:
	• entertainment;
	• legislative lobbying;
	• defense of civil or criminal fraud;
	• fines or penalties;
	• membership in social, dining, or country clubs;
	• alcoholic beverages;
	• contributions or donations;
	• advertising; and
	• promotional items.
		Costs expressly unallowable, or mutually agreed to be unallowable, shall be identified and excluded from any billing, claim, or proposal to the government.
		    Costs which become designated as unallowable as a result of contracting officer's written decision pursuant to disputes procedures shall be identified if included or used in the computation of any billing, claim, or proposal.
		    Costs directly associated with unallowable costs that would not have been incurred if not for the incurrence of the unallowable costs are also unallowable.
		    Costs of any project not contractually authorized shall be accounted for in a manner which allows ready separation from costs of authorized projects.
		    Where unallowable costs are normally part of a base(s) for the allocation of indirect expenses, the unallowable costs shall remain apart of the base(s).

Comment: Applies under modified and full coverage. 48 CFR 9904.405		

CAS 406 deals with applying a consistent 12-month accounting period, either a calendar or fiscal year.

CAS 406		
Title	**Purpose**	**Requirement**
Cost Accounting Period	To provide criteria for the selection of the time periods to be used as cost accounting periods. To reduce the effects of variations in the flow of costs within each cost accounting period. To enhance objectively, consistency, verifiability, uniformity, and comparability in contract cost measurements.	Contractor shall use its fiscal year as cost accounting period, except that: • Costs of an indirect function which exists for only a part of a cost accounting period may be allocated to cost objectives of that same part of the period. • An annual period other than the fiscal year can be used if mutually agreed upon and consistently followed by the contractor for managing and controlling its business, and appropriate accruals, deferrals, or other adjustments are made with respect to such annual period. • A transitional period other than a year (not to exceed 15 months) may be used when a change in fiscal year occurs. The same cost accounting period shall be used for accumulating costs in an indirect cost pool as for establishing its allocation base.
Comment: Applies under modified and full coverage. 48 CFR 9904.406		

CAS 407 applies to the use of a standard cost system, specifically labor and material.

CAS 407		
Title	**Purpose**	**Requirement**
Use of Standard Costs for Direct Material and Direct Labor	To improve cost measurement and cost assignment for contractors that choose to use a "standard" type accounting system.	Standard costs may be used for estimating, accumulating, and reporting costs of direct material and direct labor when: • standard costs are entered into the books of the account; • standard costs and related variances are appropriately accounted for at the level of the production unit; and • practices regarding the setting and revision of standards, use of standard costs, and disposition of variances are stated in writing and are consistently followed.
Comment: Applies under full coverage only. 48 CFR 9904-407 Does not cover the use of pre-established measures solely for estimating.		

CAS 408 generally applies to costs within the indirect cost pools, including G&A.

CAS 408		
Title	**Purpose**	**Requirement**
Accounting for Costs of Compensated Personal Absence	To improve and provide uniformity in the measurement of costs of vacation, sick leave, holiday, and other compensated personal absence and increase the probability that the measured costs are allocated to the proper cost objectives.	The costs of compensated personal absence shall be assigned to the cost accounting period or periods in which the entitlement was earned. The costs of compensated personal absence for an entire cost accounting period shall be allocated pro rata on an annual basis among the final cost objectives of the period.
Comment: Applies under full coverage only. 48 CFR 9904.408		

CAS 410 deals with the allocation of G&A costs to final cost objectives.

CAS 410		
Title	**Purpose**	**Requirement**
Allocation of Business Unit General and Administrative Expenses to Final Cost Objectives	To provide criteria for the allocation of business unit G&A expenses to business final cost objectives based on their beneficial or causal relationship. To increase the likelihood of achieving objectivity in the allocation expenses to final cost objectives and comparability of cost data among contractors in similar circumstances.	Business unit G&A expenses shall be grouped in a separate indirect cost pool which shall be allocated only to final cost objectives. The G&A expense pool shall be allocated by means of a cost input base which best represents the total activity of a typical cost accounting period (i.e., total cost input, value-added cost input, or single element cost input). Home office expenses received by a segment shall be included in its G&A expense pool. (Exceptions apply). Any costs that do not satisfy the definition of a G&A expense can remain in the G&A pool unless they can be allocated on a beneficial or causal relationship best measured by a base other than cost input.
Comment: Applies under full coverage only. 48 CFR 9904.410		

CAS 411 applies to the acquisition of materials.

CAS 411		
Title	**Purpose**	**Requirement**
Accounting for Acquisition Costs of Material	To improve the measurement and assignment of costs to cost objectives.	Contractor shall have, and consistently apply, written accounting policies for accumulating and allocating costs of material. Costs of units of a category of material may be allocated directly, provided the cost objective was specifically identified at time of purchase or production of units. Cost of material which is used solely in indirect functions or is not a significant element of production may be included in an indirect cost pool. (If significant, cost of indirect material not consumed shall be established as an asset at the end of the period.) Cost of a category of material shall be accounted for in material inventory records. Costing method for material issued from inventory shall be one of the following methods: FIFO, LIFO, weighted average, moving average, or standard cost.
Comment: Applies under full coverage only. 48 CFR 9904.411		

CAS 412 and 413 deal with pension costs.

CAS 412		
Title	**Purpose**	**Requirement**
Composition and Measurement of Pension Cost	To provide guidance for determining and measuring the components of pension costs. To enhance uniformity and consistency in accounting for pension costs and increase the probability that those costs are properly allocated to cost objectives.	Four components of defined-benefit plan costs: normal cost, part of any unfunded actuarial liability, interest equivalent on unamortized portion of liability, and adjustment for actuarial loss or gains. For defined-contribution plans, the cost is the net contribution required. For measurement of defined-benefit plan costs, an actuarial cost method is required to separately measure each of the four components listed above. Costs computed for a cost accounting period are only assignable to that period and are allocable to cost objectives to the extent that liquidation can be compelled or is actually effected.
Comment: Applies under full coverage only; however, the "Compensation for Personal Services" cost principle incorporates the standard by reference and requires compliance. 48 CFR 9904.412		

CAS 413		
Title	**Purpose**	**Requirement**
Adjustment and Allocation of Pension Cost	To enhance uniformity and consistency in accounting for pension costs. To provide guidance for adjusting pension cost by measuring actuarial gains and losses to cost accounting periods. To provide the basis on which to allocate pension cost to segments of an organization.	Actuarial gains and losses shall be calculated annually and shall be assigned to the cost accounting period for which the valuation is made and to subsequent periods. The value of all pension fund assets shall be determined under an asset valuation method which takes into account unrealized appreciation and depreciation of the market value of the assets in the pension fund. Pension cost shall be allocated to each segment having participants in a pension plan.
Comment: Applies under full coverage only; however, the "Compensation for Personal Services" cost principle incorporates the standard by reference and requires compliance. 48 CFR 9904.413		

CAS 414 and 417 are associated with the cost of capital relative to the net book value of fixed assets.

CAS 414		
Title	**Purpose**	**Requirement**
Cost of Money as an Element of the Cost of Facilities Capital	To improve cost measurement by providing for allocation of cost of contractor investment in facilities capital to negotiated contracts.	The investment base used in computing the cost of money for facilities capital shall be computed from accounting data used for contract cost purposes. The cost of money rate shall be based on rates determined by the Secretary of the Treasury pursuant to Public Law 92-41. The cost of capital committed to facilities shall be separately computed for each contract using facilities capital cost of money factors computed for each cost accounting period.

Comment: Applies under full coverage only; however, the "Cost of Money" cost principle requires compliance with this standard in order for cost of money to be allowable. 48 CFR 9904.414

CAS 417		
Title	**Purpose**	**Requirement**
Cost of Money as an Element of the Cost of Capital Assets under Construction	To improve cost measurement by providing recognition of cost of contractor investment in assets under construction. To provide greater uniformity in accounting of asset acquisition costs.	The cost of money applicable to the investment in tangible and intangible capital assets being constructed, fabricated, or developed for a contractor's own use shall be included in the capitalized acquisition cost of such assets. The cost of money rate shall be based on interest rates determined by the Secretary of the Treasury pursuant to Public Law 92-41. A representative investment amount shall be determined each period for each capital asset being contracted, fabricated, or developed giving appropriate consideration to the rate at which costs of construction are incurred.

Comment: Applies under full coverage only; however, the "Cost of Money" cost principle requires compliance with this standard in order for cost of money to be allowable. 48 CFR 9904.417

CAS 415 contains the criteria for accounting for deferred compensation, which generally flows through indirect cost pools, including G&A.

CAS 415		
Title	**Purpose**	**Requirement**
Accounting for the Cost of Deferred Compensation	To increase the probability that the cost of deferred compensation is allocated to cost objectives in a uniform and consistent manner.	The cost of deferred compensation shall be assigned to the cost accounting period in which the contractor incurs an obligation to compensate the employee. If no obligation is incurred prior to payment, the cost of deferred compensation shall be the amount paid and shall be assigned to the period in which payment is made. The measurement of the amount of cost shall be present value of future benefit to be paid by the contractor. The cost of each award (to each employee shall be considered separately unless a group basis can be measured with reasonable accuracy.
Comment: Applies under full coverage only; however, the "Compensation for Personal Services" cost principle incorporates the standard by reference and requires compliance. 48 CFR 9904.415		

CAS 416 also applies to costs in indirect cost pools, where most insurance costs are allocated.

CAS 416		
Title	**Purpose**	**Requirement**
Accounting for Insurance Costs	To increase the probability that insurance costs are allocated to cost objectives in a uniform and consistent manner.	The amount of insurance cost to be assigned to a cost accounting period is the projected average loss for the period plus insurance administration expenses. Any premium for purchased insurance shall be pro-rated among the periods covered by the policy unless the insurance was purchased specifically for and directly allocated to a final cost objective. The allocation of insurance costs to cost objectives shall be based on the beneficial or causal relationship.
Comment: Applies under full coverage only; however, the "Insurance and Indemnification" cost principle requires compliance with this standard for any contractor wishing to self-insure. 48 CFR 9904.416		

THREE

CAS 418 defines the criteria for determining and distributing indirect pool costs, except G&A.

CAS 418		
Title	**Purpose**	**Requirement**
Allocation of Direct and Indirect Costs	To improve classification of costs as either direct or indirect. To improve the allocation of indirect costs. To provide criteria for accumulating indirect costs into cost pools.	Written and consistently followed accounting policies required. Indirect costs shall be accumulated in homogeneous cost pools. Pooled costs shall be allocated to cost objectives in reasonable proportion to the beneficial or causal relationship as follows: • If cost pool costs consist of material amounts of management or supervision costs, the pool shall be allocated to a base representative of the activity being managed or supervised. • If management or supervision costs are not significant, the pool shall be allocated based on resource consumption measure.
Comment: Applies under full coverage only. 48 CFR 9904.418		

And last but not least, CAS 420 deals with the accounting for independent research and development (IR&D) and bid and proposal (B&P) costs.

CAS 420		
Title	**Purpose**	**Requirement**
Accounting for Independent Research and Development and Bid and Proposal Costs	To improve cost allocation of IR&D and B&P costs.	The basic unit for identification and accumulation of IR&D and B&P costs shall be the individual IR&D or B&P project. The individual project shall consist of all allocable costs except G&A. The IR&D and B&P cost pools shall consist of project costs and other allocable costs except G&A. The IR&D and B&P cost pools of a home office shall be allocated to segments based on a beneficial or causal relationship. IR&D and B&P cost pools of a business unit shall be allocated to the final cost objectives of that business unit based on beneficial or causal relationship. IR&D and B&P costs incurred in a cost accounting period shall not be assigned to any other period. (Exceptions apply to IR&D.)

Comment: Applies under full coverage only; however, the "IR&D and B&P" cost principle requires compliance with most of the standard. 48 CFR 9904.420.

Cost Allowability Factors

The cost principles contained in FAR Part 31 stipulate that for a cost to be allowable it must satisfy the following tests:

- *Reasonableness:* A cost is reasonable if, in nature and amount, it does not exceed that which would be incurred by a prudent person in the conduct of competitive business.
- *Allocability:* A cost is allocable if it is assignable or chargeable to one or more cost objectives on the basis of relative benefits received or other equitable relationship.

■ *Meets the Cost Accounting Standards (CAS:)* promulgated by the CAS Board if applicable; otherwise adheres to generally accepted accounting principles.
■ *Terms of the contract*
■ *Any limitations set forth*[3]

SUMMARY

In this chapter, we have discussed the basic requirements for the determination of whether a cost is deemed "allowable" or "unallowable" on a federal government contract; the applicability of the CAS to prime contractors and subcontractors; the standard format of the CAS; and the title, purpose, and requirements of each of the cost accounting standards. This is a relatively simple and high-level overview of a deep and complex topic area, filled with exceptions, deviations, and interpretations. It is intended to provide a framework for understanding, once costs are estimated, how they must be accounted for and reported in order to be deemed an allowable cost on a federal government contract or subcontract.

In Chapter 4, we will provide a comprehensive review of cost analysis tools and techniques.

QUESTIONS TO CONSIDER

1. How effectively does your organization segregate allowable costs from unallowable costs?

2. Do the contracts you currently work on require full CAS or modified CAS coverage?

3. How important is consistency in your cost estimating and cost accounting practices?

ENDNOTES

[1]   John Cibinic, Jr. and Ralph C. Nash, Jr., *Cost Reimbursement Contracting*, 3rd ed. (Chicago: CCH, 2006).

[2]   Charles Wilkins, "Cost Accounting Standards" (seminar, Market Access and FTI Consulting, Washington, DC, 2005).

[3]   Gregory A. Garrett, *Contract Negotiations: Skills, Tools, and Best Practices* (Chicago: CCH, 2005).

CHAPTER  4

COST ANALYSIS: TOOLS AND TECHNIQUES

INTRODUCTION

The purpose of cost estimating is to develop a fair and reasonable price. Although a fair and reasonable price is desired by both the buyer and the seller, the contracting parties define fair and reasonable differently, from their own perspective. The buyer may define a fair and reasonable price as the lowest price that must be paid to get the supply or service that is needed. For the seller, a fair and reasonable price may reflect the full cost to produce the supply or service, plus a reasonable profit. In determining a fair and reasonable price, price analysis, cost analysis, and profit analysis may be required. This chapter will discuss cost analysis tools and techniques. The next chapter will focus on profit analysis.

COST ANALYSIS

Cost analysis can be defined as the analysis of the various cost elements that make up the price of a supply or service. As stated in the previous chapters, price is made up of the various cost elements (such as labor, materials, overhead) and profit. Thus, cost analysis is a review of each element of cost and involves a "fair and reasonable" analysis of each cost element. The Department of Defense (DoD) defines cost analysis as:

> The review and evaluation of the separate cost elements and profit/fee in an offeror's or contractor's proposal (including cost or pricing data or information other than cost or pricing data) and the application of judgment used to determine how well the proposed costs represent what the cost of the contract should be, assuming reasonable economy and efficiency.[1]

The most common tools and techniques for conducting cost analysis include cost breakdown analysis, learning curves, economic order quantity, activity-based costing, and life-cycle costing.

COST BREAKDOWN ANALYSIS

The most common method of cost analysis is to perform a cost breakdown analysis. This can be done by developing a cost breakdown structure, which is used to break down the various elements of cost. As reflected in Figure 4-1, price is made up of cost plus profit. Within the cost component are the various cost elements that make up total cost. The most common cost elements include direct costs, such as labor, material, subcontracts, and other direct costs (ODC), and indirect costs, such as overhead and general and administrative expenses.

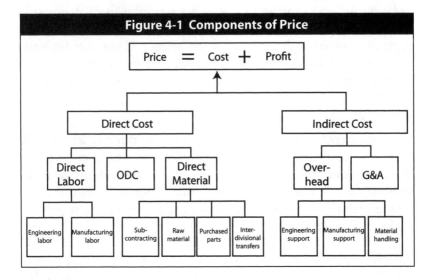

Figure 4-1 Components of Price

Labor

This cost element includes the different categories of labor (e.g., senior software engineer versus entry-level software engineer), the labor rate for each labor category, and the number of labor hours for each labor category. Labor costs are typically direct costs, meaning that they can be identified and allocated to a specific cost objective. Direct labor cost categories include direct engineering labor, direct manufacturing labor, and direct services labor.[2]

Material

This cost element includes the cost of materials used in the contracted effort. Material costs typically include raw materials, parts, subassemblies, components, and manufacturing supplies that actually become part of the product. Materials may also include collateral costs, such as freight and insurance.[3] Material costs can either be accounted for as direct or indirect costs, depending on the specific organization's accounting system. The major difference between direct materials and indirect materials is that direct material costs can be identified specifically with a final cost objective, whereas an indirect material cost is not directly identified with a single final cost objective but is identified with two or more final cost objectives or an intermediate cost objective.[4]

Subcontracts

Subcontract costs include those costs resulting from major subcontracted work that is part of the overall project. These costs are typically treated as direct costs to the project. These are typically large, unusual, or one-time costs that will benefit only the proposed contract and cost objective.

Overhead

Overhead costs are those costs that are not directly identifiable with a specific cost objective and cannot practically be assigned directly to a contract or project. Thus, overhead costs are typically indirect costs. There are different categories of overhead costs, which include engineering overhead, manufacturing overhead, and material overhead.

Another type of indirect costs are general and administrative (G&A) costs. G&A costs are management, financial, and other expenses related to the general management and administration of the business unit as a whole. To be considered a G&A expense of a business unit, the expenditure must be incurred by, or allocated to, the general business unit. Examples of G&A costs include salaries, staff services, and selling and marketing expenses.[5]

In conducting a cost breakdown analysis of labor, material, subcontracts, and overhead costs, a focus should be on the reasonableness of the estimated costs. A cost is determined reasonable if, in its nature and amount, it does not exceed what a prudent person would incur in the conduct of competitive business.[6] The DoD *Contract Pricing Reference Guides* list the following four questions that focus on determining the reasonableness of any estimated costs:

- Is the type of cost generally recognized as necessary in conducting business?
- Is the cost consistent with sound business practice, law, and regulation, and are purchases conducted on an "arm's-length" basis?
- Does the offeror's action reflect a responsible attitude toward the government, other customers, the owners of the business, the employees, and the public at large?
- Are the offeror's actions consistent with established practices?[7]

The answers to these questions should provide useful information to enable the analyst to make an informed determination, based on cost data and judgment, on the reasonableness of the estimated costs. Using a cost breakdown structure, you can perform a cost breakdown analysis by focusing on the major elements of cost, such as labor, material, subcontracts, and overhead.

LEARNING CURVE TECHNIQUE

The learning curve technique is a tool used to analyze and estimate direct labor hours, specifically manufacturing labor hours in contracts that are labor intensive. The learning curve theory states that "each time cumulative production doubles, the total manufacturing time and cost falls by a constant and predictable amount." The focus here is on the constant reduction in time required over successive doubled quantities of units produced, which is called the *rate of learning*.[8] The slope of the learning curve is the difference between 100 percent and the rate of learning.

The learning curve technique is based on the results of empirical studies that showed that the time required to perform a task decreases each time the task is repeated, the amount of improvement decreases as more units are produced, and the rate of improvement is consistent enough to allow it to be used as a prediction tool.[9]

The learning curve can be used in two different models—the cumulative average cost curve and the unit curve. The cumulative average cost curve plots cumulative units against the average cost or average hours required per unit for all units produced. The unit cost curve plots cumulative units produced against the actual hours required to produce each unit.[10]

Table 4-1 Learning Curve Illustration				
Units Produced	Labor Hours Per Unit at Doubled Quantities	Difference in Labor Hours Per Unit at Doubled Quantities	Rate of Learning (%)	Slope of Learning Curve (%)
1	100,000			
2	80,000	20,000	20	80
4	64,000	16,000	20	80
8	51,200	12,800	20	80
16	40,960	10,240	20	80
32	32,768	8,192	20	80

Source: Adapted from Department of Defense, *Contract Pricing Reference Guides,* Vol 2, Chapter 7. Accessed at http://www.acq.osd.mil/dpap/contractpricing/vol2chap7.htm.

As illustrated in Table 4-1, the first unit required 100,000 labor hours to produce. As the units produced doubles, the number of labor hours required to produce that doubled quantity is reduced by a constant rate, in this case 20 percent. Thus, the rate of learning is 20 percent, and the slope of the learning curve is 80 percent (100 percent minus the rate of learning). It should be noted that although the amount of labor-hour reduction between doubled quantities is constantly declining (20,000, then 16,000, then 12,800, and so on), the rate of learning remains constant at 20 percent.[11]

Kerzner discusses the following sources of learning that contribute to the learning curve theory. It should be noted that these sources of learning are interrelated and do not operate independently of each other. These sources of learning include labor efficiency; work specialization and methods improvement; new production processes; better- performing production equipment; changes in resource mix, product standardization or design; and incentives or disincentives.[12]

Before conducting a cost analysis using the learning curve method, you should first ensure that the specific situation is appropriate for its use. Some critical questions to ask in ensuring that the application of the learning curve is appropriate include:

- Is there a significant amount of manual labor involved in the production process?
- Is there an uninterrupted production process?
- Does the production process involve complex items?
- How extensive are major technological changes involved in the production process?
- Is there a continuous pressure to improve production efficiencies?[13]

ECONOMIC ORDER QUANTITY METHOD

The economic order quantity (EOQ) method generally is used for determining the procurement order size that will minimize the total cost of acquisition and carrying inventory. Thus, the total cost of acquisition and carrying inventory consists of the separate indirect acquisition costs and carrying costs.

The acquisition costs reflect the cost of acquiring the material, and the carrying costs reflect the cost of carrying the material in inventory. The EOQ concept states that the sum of all indirect costs associated with inventory will be minimized on an annual basis if the material is ordered in the quantity that corresponds with the lowest point on the total cost curve.[14]

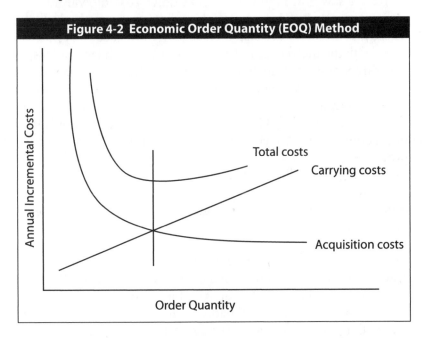

Figure 4-2 Economic Order Quantity (EOQ) Method

As illustrated in Figure 4-2, the economic order quantity is that quantity that corresponds with the lowest point on the total cost curve, which is also the point where the acquisition cost curve intersects with the carrying cost curve. Also reflected in Figure 4-2, quantities ordered in excess of the EOQ will result in carrying costs that exceed acquisition costs, and quantities ordered less than EOQ will result in acquisition costs that are higher than carrying costs.

Although the EOQ method is used for determining the optimum order quantity for inventories, it can also be used to determine the economic production lot sizes in a manufacturing operation. In addition, given the robustness of the EOQ model, this tool can be quite effective as part of a cost analysis on a contractor's cost proposal for production contracts. Some considerations that need to be addressed in using the EOQ model include the following:

1. Is the monthly demand for the supply constant throughout the year?
2. What is the lead time for the delivery of the supply?
3. Are quantity <u>discounts</u> included in the acquisition costs?

ACTIVITY-BASED COSTING TECHNIQUE

We previously stated that price consists of cost plus profit. In addition, we saw how Figure 4-1 breaks down cost into various cost elements, such as labor, materials, subcontracts, and overhead. These cost elements are classified as either direct costs or indirect costs, with the indirect costs being determined as a factor of a specific direct cost pool, such as direct labor. Indirect costs include such cost elements as engineering overhead, materials overhead, manufacturing overhead, and G&A. Typically, indirect costs represent approximately 30 to 40 percent of an organization's total production costs.[15] Back in the days when most manufacturing processes were labor intensive, indirect costs were traditionally derived from the direct labor cost pool. However, today, with labor costs accounting for approximately 10 percent of total costs, they are becoming less appropriate from which to determine indirect costs.[16]

Activity-based costing is a tool that is used to more accurately and realistically allocate indirect costs to their appropriate cost drivers. As illustrated in Figure 4-3, in activity-based costing, indirect costs, such as manufacturing overhead, are divided into cost pools that reflect the various activities that drive those costs, such as unit-level activities, batch-level activities, and product-level activities. By identifying and tracking the cost drivers behind indirect costs, activity-based costing not only enables a more accurate allocation of indirect costs, but it also allows the identification of any non-value- adding activities in the associated business processes. Once the non-value-adding activities are identified, they can then be eliminated or reduced. The use of activity-based costing is part of the overall activity-based management, which is focused on continuous improvement and business process reengineering.[17]

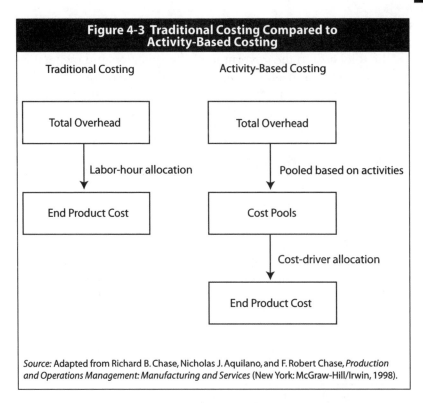

Figure 4-3 Traditional Costing Compared to Activity-Based Costing

Traditional Costing

Activity-Based Costing

Total Overhead

Labor-hour allocation

End Product Cost

Total Overhead

Pooled based on activities

Cost Pools

Cost-driver allocation

End Product Cost

Source: Adapted from Richard B. Chase, Nicholas J. Aquilano, and F. Robert Chase, *Production and Operations Management: Manufacturing and Services* (New York: McGraw-Hill/Irwin, 1998).

As today's organizations become more capital intensive and less labor intensive, the issue of indirect cost allocation continues to be a critical factor, especially when it comes to cost estimating and cost analysis. Even minor inaccuracies in overhead cost estimating can have a significant impact on total costs. In conducting an activity-based cost analysis, it is imperative that the analyst have a thorough understanding of the following:

■ The company's accounting system and the system used for estimating and allocating overhead costs.

■ The company's direct and indirect cost structure, as well as its overhead cost structure.

LIFE-CYCLE COSTING METHOD

The Department of Defense's push for acquisitions based on best value, and not necessarily based on lowest price, has increased the emphasis on life-cycle costing. Life-cycle costing focuses on the total cost of a system or service over its entire life cycle. The Department of Defense defines a system's life-cycle as "all phases of the system's life including research, development, test, and evaluation (RDT&E), production, deployment (inventory), operations and support (O&S), and disposal." The DoD defines life-cycle cost as "the total cost to the government of acquisition and ownership of a system over its useful life. It includes the cost of development, acquisition, operations, and support (to include manpower), and where applicable, disposal."[18] Figure 4-4 illustrates the DoD's composition of life-cycle costs.

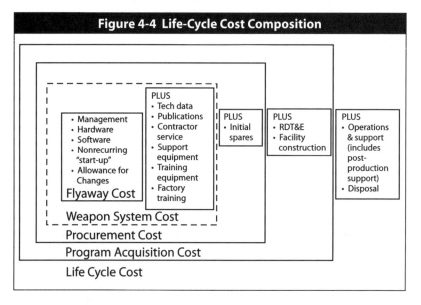

Figure 4-4 Life-Cycle Cost Composition

As can be seen from Figure 4-4, a DoD weapon systems life-cycle cost is composed of *weapon system cost* (which includes flyaway cost plus tech data, publications, contractor service, support equipment, training equipment, and factory training), *procurement cost* (which includes initial spares), *program acquisition cost* (which includes RDT&E and facility construction), plus operations and support, which includes post-production support and disposal.

The importance of using a life-cycle perspective becomes clear once we realize the significance of the operations and support costs in terms of the total life-cycle costs of a typical DoD acquisition program. Figure 4-5 illustrates that only approximately 28 percent of a system's total life-cycle cost is derived from the actual acquisition cost (RDT&E and production), while the remaining 72 percent of total life-cycle costs are incurred during the O&S and disposal phases of the system's life cycle.

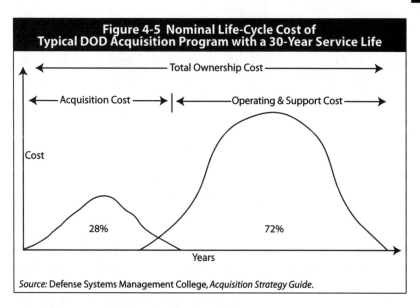

Figure 4-5 Nominal Life-Cycle Cost of Typical DOD Acquisition Program with a 30-Year Service Life

Source: Defense Systems Management College, *Acquisition Strategy Guide.*

In addition, the significance of focusing on life-cycle costs also becomes clear when we see that a system's life-cycle costs are determined early in its life cycle. As can be seen in Figure 4-6, approximately 85 percent of a system's total life-cycle cost is determined once the requirement has been set and the design has been established. Figure 4-6 illustrates that although minimal costs have actually been *spent* at the requirements phase of the acquisition process, approximately 85 percent of total life-cycle costs have already been *determined* by this phase.

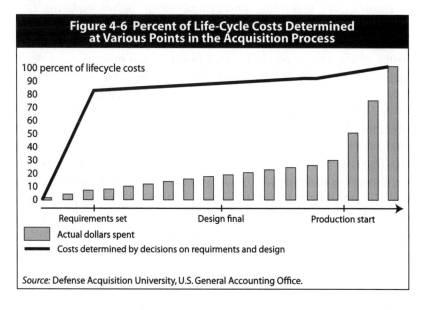

Figure 4-6 Percent of Life-Cycle Costs Determined at Various Points in the Acquisition Process

Source: Defense Acquisition University, U.S. General Accounting Office.

Life-cycle cost analysis has been defined as "the systematic ana-lytical process of evaluating various alternative courses of action early on in a project, with the objective of choosing the best way to employ scarce resources."[19] Thus, life-cycle analysis includes evaluating alternative design configurations, manufacturing pro-cesses, operations concepts, and logistics support options. Kerzner identifies the following steps in conducting a life-cycle analysis:

1. Define the problem to determine the information needed.
2. Define the requirements of the cost model being used.
3. Collect historical cost relationship data.
4. Develop life-cycle estimate and test results.[20]

Obviously, trying to estimate the cost of a system during its entire life cycle entails a lot of uncertainty. Imagine trying to conduct a life-cycle cost analysis on the Air Force B-52 bomber, now in its 52nd year of operation and programmed to operate until the year 2020. Various cost estimating methods, as discussed in Chapter 1, must certainly be used, along with specific software programs designed for this purpose. Some of the challenges involved in conducting a life-cycle analysis include changing requirements and the lack of a disciplined systems engineering approach during the acquisition phase of the system.

Kerzner identifies the following common errors made during life-cycle cost analysis, which include omission and/or misinterpretation of data, lack of a systematic structure, usage of the wrong techniques or misusing the technique, and estimation of the wrong items.[21]

Today's organizations are becoming increasingly aware of the signifi-cance of life- cycle costs in their acquisition and procurement deci-sions. Due to its nature, life-cycle costing entails a lot of uncertainty, especially for high-tech and never-before-used systems and services. Thus, the cost estimating method used will have a critical impact on successful life-cycle cost analysis. In conducting a life-cycle cost analysis, it is imperative that the analyst consider the following:

- The envisioned life cycle of the new system or service (RDT&E, production, deployment [inventory], O&S, and disposal).
- The stability of the requirement, design, and concept of O&S of the newly acquired system.
- The availability of historical cost data (for all life-cycle phases) for systems or services similar to the one currently being ac-quired and analyzed.

Summary

As stated at the beginning of this chapter, the purpose of cost estimating is to develop a fair and reasonable price, from either the buyer's or seller's perspective. In determining a fair and reasonable price, price analysis, cost analysis, and profit analysis may all be required, depending on the specific situation. Cost analysis is used to review each element of cost and involves a "fair and reasonable" analysis of each cost element. This chapter discussed the most common cost analysis tools and techniques—cost breakdown analysis, learning curve technique, economic order quantity, activity-based costing, and life-cycle costing. Each of these tools and techniques is designed to serve a specific purpose in analyzing the various elements of cost in ensuring that the costs are fair and reasonable. In addition, each cost analysis tool and technique has its own strengths and weaknesses that should be considered before using it for any specific cost analysis. Table 4-2 provides a summary of these cost analysis tools and techniques, along with the purpose and specific factors to consider in using each method.

Table 4-2 Summary of Cost Analysis Tools		
Cost Analysis Tool	Pupose	Factors to Consider
Cost Breakdown Analysis	Break down the various cost elements (labor, material, subcontracts, overhead) in order to determine the reasonables of each of the estimated costs.	Are the estimated costs generally recognized as necessary and consistent with established business practices? Are purchases conducted on an "arm's-length" basis?
Learning Curve Technique	Analyze and estimate direct labor hours. Determine reduction in labor hours based on the doubling of quantities produced.	Do the labor hours reflect a labor-intensive, uninterrupted production process involving complex items? Is there a continuous pressure to imporve production efficiencies?
Economic Order Quantity	Determine the procurement order or production lot size that minimzies the total cost of acquisition and carrying inventory.	Do the costs reflect a constant monthly demand throughout the year? How do lead time and quantity discounts affect the EOQ model?
Activity Based Contracting	Accurately and realistically allocate indirect costs to their appropriate cost drivers based on an analysis of the activities that drive those costs.	Do you have a thorough understanding of the company's accounting system, and the system used for estimating and allocating overhead costs, as well as the company's direct and indirect cost structure, and its overhead cost structure?
Life-Cycle Costing	Analyzing the total cost of acquisition and ownership of a system over its useful life. It includes the cost of development, acquisition, operations, support, and disposal.	Do you understand the envisioned life-cycle of the new system or service? Is the requirement, design, and concept of operations and support of the new acquired system stable? Is there available historical cost data (for all life-cycle phases) for systems or services similar to the one currently being acquired and analyzed?

RECOMMENDATIONS

The beginning of this chapter defined cost analysis as the review and evaluation of the separate cost elements and profit/fee and the application of judgment used to determine how well the proposed costs represent what the cost of the contract should be, assuming reasonable economy and efficiency. Thus, cost analysis combines analytical techniques and judgment. Knowledge of the available cost analysis tools and techniques and how to use them is only half of the challenge. The other half is being able to apply proper business judgment to the application of these tools. Just as a master craftsman must know which tool is the right tool for the right job, the competent cost analyst must also know which cost analysis tool is the right tool for the required analysis. In conducting a cost analysis, it is recommended that a toolbox approach be used. We need to be familiar with and knowledgeable about the various cost analysis tools available and how to use them, but more important, we need to know which is the right tool for the right job. The use of judgment in selecting the appropriate tool and in analyzing the resulting data will continue to be a key in conducting an effective cost analysis.

Just as in other professions and disciplines, the area of cost analysis and cost estimating is changing along with advances in computing technology and software programs. These advancing technologies are becoming enablers for even greater and expanded uses of the various cost analysis tools. The need for continuous learning in current cost estimating and analysis capabilities will continue with current advances in technology. Professional associations such as the Society of Cost Estimating and Analysis (SCEA) provide a wealth of training, education, and certification programs in the area of cost estimating and analysis.[22] Taking advantage of these sources of knowledge will be critical to achieving the required level of competence in cost estimating that is needed in today's business environment.

In the next chapter, we will provide you an excellent discussion of the numerous profit analysis tools and techniques.

QUESTIONS TO CONSIDER

1. Which cost analysis tools and techniques does your organization use when conducting a cost analysis?

2. Does your organization provide policies or guidance on which cost analysis tool to use in specific cost analysis situations?

3. What type of computing technology or software programs does your organization use for conducting cost analyses?

4. Does your organization provide or support training and education courses and seminars on cost analysis tools and techniques?

ENDNOTES

[1] Department of Defense, *Contract Pricing Reference Guides*, Vol. 3, Chapter 1. Accessed at *http://www.acq.osd.mil/dpap/contractpricing/chap-index.htm*.

[2] Ibid.

[3] Ibid.

[4] Ibid.

[5] Ibid.

[6] Ibid.

[7] Ibid.

[8] Harold Kerzner, *Project Management: A Systems Approach to Planning, Scheduling, and Controlling*, 9th ed. (Hoboken, NJ: Wiley, 2005).

[9] Ibid.

[10] David N. Burt, Donald W. Dobler, and Stephen Starling, *World Class Supply Management: The Key to Supply Chain Management*, 7th ed. (New York: McGraw-Hill/Irwin, 2002).

[11] DoD, Contract Pricing Reference Guides, Vol. 3, Chapter 1.

[12] Kerzner, *Project Management*.

[13] DoD, Contract Pricing Reference Guides, Vol. 3, Chapter 1.

[14] Donald W. Dobler and David N. Burt, *Purchasing and Supply Management: Text and Cases*, 6th ed. (New York: McGraw-Hill, 1996.)

[15] Burt, et al., *World Class Supply Management*.

[16] Ibid.

[17] Michiel R. Leender, P. Fraser Johnson, Anna Flynn, and Harold E. Fearon, *Purchasing and Supply Management*, 13th ed. (New York: McGraw-Hill/Irwin, 2005).

[18] *Glossary of Defense Acquisition Acronyms and Terms*, 12th ed. (Fort Belvoir, VA: Defense Acquisition University Press, July 2005).

[19] Kerzner, *Project Management*.

[20] Ibid.

[21] Ibid.

[22] For more information on SCEA, see http://www.sceaonline.org/index.cfm.

CHAPTER  5

PROFIT ANALYSIS: TOOLS AND TECHNIQUES

Introduction

As was discussed in the previous chapter, developing a fair and reasonable price is extremely important in cost estimations from both the buyer's and seller's perspectives. In determining a fair and reasonable price, in addition to other key factors, profit analysis is essential. While there are a myriad of ways to measure the success of a business, one significant and fundamental measure is profitability. In arriving upon a suitable profit or fee, accurately conducting a risk versus reward analysis is crucial. One fundamental objective of a business is to consistently earn a profit. As mentioned earlier, from the seller's perspective, maximizing both sales revenue and profitability in a consistent manner is critical. From a buyer's perspective, ensuring that a fair price is paid for goods and services is important. This chapter will discuss profit analysis, profitability, and measures of profitability as well as recommendations and questions to consider.

Profit Analysis

Profit analysis is extremely important to different stakeholders who have different perspectives of profit. For example, stockholders have a great interest in profit analysis because they receive revenue in the form of dividends from the corporations in which they invest. Creditors find profit analysis of vital importance since profits are a source from which debt is paid. Furthermore, because profits help finance the operations of a business, managers use profit analysis to measure the income or operating performance of a business.[1] In addition, competitors are interested in profit analysis for comparison purposes in the performance and efficiency of businesses that are operating in the same industry.[2]

Without profit, it would be difficult for a business to purchase updated equipment, construct or acquire buildings, or obtain additional working capital through either loans or sale of stock. However, an unhealthy emphasis on profit that does not consider risk could jeopardize a business' potential for continued existence. When analyzing a prospective investment, managers must consider possible risk associated with the prospective profit.[3]

In attempting to determine the appropriate rate of return or profitability for goods or services, it is important to consider the four principles for profit analysis set forth by the Department of Defense

(DoD). The principles were set forth by acquisition regulations in order to encourage effective and economical contract performance and to draw exemplary contractors to defense contracting.[4] The four principles of profit analysis are as follow:

- Motivate contractors to undertake more difficult work requiring higher skills and reward those who do so.
- Allow contractors an opportunity to earn profits commensurate with the extent of the cost risk they are willing to assume.
- Motivate contractors to provide their own facilities and financing and establish their competence through development work undertaken at their own risk and reward those who do so.
- Reward contractors for productivity increases.[5]

In government, contracting officers conducting a profit analysis should acknowledge efficient and effective contractor effort and the risk that the contractor is willing to take in a particular contract. In efforts to meet the goal of motivating effective contractor performance, contracting officers should not merely focus on the negotiation of the lowest possible profit, especially if that profit is based on just applying a randomly determined percentage to the total product cost. Of course, the higher the potential profits, the higher will be the risk involved. Businesses that choose to accept the higher risk will do so in hopes of reaping the reward of potentially higher profits.[6]

PROFITABILITY

It is important to distinguish between profit and profitability. The *profit* or earnings of a business will be found on its income statement. If the income is greater than expenditures, the business is considered to have earned a profit. If the income is less than expenditures, the business is considered to have sustained a loss for that particular operating period.

For government contracts, the *Contract Pricing Reference Guides* provide guidelines for profit/fee ceilings. When preparing the profit/fee calculations, contracting officers must take into consideration the distinctive conditions of each individual negotiation. In addition, the contract fee must not exceed the statutory limits that apply to cost-plus-fixed-fee contracts as illustrated in Table 5-1.[7]

Table 5-1 Statutory Limits on Contract Fee	
Type of Contract	**Statutory Fee Limitation**
Experimental, developmental, or research work performed under a cost-plus-fixed-fee contract	15% of estimated contract cost
All other cost-plus-fixed-fee contracts	10% of estimated contract cost

Profitability, on the other hand, is measured by utilizing ratios that incorporate profit or earnings with a minimum of one other number from the financial statements such as the income statement or the balance sheet.[8] In essence, profitability is the capability of a business to offer its investors a certain rate of return on their investment.[9] Additionally, profitability ratios evaluate the operating or income performance of a business.[10] A few profitability ratios will be discussed in subsequent sections.

In order to firmly grasp the concept of profitability, the ability to differentiate between absolute and relative profitability is necessary. *Absolute profitability* assesses the effect of adding or dropping a certain business segment or product on the overall earnings or profits of the business, with no additional changes. In contrast, *relative profitability* deals with the ranking of products and other business segments to establish which segment or product should be prioritized. Relative profitability is particularly useful if a business has several profitable opportunities that cannot be pursued all at once.[11]

Usually, the relative profitability of projects or segments can be evaluated by using the profitability index. The profitability index, a variation of the net present value, is a viable approach to capital budgeting. The profitability index can be computed as follows:[12]

Profitability Index = Present Value of Cash Inflows/
Present Value of Cash Outflows

For a project to be acceptable, a profitability index of 1 or greater is required. When a business does not have the available resources to fund all of the potential projects that have a positive net present value, the profitability index can bring some helpful insights into the decision-making process.[13]

MEASURES OF PROFITABILITY

In government contracting, financial analysis is comprised of evaluating the financial capability of potential contractors, analyzing the consequences that government financing decisions could have on the financial management of contractors, and reviewing the necessity for government protection due to performance problems stemming from the financial problems of contractors.[14]

The starting point for assessing and measuring profitability is generally the annual report of a business, which includes financial statements such as the income statement and the balance sheet. The income statement shows all of the sales and service revenues earned by a business during a specific period of time as well as all of the expenses or costs incurred to produce that particular revenue. A balance sheet is a snapshot of a business that portrays the financial position of a company at a specific point in time and is comprised of assets, liabilities, and stockholders' (owners') equity.[15] Assets are considered to be the economic resources owned by a business that provide future benefits by helping to generate revenues. Liabilities are the claims by external creditors against the assets of a business. Owners' (stockholders') equity is the owners' financial claim against the assets of a business.[16]

When conducting a financial analysis, the contracting officer has the responsibility of determining whether poor finances could possibly hinder future contract performance. In order to properly conduct a financial analysis, contracting officers must comprehend the relationship between assets, liabilities, and owners' equity, which are shown on the balance sheet of a business. The relationship is illustrated when reviewing the following accounting equation, which should always balance:[17]

$$\text{Assets} = \text{Liabilities} + \text{Owners' (Stockholders') Equity}$$

An in-depth analysis of the financial strength of a business generally is comprised of various comparisons, including comparisons within the same business over a period of years to identify trends, comparisons between other businesses in the same industry, and comparisons against the industry itself. It is also important to remember that different types of businesses will have different financial structures.[18]

Overall, financial ratio analysis assists managers in evaluating a business' past performance as well as estimating its future performance.[19] The following sections will illustrate some of the many ratios available for use in analyzing the performance of a business.

Return on Investment

The return on investment (ROI) evaluates the earnings performance of a business. It measures the income earned on the capital invested by the business and measures how well the business uses its assets or investments.[20] In its simplest form, ROI is calculated by merely dividing income by the invested capital:[21]

$$ROI = Income/Invested\ Capital$$

However, depending on how the ROI measure is intended to be used, there could be different definitions of income and invested capital. For example, income could be only the income provided by the particular investment, gross profit, net income, operating income, or earnings before interest and taxes. Invested capital could be only the amount of the particular investment, stockholders' equity, or in other cases, total assets, which includes the total capital provided by both sources of financing, debt and equity.[22]

The rate of return quantifies a business' return on investment. Contracting officers generally use the following formula for calculating the rate of return:[23]

$$Rate\ of\ Return\ =\ \frac{Gross\ Profit}{Fixed\ Assets + Net\ Working\ Capital}$$

Gross profit is calculated by subtracting the cost of selling the products or services (also known as cost of goods sold) from the sales or service revenue, the amount that a business earns for the goods it sells or the services it provides.[24]

$$Revenue - Cost\ of\ Goods\ Sold = Gross\ Profit$$

Fixed assets are generally the long-term assets of a business, such as buildings and equipment, while net working capital, a measure of liquidity, is calculated by subtracting current liabilities from current assets. *Current assets* refers to cash, accounts receivable, and inventories, whereas *current liabilities* include debt that is due within a year, such as accounts payable and short-term notes payable.

The rate of return is normally used to evaluate potential investments within a business where a higher ratio could signify a comparatively better and more profitable use of the business' assets or investments.[25] If the calculated ROI exceeds the predetermined required rate of return (also known as the *cost of capital rate* or *hurdle rate*) of a business, then the investment or project should be considered for acceptance.[26] Because ROI is sometimes considered to be a type of return on capital, it tends to measure the ability of a business to reward providers of long-term finances as well as to draw providers of future potentially needed funds.[27]

Two types of risk that businesses need to address and that are associated with potential investments include business risk and financial risk. Whereas *business risk* deals with the inability of a business to remain competitive and sustain stability and earnings growth, *financial risk* refers to the inability of a business to meet its liability or debt obligations as they come due.[28]

When analyzing a contractor's proposal, the facilities investment cost of money is considered because it has an influence on profit.[29] Whenever managers assess potential new investments or projects, they will approximate the amount of possible revenue that could be made from the investment as well as the probable costs associated with earning that particular revenue.[30] Successful managers want to make sure that the investments will be worthwhile and profitable for the business.

While there are several methods of calculating the ROI, one frequently used measurement for ROI is profit margin multiplied by the asset turnover rate, also known as *return on assets*, which will be discussed in the next section.

Return on Assets

Generally, a business acquires assets in an effort to create potential income, which in turn produces a profit.[31] A ratio that is useful in analyzing the overall profit performance of a business is the return on assets (ROA).[32] ROA is also referred to as *return on invested capital.* Invested capital includes total financing, which is comprised of both owner (equity) and non-owner (debt) financing.[33]

The total assets, as shown on the balance sheet, represent the total amount of physical and financial resources or assets that a business had available for use during the operating period to create the profit shown on the income statement.[34] ROA measures how well a business is utilizing its resources or assets to create earnings.[35]

Return on assets (investment) can be calculated in two different ways:

1. Return on Assets = Net Income/Average Total Assets

2. Return on Assets = Profit Margin × Asset Turnover

    Profit Margin = Net Income/Sales

    Asset Turnover = Sales/Average Total Assets

The first method is the most basic form of the ROA calculation. The second method is referred to as the DuPont measurement system of analysis, which was first developed by DuPont's managers to assist business managers in the decision-making process. A high profit margin, an income statement ratio, indicates the business is adequately controlling its costs.[36] In calculating average total assets, beginning total assets are added to ending total assets and divided by two. A higher asset turnover indicates more sales dollars are being created by each asset dollar, indicating the business is operating in a more efficient manner.[37]

The DuPont analysis method offers managers more detailed analyses that could provide insights regarding areas of the operations of a business needing management attention and improvement, which in turn could lead to efforts to enhance the competitive advantages of a business.[38] It is important to note that the DuPont analysis system is widely applied to both ROI and ROA, which are sometimes used interchangeably.

The DuPont measurement system of financial control concentrates on return on investment or assets by focusing on two components, which include a measurement to evaluate efficiency and a turnover measurement that analyzes the productivity of a business. The profit margin, a ratio of income to sales (also called *return on sales* or *sales margin*), measures efficiency. It represents the ability of a business to control its costs at a particular level of sales. The asset turnover, a ratio of sales to total assets (investment) (also called *asset turnover*) measures productivity. It shows the capability of a business to produce sales from a certain level of investment (assets).[39] For example, when analyzing the efficiency ratio of operating income to sales, the different cost elements, such as manufacturing, selling, and administrative, and their relationship to sales can be easily examined. Ordinarily, industry competition, economic circumstances, debt financing usage, and other business operating attributes could cause the profit margin to differ within as well as between industries.[40] Figure 5-1 illustrates the ROA DuPont method:[41]

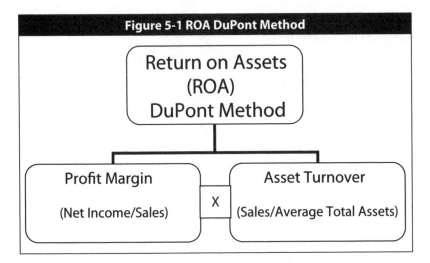

Figure 5-1 ROA DuPont Method

Return on Assets (ROA) DuPont Method

Profit Margin

(Net Income/Sales)

X

Asset Turnover

(Sales/Average Total Assets)

In evaluating the productivity ratio of sales to total assets (investment), managers can monitor the turnover measures, which include working capital elements such as inventory, accounts receivable, and cash as well as long-term or permanent asset (investment) elements such as equipment and buildings The ability to evaluate these different elements can assist managers in their decision-making process to pinpoint where improvements may be necessary.[42]

Since a business may spend over half of its total dollars in purchasing, this fact has a high significance in the profit-making prospects of the purchasing and supply function of a business. Purchasing costs can contribute to the ROI (or ROA) of a business by increasing both the profit margin and the asset turnover rate. In other words, each dollar saved in purchasing is equal to a new dollar of profit. However, because expenses are deducted from sales to arrive at a profit, it is essential to understand that an additional dollar of income from sales is not necessarily a new dollar of profit.[43]

Generally, higher efficiency signifies higher profitability as well as a business' ability to turn its resources or assets into cash to meet current liabilities or debt. It is vitally important to analyze a contractor's trends over a period of time. If a contractor becomes less efficient in utilizing its resources and assets, it may be an indication that the contractor may be experiencing decreasing profits and in turn increasing its dependence on borrowing as a source of funds to sustain its operations.[44] Even though there are several variations of ROA, it is considered one of the most widely used financial ratios.

Internal Rate of Return

The internal rate of return (IRR), expressed as a percentage, is an approach widely used in capital budgeting to evaluate capital investment proposals. The essential assessment issue in dealing with a capital investment or a long-term asset is whether or not the investment's future benefits warrant its initial cost.

When the IRR is used to analyze an investment or project, the IRR is compared with a predetermined hurdle rate, which is the minimum rate of return that management is willing to accept. As illustrated in Figure 5-2, if the IRR is higher than the hurdle rate, the project is accepted. If the IRR is lower than the hurdle rate, the project is rejected. The selection of the hurdle rate is subjective in nature, and the management of a business must analyze different potential capital investments to choose the correct rate. In addition, the hurdle rate is usually different for various individual projects depending on the risk that management is willing to take.[45]

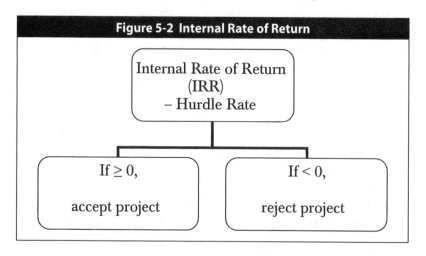

Figure 5-2 Internal Rate of Return

Internal Rate of Return
(IRR)
– Hurdle Rate

If ≥ 0,

accept project

If < 0,

reject project

The IRR is the discount rate that makes the investment's net present value equal to zero and is the actual rate of return projected from an investment.[46] There are two main methods that can be used to compute the IRR. The first method involves the use of a present value table. The IRR is calculated by first computing the present value factor of the investment or project:

Present Value Factor = Required Initial Investment/Annual Net Cash Inflows

Next, the IRR calculation involves finding the present value factor in the present value of an annuity of 1 table, which may fall between two factors on the table. Once the calculated present value factor is found in the table for the number of periods of the project life, the IRR can be approximated. The second method of calculating the IRR is done using a financial calculator, which would provide a more precise figure.

However, the IRR has a few disadvantages. First, the IRR makes the erroneous assumption that a business will reinvest a project's cash flows at the project's internal rate of return. Second, the IRR can produce vague results, especially when analyzing opposing projects in circumstances where a lack of sufficient funds keeps the business from investing in all of the potential projects with a positive net present value.[47] Third, another limitation of the IRR is that it ignores the varying risks over the life of a project.[48]

The tax effect on capital budgeting decisions includes the fact that a business must pay taxes on any net benefits generated by the investment in long-term assets. In addition, a business can use the depreciation related to the capital investment to decrease its taxable income and offset part of the taxes. The method of depreciation that tax laws use to allow a business to depreciate the acquisition costs of their long-term assets as tax-deductible expenses may differ from business to business.[49]

Overall, the IRR is an excellent profitability measurement that reflects the time value of money and allows for comparisons between dissimilar projects or investments.[50] The following section will address measured operating income.

Measured Operating Income (MOI)

In measuring profitability, it is vitally important to be able to measure operating income and the earning power of a business. Core operating income includes sales and service revenue less cost of goods sold, and less selling, general, and administrative expenses, also referred to as *operating expenses*.[51] In other words, operating income includes revenue and expenses from the ordinary operations of a business and excludes such items as other revenue (losses), extraordinary items, and income from discontinued operations.[52] Earning power is the capability of a business to create profits and increase its future assets.[53]

Operating income is also called *operating profit* or *income from operations*. A multi-step income statement usually lists the operating expenses, which relate to the ongoing operations of a business and offset the related operating income. For measurement purposes, when analyzing trends of income, it is important to compare the operating income over time or between businesses in order to concentrate on the factors of selling the product or service and controlling the related costs. For example, if a business included revenue from the sale of a business segment, which is not considered revenue from the day-to-day operations of the business, to offset ordinary operating expenses, it would in essence be showing a deceptive or misleading operating income amount. Therefore, it is important for a business to show its non-operating income and expenses in a separate section of the income statement.[54]

Accrual-based accounting refers to the recognition of revenue when it is earned and the recognition of expenses when they are incurred to earn that revenue, regardless of the timing of the cash receipt or payment. Under generally accepted accounting principles (GAAP), this matching principle requires that expenses be recognized, or shown on the income statement, in the same period as the revenue that the expenses helped create.[55] Accrual accounting is considered to better match economic benefit with economic effort, which in turn yields a measure of operating performance (accrual earnings) that gives a practical and realistic picture of past economic transactions. However, it is imperative to be aware that reported accrual accounting income may not always paint an accurate picture of the underlying economic performance of a business for a particular period of time due to various reasons, including the issue of income recognition.[56]

FIVE

In a competitive environment, the amount of profit realized by a business will depend on its capability of controlling and reducing its costs. Government buyers are usually concerned with obtaining a fair and reasonable price based on sufficient market competition. On the other hand, when there is no competitive market in existence, the market constraints placed on cost and profit are not present; therefore, cost analysis and profit analysis are absolutely critical.[57]

Operating income or operating profit can be calculated as follows:[58]

> Gross Profit – Operating Expenses = Operating Income or Profit

Measuring operating income is one of the key factors of performance measurement of a business in order to succeed financially from the financial perspective of the balanced scorecard, which is an integrated set of performance measurements organized around four distinctive perspectives to include financial, customer, internal, and innovation and learning.[59] At the organizational level, MOI is one measure that is used to quantify the value that has been produced or lost from the ongoing operations of a business. The following section will discuss days of sales outstanding.

Days of Sales Outstanding

Accounts receivable, a current asset shown on the balance sheet, is the business account that includes the sales of products and services sold to clients or customers on credit or on account.[60] For better cash flow, a business must convert its accounts receivables into cash. The days of sales outstanding (DSO) (also known as *days' sales in receivables* or *collection period*) indicates how many days' sales remain in accounts receivables waiting to be collected.[61]

There are different methods of calculating DSO. One widely used method of computing DSO is as follows:[62]

> Average Net Accounts Receivables/(Net Sales/365 Days) = Days of Sales Outstanding

Overall, DSO measures how long, on average, it takes a business to collect its accounts receivables. Generally, outstanding receivables should not be allowed to exceed credit terms by 10–15 days.[63]

Another method of computing DSO is by dividing 365 by the accounts receivable turnover, which is net credit sales divided by average accounts receivable. The accounts receivable turnover reflects the number of times that receivables turn over within a year. The DSO is a good indicator for analyzing customer payment patterns.[64]

It is essential to understand that profit is not the same as cash. The profit shown on the income statement is not necessarily represented by cash at the end of the operating and reporting period. When using accrual-based accounting, if a business shows a profit in the income statement, it does not necessarily mean that the cash has been collected and is available for use by the business yet. Sales revenue on an income statement usually includes both cash and credit sales. When a business offers its clients or customers credit terms, the business is actually making a loan to its customers until payment is received from those customers sometime in the future. Consequently, when a sale is made, it is included in the income statement for the operating period; however, cash may not have been received yet related to that sale. The timing difference between the recognition of an economic event or transaction and the related cash receipt can have critical and important implications for a business.[65]

Depending on the credit terms, a high DSO may indicate that a business is encountering difficulties in collecting cash from its clients or customers. If this is a recurring and consistent problem, a business may be facing a going concern issue, which means that it may not be able to sustain its operations to remain in business.[66]

Weighted Guidelines Method

Since 1963 when the DoD initially issued the weighted guidelines method (WGM) to be used in establishing profit objectives, there have been changes to the profit policy. The WGM, similar to the commercial marketplace, offers the promise of various degrees of rewards based on the cost risks assumed by the contractor, the contractor's performance, and other factors unique to the contract.[67]

Effective April 26, 2002, the new profit policy changes had the effect of reducing the weight on facilities investment, adding general and administrative expenses to the cost base utilized in arriving at the profit objectives, increasing the importance of performance risk, and encouraging contractors in cost reduction efforts. The contracting officer has flexibility in determining the best method of evaluating the contractor's efforts to reduce costs that benefit the contract and may increase the prenegotiation profit objective to reward the contractor's efforts.[68]

Over the years, the current DoD weighted guidelines method of profit policy has undergone many studies resulting in differing outcomes as to the effectiveness of this profit policy and measurement analysis within DoD. Overall, when appropriately used, the WGM will reward contractors with profits proportionate to the risks assumed and the unique conditions of each contract. In general, the WGM provides a guide for properly documenting the profit objective and makes sure that a contractor's effort, risk assumed, facility investment, and other unique factors particular to the contract are considered in the profit/fee determination.[69]

It is mandatory for DoD contracting officers to use the structured WGM for profit/fee analysis when cost analysis is used in determining the reasonableness of price in a contract. The WGM outlines a structure for profit/fee analysis that involves the designation of ranges for objective values and norm values that can be tailored to fit the unique conditions of a particular contract. Figure 5-3 illustrates the Weighted Guidelines Form (DD Form 1547), which provides the structure for DoD profit/fee analysis and reporting.[70]

Figure 5-3 DD Form 1547

RECORD OF WEIGHTED GUIDELINES APPLICATION			REPORT CONTROL SYMBOL DD-A&T(Q)1751	

1. REPORT NO.	2. BASIC PROCUREMENT INSTRUMENT IDENTIFICATION NO.			3. SPIIN	4. DATE OF ACTION
	a. PURCHASING OFFICE	b. FY	c. TYPE PROC INST CODE	d. PRISN	a. YEAR b. MONTH

5. CONTRACTING OFFICE CODE	ITEM	COST CATEGORY	OBJECTIVE
6. NAME OF CONTRACTOR	13.	MATERIAL	
	14.	SUBCONTRACTS	
7. DUNS NUMBER 8. FEDERAL SUPPLY CODE	15.	DIRECT LABOR	
	16.	INDIRECT EXPENSES	
9. DOD CLAIMANT PROGRAM 10. CONTRACT TYPE CODE	17.	OTHER DIRECT CHARGES	
	18.	SUBTOTAL COSTS *(13 thru 17)*	
11. TYPE EFFORT 12. USE CODE	19.	GENERAL AND ADMINISTRATIVE	
	20.	TOTAL COSTS *(18+19)*	

WEIGHTED GUIDELINES PROFIT FACTORS

ITEM	CONTRACTOR RISK FACTORS	ASSIGNED WEIGHTING	ASSIGNED VALUE	BASE *(ITEM 20)*	PROFIT OBJECTIVE
21.	TECHNICAL	%			
22.	MANAGEMENT/COST CONTROL	%			
23.	PERFORMANCE RISK (COMPOSITE)				
24.	CONTRACT TYPE RISK				
25.	WORKING CAPITAL	Costs Financed	Length Factor	Interest Rate %	

	CONTRACTOR FACILITIES CAPITAL EMPLOYED	ASSIGNED VALUE	AMOUNT EMPLOYED	
26.	LAND			
27.	BUILDINGS			
28.	EQUIPMENT			

29.	COST EFFICIENCY FACTOR	ASSIGNED VALUE	BASE *(Item 20)*	
30.	TOTAL PROFIT OBJECTIVE			

NEGOTIATED SUMMARY

		PROPOSED	OBJECTIVE	NEGOTIATED
31.	TOTAL COSTS			
32.	FACILITIES CAPITAL COST OF MONEY *(DD FORM 1861)*			
33.	PROFIT			
34.	TOTAL PRICE *(Line 31 + 32 + 33)*			
35.	MARKUP RATE *(Line 32 + 33 divided by 31)*	%	%	%

CONTRACTING OFFICER APPROVAL

36. TYPED/PRINTED NAME OF CONTRACTING OFFICER *(Last, First, Middle Initial)*	37. SIGNATURE OF CONTRACTING OFFICER	38. TELEPHONE NO.	39. DATE SUBMITTED *(YYYYMMDD)*

OPTIONAL USE

96.	97.	98.	99.

DD FORM 1547, JUL 2002   PREVIOUS EDITION IS OBSOLETE.

FIVE

As illustrated in Table 5-2, for profit/fee analysis, the factors for performance of risk analysis include technical and management/cost control. Items 21 through 23 of DD Form 1547 are intended to reward contractors who assume more performance risk in the contracts that they accept. In order to evaluate performance risk, contracting officers need to analyze the risk associated with satisfying the requirements of the contract. Table 5-2 outlines factors that should be taken into consideration when analyzing each type of risk.[71]

Table 5-2 Factors for Performance Risk Analysis	
Risk Type	Examples of Factors to Be Considered
Technical	• Technology being applied or developed by the contractor • Technical complexity • Program maturity • Performance specifications and tolerances • Delivery schedule • Extent of warranty or guarantee
Management/cost control	• Contractor's management and internal control systems • Management involvement expected under the contract • Resources applied and value added by the contractor • Contractor support for federal socioeconomic programs • Expected reliability of cost estimates • Adequacy of management's approach to controlling cost and schedule • Other factors affecting contractor's ability to meet cost targets

The DD Form 1547 contains numerous evaluation factors and can be complex. The actual detailed steps and instructions for completing DD Form 1547 are beyond the scope of this chapter. Overall, the form is divided into five parts to include contractor effort, contractor risk, facilities investment, special factors, and cost of money offset. Different profit weight ranges are assigned to each profit/fee factor. It is important to note that fixed-price contracts with financing usually have lower profit/fee ranges than fixed-price contracts with no financing. When the government provides financing, the contractor would be likely to assume less financial risk. When assigning values, the contracting officer should assign a profit/fee value consistent with the value for performance risk. The contracting officer signs and dates the DD Form 1547 after the completion of the negotiation.[72]

Earnings Before Interest, Taxes, Depreciation, and Amortization

One measure of profitability currently being utilized is that of earnings before interest, taxation, depreciation, and amortization (EBITDA). The main argument for using this measure is that it eliminates all of the minor items in order to focus on the true profitability of a business without being influenced by capital structures, tax systems, or methods of depreciation. While EBITDA can be very useful as part of a detailed analysis of a business, it is important to note that EBITDA ignores the cost of fixed assets used in a business as well as depreciation, interest, and taxes. For example, a business showing an after-tax loss from a large investment in fixed assets that were financed by equal amounts of debt could look rather healthy on an EBITDA basis.[73] Therefore, a careful evaluation of a business using EBITDA should be made in the total profitability analysis.

The calculation for EBITDA is as follows:[74]

> Net Income − (Interest Expense + Tax Expense + Depreciation Expense + Amortization) = EBITDA

In the 1980s, EBITDA superseded EBIT (earnings before interest and taxes) as a financial yardstick for measuring the cash flow of a business. EBITDA removes depreciation and amortization from the profit calculation, which are non-cash items comprising a majority of the expenses for many businesses. Those in favor of using EBITDA believe that it is an accurate measure of cash flow. On the other hand, those who criticize the use of EBITDA disagree that it measures cash flow, because EBITDA ignores the working capital growth cash requirements as well as cash necessary for replacement of outdated assets such as obsolete equipment. In addition, because EBITDA does not consider whether operating revenues and expenses directly affect cash, the quality of the earnings is not properly reflected, which can result in the possible manipulation of earnings through aggressive accounting policies relating to both revenue and expenses. Furthermore, non-GAAP earnings like EBITDA overlook certain business expenses or costs, such as depreciation, which can result in a faulty representation of the profitability of a business.[75]

SUMMARY

As discussed earlier, profitability ratios evaluate the operating or income performance of a business. This chapter covered profitability and profit analysis measures that include ROI, ROA, IRR, MOI, DSO, WGM, and EBITDA. While financial ratios are a powerful tool for analyzing the performance and profitability of a business, it is important to keep in mind that there is no one correct method of computing financial ratios. For various reasons, companies may include or exclude certain numbers or use different numbers in their calculations to arrive at the ratios. Because companies may use different terminology for the same item on financial statements, it is important to understand exactly how the numbers were derived. Financial ratios can assist managers in asking the right questions, but they cannot provide the answers. Ratio analyses help shed light on the overwhelming amount of information and data on financial statements. In addition, it is wise to be cautious of accounting discrepancies or distortions that could obscure the interpretation of financial ratios.[76]

As part of the decision-making process in evaluating new prospects or investments, profitability measures are indeed useful and appropriate tools. Ratio analyses assist managers by giving meaning and significance to the numbers on financial statements.[77] For example, for profitability analysis, ROA is broken down into meaningful components using the DuPont system of financial analysis.

It is important to analyze a business using various methods, including both the financial aspects of the business as well as the nonfinancial features of the business as a whole. Over the years, financial ratio analysis has become more popular; however, it is important to make sure that the ratios utilized in profit analysis are meaningful and can contribute to the analysis and evaluation of the performance of a business as well as to the overall long-term financial health of the business.

Table 5-3 summarizes the various measures of profitability discussed in this chapter.

Table 5-3 Summary of Analytical Measures of Profitability		
Ratio or Other Measure	Method of Calculation	Implication
Profitability index (PI)	Present Value of Cash Inflows/ Present Value of Cash Outflows	Capital budgeting method for evaluating projects. PI of 1 or better is required.
Return on investment (ROI)	Income/Invested Capital	It measures the income earned on the capital invested.
Return on assets (ROA)	Income/Average Total Assets OR Profit Margin × Asset Turnover	It measures return on total investment in a business. It measures both efficiency and the productivity of assets.
Internal rate of return (IRR)	*Method 1:* Use of present value table: Present Value Factor = Required Initial Investment/ Annual Net Cash Inflows *Method 2:* Use of financial calculator	An approach that is used in capital budgeting to evaluate capital investment proposals.
Measured operating income (MOI)	Gross Profit - Operating Expenses	It measures the profitability of a business' basic business activities.
Days of sales outstanding (DSO)	Average Net Accounts Receivables/(Net Sales/365 Days)	It measures how long, on average, it takes a business to collect its accounts receivables.
Weighted guidelines method (WGM)	DD Form 1547	DoD method for determining the profit objectives of a contract.
Earnings before interest, taxes, depreciation, and amortization (EBITDA)	Net Income - (Interest Expense + Tax Expense + Depreciation Expense + Amortization)	It measures the cash flow of a business.

RECOMMENDATIONS

To fully evaluate the effectiveness and operating performance of a business, contracting officers need to look beyond the mere numbers on financial statements such as sales revenue, profits, and total assets. They must possess the ability to understand how the numbers on the financial statements can be useful for evaluating and measuring performance, especially profitability. When used in conjunction with other business assessment processes, comparative ratio analysis is one powerful method that can help tremendously to assist in identifying and quantifying the strengths and weaknesses of the business, in analyzing the profitability of the business, in reviewing the financial position of the business, and in considering and understanding the impending risks that a business may be assuming.[78]

In evaluating a business for profitability purposes, two major issues must be addressed. First, the capability of the business to produce a profit from its operations must be analyzed. The profit margin, part of ROA, is a good indicator of the profitability level of the operations of a business. Second, the utilization of available assets and capital to produce a profit needs to be assessed. The major reason for a business to maintain assets is to sustain its operations and to aid in the production of current and future profits. When making comparisons, three to five years of financial data are recommended.[79]

Because of different accounting policies and the flexibility given to businesses in the preparation of their financial statements, a financial analysis needs to take into consideration various GAAP limitations, the business environment, competitive issues, and business strategies.[80] The notes to financial statements usually disclose other valuable information to assist in evaluating and measuring the profit performance of a business.

As in cost analysis, profit analysis involves both analytical techniques and judgment. Properly applying the appropriate profitability measurements to each unique situation is the key to conducting an effective profit analysis. In Chapter 6, we will discuss contract pricing strategies, methods, and best practices.

QUESTIONS TO CONSIDER

1. Which profit analysis tools and techniques does your organization use when conducting a profit analysis for performance measurement?

2. Does your organization provide profit policies or guidance on which profit analysis tool to use when considering potential investments and potential contracts?

3. Is your organization actively monitoring its profitability over the years and making comparisons with industry averages?

4. Does your organization offer or support any training on profit analysis tools and techniques?

5. Does your organization provide adequate education for the completion of DD Form 1547 to ensure that contracting officers are familiar with the new changes?

ENDNOTES

[1] Charles H. Gibson, *Financial Reporting and Analysis: Using Financial Accounting Information*, 10th ed. (Mason, OH: Thomson South-Western, 2007).

[2] Bob Vause, *Guide to Analyzing Companies*. (London: The Economist Newspaper Ltd., 2005).

[3] Joseph L. Brittelli, Patrick J. Lynch, and Peggy Emmelhainz, *Principles of Contract Pricing*, 4th ed. Course number 6610018383. Extension Course Institute, Air University. Wright-Patterson AFB, OH: School of Systems and Logistics, AFIT.

[4] Ibid.

[5] Ibid., 85.

[6] Ibid.

[7] "Analyzing Profit or Fee: DOD Weighted Guidelines Method", DoD Defense Procurement and Acquisition Policy. *Contract Pricing Reference Guides*, August 26, 2005. http://www.acq.osd.mil/dpap/contractpricing/vol3chap11.htm; FAR 15.404-4(a)(3) and 15.404-4(c)(4) (accessed January 6, 2007).

[8] Vause: *Guide to Analyzing Companies*.

[9] Charles T. Horngren, Gary L. Sundem, John A. Elliott, and Donna R. Philbrick, *Introduction to Financial Accounting*. 9th ed. (Upper Saddle River, NJ: Pearson, 2006).

[10] Jane L. Reimers, *Financial Accounting*. (Upper Saddle River, NJ: Pearson, 2007).

[11] Ray H. Garrison, Eric W. Noreen, and Peter C. Brewer, *Managerial Accounting*, 11th ed. (New York: McGraw-Hill/Irwin, 2006).

[12] Anthony A. Atkinson, Robert S. Kaplan, Ella Mae Matsumura, and S. Mark Young, *Management Accounting*, 5th ed. (Upper Saddle River, NJ: Pearson, 2007).

[13] Ibid.

[14] "Performing Financial Analyses", DoD Defense Procurement and Acquisition Policy. *Contract Pricing Reference Guides*, August 26, 2005. http://www.acq.osd.mil/dpap/contractpricing/vol4chap9.htm; FAR 9.104-1, 28.103-2(3), and 32.006-4(d)(3) (accessed January 6, 2007).

[15] Reimers, *Financial Accounting*.

[16] "Performing Financial Analyses," *Contract Pricing Reference Guides*.

[17] Ibid.

[18] Ibid.

[19] Reimers, *Financial Accounting*.

[20] Gibson, *Financial Reporting and Analysis*.

[21] Horngren, et al., *Introduction to Financial Accounting*.

21   Ibid.

22   "Performing Financial Analyses," *Contract Pricing Reference Guides*.

23   Reimers, *Financial Accounting*.

24   "Performing Financial Analyses," *Contract Pricing Reference Guides*.

25   Michael L. Werner and Kumen H. Jones, *Introduction to Accounting: A User Perspective*, 2nd ed. (Upper Saddle River, NJ: Pearson, 2004).

26   Gibson, *Financial Reporting and Analysis*.

27   Stanley B. Block and Geoffrey A. Hirt, *Foundations of Financial Management*, 11th ed. (New York: McGraw-Hill/Irwin, 2005).

28   Brittelli, et al., *Principles of Contract Pricing*.

29   Reimers, *Financial Accounting*.

30   Ibid.

31   Vause, *Guide to Analyzing Companies*.

32   Thomas R. Dyckman, Peter D. Easton, and Glenn M. Pfeiffer, *Financial Accounting*. (Cambridge Business Publishers, 2007.)

33   Vause, *Guide to Analyzing Companies*.

34   Reimers, *Financial Accounting*.

35   Block, et al., *Foundations of Financial Management*.

36   "Performing Financial Analyses," *Contract Pricing Reference Guides*.

37   Dyckman, et al., *Financial Accounting*.

38   Atkinson, et al., *Management Accounting*.

39   Gibson, *Financial Reporting and Analysis*.

40   Dyckman, et al., *Financial Accounting*.

41   Atkinson, et al., *Management Accounting*.

42   Donald W. Dobler and David N. Burt, *Purchasing and Supply Management: Test and Cases*. (New York: McGraw-Hill, 1996).

43   "Performing Financial Analyses," *Contract Pricing Reference Guides*.

44   Kermit D. Larson, John J. Wild, and Barbara Chiappetta, *Fundamental Accounting Principles*, 15th ed. (New York: McGraw-Hill, 1999).

45   Atkinson, et al., *Management Accounting*.

46   Ibid.

47   Larson, et al., *Fundamental Accounting Principles*.

48   Atkinson, et al., *Management Accounting*.

49   Larson, et al., *Fundamental Accounting Principles*.

50   Dyckman, et al., *Financial Accounting*.

51   "Analyzing Your Financial Ratios" (n.d.) http://www.va-interactive.com/inbusiness/editorial/finance/ibt/ratio_analysis.html#4 (accessed December 27, 2006).

52   Reimers, *Financial Accounting*.

[53] Horngren, et al., *Introduction to Financial Accounting.*

[54] Reimers, *Financial Accounting.*

[55] Lawrence Revsine, Daniel W. Collins, and W. Bruce Johnson, *Financial Reporting and Analysis*, 3rd ed. (Upper Saddle River, NJ: Pearson, 2005).

[56] Brittelli, et al., *Principles of Contract Pricing.*

[57] Reimers, *Financial Accounting.*

[58] Werner, et al., *Introduction to Accounting.*

[59] "Analyzing Your Financial Ratios."

[60] Walter T. Harrison and Charles T. Horngren, *Financial Accounting*, 6th ed. (Upper Saddle River, NJ: Pearson, 2006).

[61] Ibid., 622.

[62] "Analyzing Your Financial Ratios."

[63] Revsine, et al., *Financial Reporting and Analysis.*

[64] Vause, *Guide to Analyzing Companies.*

[65] Robert W. Ingram and Thomas L. Albright, *Financial Accounting: A Bridge to Decision-Making*, 6th ed. (Mason, OH: Thomson South-Western, 2007).

[66] Paul M. Truger, "Defense Contract Profits: Weighted Guidelines Method," Journal of Accountancy 119 (February 1965): 45-50.

[67] "Changes to Profit Policy," Defense Federal Acquisition Regulation Supplement, April 26, 2002. http://www.acq.osd.mil/dpap/dars/dfars/changenotice/docs/2000d018f.pdf (accessed January 13, 2007).

[68] Brittelli, et al., *Principles of Contract Pricing.*

[69] "Analyzing Profit or Fee: DOD Weighted Guidelines Method", DoD Defense Procurement and Acquisition Policy. *Contract Pricing Reference Guides*, August 26, 2005. http://www.acq.osd.mil/dpap/contractpricing/vol3chap11.htm; FAR 15.404-4(a)(3) and 15.404-4(c)(4); DFARS 215.404-4(b), 215.404-71-2(c), and 215.404-71-4(c) (accessed January 6, 2007).

[70] Ibid; DFARS 215.404-71-2.

[71] Ibid.

[72] Vause, *Guide to Analyzing Companies.*

[73] Revsine, et al., *Financial Reporting and Analysis.*

[74] Ibid.

[75] Ibid.

[76] Horngren, et al., *Introduction to Financial Accounting.*

[77] "Analyzing Your Financial Ratios."

[78] Vause, *Guide to Analyzing Companies.*

[79] Dyckman, et al., *Financial Accounting.*

CHAPTER **6**

CONTRACT PRICING STRATEGIES, METHODS, AND BEST PRACTICES

INTRODUCTION

So, what is price? What constitutes a fair and reasonable price? How do you develop the right price? The answer to all three of these questions is, "It depends." No, we are not trying to be difficult; rather, price is a flexible item that is dependent upon numerous factors. Price should be a derivative of your people, processes, performance, and competition. Price should be adjusted by your business strategy, given the marketplace your organization is operating in as either a buyer or a seller. In this chapter, we shall examine the following aspects of price: the two most common pricing strategies (lowest-price-technically-acceptable and best value), and the three major methods for determining price (cost-based pricing, value-based pricing, and activity-based pricing).

Price is an essential element for both buyers and sellers. Buyers care about price, because they have a limited budget and they want to ensure their selected seller is sufficiently motivated to achieve excellence. Likewise, sellers care about price because they want to ensure they are able to cover their actual costs, achieve a reasonable profit, and ensure customer satisfaction. So, let us now discuss how organizations develop the right price.

TWO MOST COMMON PRICING STRATEGIES

Clearly, in both the public and private sectors the two most common pricing strategies are the lowest-price-technically-acceptable (LPTA) strategy and the best-value strategy.

LPTA Pricing Strategy

Simply stated, the LPTA strategy is typically used by buyers when there are multiple sellers, usually providing commercially available off-the-shelf products and services. LPTA is the right pricing strategy if there is no real differentiator other than price. Said differently, if all of the products and/or services being considered for purchase are basically the same in terms of quality, schedule, reputation, and technical capability/features, then price should be the key attribute for purposes of source selection and contract award.

From a seller's perspective, LPTA is the appropriate pricing strategy in most markets when their products and/or services offer no real value differentiator from their competitors' products and/or services. LPTA is based on a simple strategy: The lowest price wins the deal. However, LPTA does not necessarily assure either party of a fair and reasonable price.

In reality, sometimes all of the sellers in the marketplace have overly high prices, based upon supply and demand, and even the lowest price can still be perceived by the buyer as too expensive. Likewise, sellers may at times feel they are being squeezed by their competitors and customers to drive their prices so low, in order to get the deal, that they are forced to lose money. Both buyers and sellers must properly evaluate the market to ensure when it is truly appropriate to use the LPTA pricing strategy. For both buyers and sellers it is important to remember that the lowest price is not always the best deal or the right price.

Best-Value Pricing Strategy

The term *best value* can have several meanings, depending on one's particular perspective. The federal government defines best value as the expected outcome of an acquisition that in the government's estimation provides the greatest overall benefit in response to the requirement. Best value is usually associated with the source selection process. However, the concept can also be applied to other situations.

In all situations, best value is intended to serve as a tool for the buyer and seller to establish a proper balance between factors such as price, quality, and technical and past performance. Best value applies to products and services already developed, as opposed to value analysis, which examines trade-offs during the design and/ or production process.

Perhaps it would be more helpful to define best value in terms of what it is and what it is not. Best value *is* a disciplined, balanced approach, an assessment of trade-offs between price and performance, a team effort, an evaluation of qualitative and quantitative factors, and an integrated risk assessment. Best value *is not* price cutting, uncompensated overtime, accounting gimmicks, specials, one-time discounts, the shifting of all price and performance risk to the supplier, or an excuse not to properly define requirements.

For our purposes, best value is a determination of which offer presents the best trade-off between price and performance, where quality is considered an integral performance factor. The best-value decision can be made using a variety of qualitative and quantitative management tools. Best-value contracting is intrinsically tied to the process of contract negotiations for several reasons. First of all, to be successful, negotiations must focus on some specific quantifiable objective. Best value offers a meaningful objective to each negotiation party. In addition, contract negotiation typically requires trade-offs among a variety of interrelated factors. Using best-value techniques helps contract management professionals assess the impact of these trade-offs to ensure a successful negotiation session. These techniques also help determine the range of values (e.g., cost, production, quality requirements, life-cycle cost) where trade-offs can be made while preserving the optimal balance between price, performance, and quality. Lastly, best value establishes realistic negotiation objectives up front.

For example, best-value contracting techniques can discourage the use of unrealistic initial negotiation positions by suppliers seeking to win a contract with practices such as uncompensated overtime or unrealistically low initial prices. To be successful, best-value contracting must be an integral part of the acquisition strategy planning process; this means early planning must occur. Best-value contracting also requires a team effort among various disciplines such as engineering, accounting, legal, manufacturing, and contracts, to clearly identify all acquisition requirements and determine the optimum trade-offs among various factors.

Trade-offs Decision Making

Trade-offs in making a best-value decision should always consider the objectives of both the buyer and seller, which was discussed previously. Trade-offs may have to be revisited as negotiations progress, since the needs of the buyer and seller will be revealed (usually incrementally) during the course of negotiations. The level of analysis in a best-value trade-off decision depends on the complexity of the particular procurement. Low-technology procurements usually require a simple, straightforward trade-off approach, because price is normally the primary factor. However, high-technology procurements normally require more sophisticated trade-off analysis tools, because price is usually secondary to technical and quality concerns.[1]

Because of the many types of contracting situations, there is no single, preferred way to determine best value. Rather, a combination of techniques should be used, preferably integrating quantitative and qualitative factors. The use of a team approach helps with making the necessary trade-offs rationally (see Figure 6-1).

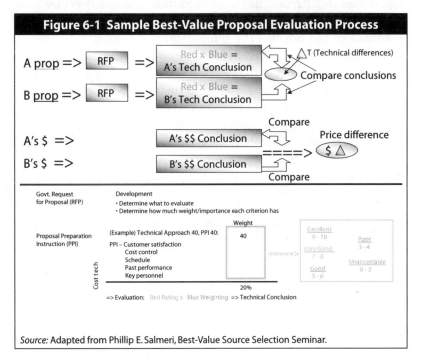

Figure 6-1 Sample Best-Value Proposal Evaluation Process

Source: Adapted from Phillip E. Salmeri, Best-Value Source Selection Seminar.

The Evolution of Best-Value Pricing

The practice of best-value pricing has continued to grow in importance over the past decade in both the public and private sectors. First of all, the federal regulatory environment has continually evolved, gradually allowing for increased best-value pricing techniques. Government contractors have responded to these changes by offering best-value pricing as part of an overall value-based cost and technical approach. This has helped make government contractors more efficient and competitive. In addition, the items and services to be purchased have continued to become more technical and complex (e.g., sophisticated consulting, advanced hardware, software, and professional services). This has often made quality and past performance factors more important than price-related factors. Also, the emphasis on making best-value purchasing decisions will increase as the government refines its attempts to obtain more value for its money. Finally, the continual improvement in increasing the professional qualifications and credentials of both government and industry acquisition workforce personnel has fostered the use of best value on both sides.

The commercial sector has long used best-value contracting techniques as a means to remain competitive and profitable. The federal government has not had the same degree of flexibility to employ best-value techniques, because it must comply with various requirements that have no material bearing on the business aspects of the contract but are mandated by law to be included in all federal acquisitions as a matter of public policy. As a result, best-value pricing implementation has not achieved its full potential in the government contracting arena.[2] Too often, best-value pricing really becomes a modified version of LPTA, where the buyer will agree to pay just slightly more than the LPTA for higher overall value. (See Tables 6-1 and 6-2 for checklists of best-value dos and don'ts).

Table 6-1 Checklist of Best-Value "Dos"
Do:
☐ develop or obtain proven best-value pricing tools.
☐ select best-value measurement tools that are easy to understand and use.
☐ ensure that quality factors do not become secondary to cost issues, except for noncomplex acquisitions.
☐ consider using automation tools for best-value decision making.
☐ tailor best-value measurement tools to specific procurement situations, realizing that complexity increases with the size and scope of the acquisition.
☐ use a contract type that fairly allocates risks.
☐ provide contract incentives for superior (quality) performance.
☐ implement guidance throughout the agency or company.
☐ continue to improve techniques.
☐ make each best-value decision a team effort between contracts, finance, engineering, production, quality assurance, and other related offices.
☐ ensure that a best-value approach supports the overall negotiation strategy.
☐ realize the best-value approach works only if you know what you're buying.
☐ document the rationale for best-value decisions.
☐ allow flexibility for trade-offs.
Source: Richard J. Hernandez, "Negotiating a Quality Contract" (National Contract Management Association National Education Seminar, 1992).

Table 6-2 Checklist of Best-Value "Don'ts"

Don't:

☐ use (1) the low bid or (2) the lowest-cost-technically-acceptable offer as a substitute for best value when best value is applicable.

☐ expect to make a good best-value decision without clearly defining your approach up front.

☐ attempt to implement best-value contracting without properly training acquisition personnel.

☐ forget to research all relevant issues, especially technical factors.

☐ make best-value decision tools unnecessarily complex.

☐ allow for such practices as a "buy-in" or uncompensated overtime.

☐ use auctioning, technical leveling, or technical transfusion techniques as a substitute for best-value contracting.

☐ forget to formalize the elements of the best-value agreement as soon as possible after contract negotiations.

☐ allow an offeror's low initial price to overshadow life-cycle cost considerations.

☐ expect to obtain the maximum level of economy when buying noncommercial off-the-shelf items.

Source: Richard J. Hernandez, "Negotiating a Quality Contract" (National Contract Management Association National Education Seminar, 1992).

MAJOR METHODS FOR DETERMINING PRICE

There are three major methods for determining price: cost-based pricing, value-based pricing, and activity-based pricing.

Cost-Based Pricing

Cost-based pricing (CBP) is a relatively straightforward method of pricing. Using CBP, a seller must have an accurate and acceptable cost estimating and accounting system whereby it can estimate its future costs, then apply a desired margin, profit, or fee to yield a fair and reasonable price. The two most common challenges faced by sellers when using CBP are creating an adequate cost estimating and accounting system and applying an appropriate profit or fee structure that properly balances opportunity versus risk. In the private sector, there are generally accepted accounting principles (GAAP) that are followed and audited to ensure companies have adequate cost estimating and accounting systems. There are no real stringent rules for commercial companies on applying an appropriate profit or fee structure.

However, when dealing in the public sector, the U.S. government has numerous rules and regulations to ensure companies doing business with the government have adequate cost estimating and accounting systems (especially when using cost-type contracts), apply appropriate profit/fee structures, and practice truth in negotiations.

As discussed in Chapters 1 and 2, the primary goal of a cost estimating and accounting system is to ensure that costs are appropriately, equitably, and consistently estimated and then allocated to all final cost objectives (i.e., individual contracts, jobs, or products). The federal government essentially requires a company to maintain, and consistently apply, any generally accepted accounting method that is adequate, efficient, reliable, and equitable, but not necessarily exact and specific, and not biased against the government. The government does not require companies to adopt separate or necessarily complex accounting systems. Consequently, contractors are free to develop and use the type of cost estimating and accounting system most appropriate for their businesses. However, consistent application of this approach is vital.

Although the use and design of certain specific cost estimating accounting records and practices may vary from company to company, at a minimum, the record-keeping system for any company doing business with the government must include a general ledger, a job-cost ledger, labor distribution records, time records, subsidiary journals, a chart of accounts, and financial statements.[3]

To determine whether a company's accounting system is acceptable, a government auditor will generally go through a checklist, asking questions similar to those found in the accounting system questionnaire (see Table 6-3).

Table 6-3 Government Auditor Accounting System Questionnaire	Yes	No
Is the system in accord with generally accepted accounting principles (GAAP)?	☐	☐
Will the system be able to identify and segregate direct costs from indirect costs and allocate these costs equitably to specific contracts on a consistent basis?	☐	☐
Is the system that accumulates costs integrated with, and reconcilable to, the general ledger?	☐	☐
Do the timekeeping and labor distribution systems appropriately identify direct and indirect labor charges to intermediate and final cost objectives?	☐	☐
Will the system be able to determine the cost of work performed at interim points (at least monthly) because of routine posting of costs to the books of account?	☐	☐
Will the system be able to identify and segregate unallowable costs as required by FAR Part 31 and any contract terms?	☐	☐
If required by the contract, will the system be able to identify costs by contract line item or by unit?	☐	☐
Will the system be able to segregate preproduction costs from production costs?	☐	☐
Is the system capable of providing the necessary information required by FAR 52.232-20, Limitation of Cost (Also -21 and -22), or FAR 52.216-16, Incentive Price Revision—Firm Target?	☐	☐
Is the system able to provide the necessary data for recovery of costs, using progress payments?	☐	☐
Is the accounting system designed? Are the records maintained in such a manner that adequate, reliable data are developed for use in pricing follow-on contracts?	☐	☐
Is the accounting system currently in full operation?	☐	☐

Source: Jeffrey A. Lubeck, "Beyond an 'Adequate' Accounting System," Contract Management Magazine, May 2004.

Accounting information can, and should, be used in more ways than merely to produce financial statements and job-cost reports. Only after identifying activities that are important to your business and beginning to measure them can you encourage the rest of your team to support your goals. A business that provides clear expectations and real-time performance feedback can be managed on a real-time basis and, therefore, has greater control over its destiny.[4]

Adequate Cost Estimating

As discussed in Chapter 1, developing a sound cost estimate requires a coordinated effort by a team of qualified seller personnel who understand how to extract and price requirements presented in the buyer's request for proposal (RFP). At a minimum, the team should consist of a program manager, technical manager, contract manager, accounting/finance manager, and a senior executive responsible for final review and submission of the proposal to the buyer. Depending on the company's size, the magnitude of the proposal, and the types of costs being estimated, the estimating team also may include representatives of the purchasing, legal, human resources, operations, and other teams.

All personnel with any responsibility for preparing a proposal to the U.S. government should be well versed in the guidelines contained in the Federal Acquisition Regulation (especially FAR 15.4–Contract Pricing). All team members should have adequate experience and knowledge of the particular requirements of pricing function to which they have been assigned. Responsible personnel should know where to obtain the most relevant and current data and be aware of the turnaround time allowed for submission of the proposal.[5]

A proposal preparation system that entrusts one person with the sole authority for translating the RFP into requirements, pricing those requirements, and reviewing and submitting the final proposal is an accident waiting to happen. Omission of key personnel in the estimating process can result in cost and delivery projections that do not consider current and future business decisions and company plans. In other words, the proposal may not realistically represent the company's ability to deliver the product or services within the estimated cost or required delivery timelines.

Including personnel who are familiar with various components of the business operations will reduce the risk that a proposal will be overstated or understated. Even in small companies with few employees, in which officials wear several hats of responsibility, it is just as important that the estimating system involve at least two or three qualified persons to better ensure an accurately priced final product.

Finally, a forward-pricing proposal should minimize the use of judgmental estimates and maximize the use of factual data when such data are available and relevant. Developing extensive price requirements with judgmental estimates does not provide the visibility required by the government to evaluate the reasonableness of a proposal. Judgmental estimates add time to the government audit and cost analysis and sometimes result in adverse audit opinions because of a lack of verifiable data. The typical cost elements in Table 6-4 are examples of verifiable proposal supporting data.

Table 6-4 Examples of Verifiable Proposal Supporting Data	
Direct labor hours	Labor-hour history of the same or similar projects Company or industry standards
Bill of direct materials	Material planning documents Engineering blueprints
Direct labor rates	Labor cost history for the same or similar project Average labor rates from payroll data Market wage or salary survey information
Direct materials	Purchase history of same or similar items Vendor quotations Vendor catalogs
Indirect rate	Historical annual indirect rates Budgetary/provisional rates

Source: Darryl L. Walker, "Is Your Estimating System Asking for Trouble?" *Contract Management Magazine,* May 2004.

In selecting the proposal resources for developing and pricing RFP requirements, the supplier must be careful to use the most current, accurate, and complete information, especially if the government requires submission of cost or pricing data. This means selecting the data most relevant to the proposal being prepared and ensuring that the source information is as current as possible. Even if the proposal is not specifically subject to the Truth in Negotiations Act, companies have an obligation to prepare reasonable estimates and, in that pursuit, should rely on up-to-date, relevant, and factual data when possible.

It goes without saying that estimating techniques must be relevant to the specific RFP requirements. Supplier techniques should be consistent among all bids and proposals, except in cases in which those techniques clearly will not produce the most accurate cost estimate for the RFP's scope of work.[6]

Cost Proposal Package:
Information Required for U.S. Government Prime Contracts

A U.S. government prime contract cost proposal requiring cost or pricing data must follow the format shown in FAR 15.408, Table 15-2. This information may be helpful in assessing the adequacy of a proposal.

1. First Page of Proposal–Table 15-2, Item I.A lists 11 separate informational requirements:
   a. Solicitation/contract no.
   b. Offeror name and address
   c. Contact point and phone number
   d. Name of contract administration office

e. Type of contract option (i.e., new contract, change order, letter contract, etc.)

f. Date of submission

g. Name, title, and signature of authorized representative

h. Proposed cost, fee, and total

i. What government property is required

j. Cost accounting standards
   i. Whether organization is subject to CAS
   ii. Whether a Cost Accounting Standards Board Disclosure Statement has been submitted and determined adequate
   iii. Any notifications of material noncompliance with CAS or Disclosure Statement and whether proposal is consistent with CAS and disclosed practices—no need to disclose "technical" noncompliances

k. Statement that proposal reflects estimated/actual costs and that contracting officer/authorized representatives have access to records

2. Summary of Cost and Detailed Support—Table 15-2, Items I.C–G, II, and III

3. Disclosure Narrative—Table 15-2, Items I.C–G
   a. Helps protect against defective pricing allegations
   b. Describes the basis of estimates
      i. Specific discussion by cost category (direct materials, direct labor, other direct costs, overhead, etc.)
      ii. Discusses assumptions made and the rationale such as judgmental factors, applied and mathematical or other methods used in the estimate
      iii. Method used in projecting from known data
      iv. Includes the nature and amount of contingencies in the proposed price
   c. Discloses significant cost or pricing data in narrative form
      i. Discusses key data used in cost estimating
      ii. Discloses cost data not used in cost estimating and states why they were not used

4. Disclosure Index—Table 15-2, Item I.B
   b. Helps protect against defective pricing claims by listing all available cost or pricing data, or other information accompanying the proposal or identified in the proposal, appropriately referenced.

   b. Index should specifically identify all reports and documents. Should include:
      i.   Specific report name and/or number
      ii. Date of most recent report
      iii. Physical location of data
   c. Includes items such as:
      i.   General ledger
      ii. Payroll register
      iii. Vendor invoice
      iv. Accounts payable history, etc.
   d. Future additions and/or revisions up to the date of agreement on price must be annotated on a supplemental index.

Understanding the Truth in Negotiations Act

Congress enacted the Truth in Negotiations Act (TINA) as Public Law 87-653 (10 U.S.C. 2306) in December 1962. The TINA has been viewed as one of the most significant pieces of procurement legislation. The original act covered only contracts entered into by the Department of Defense and the National Aeronautics and Space Administration (NASA). Civilian agencies subsequently adopted the same statutory provisions under their own regulations. The statutory disparity between the various government agencies was addressed by the 1984 Competition in Contracting Act (CICA), which required that the TINA apply to all government contracts. This remedy has significantly decreased the number of disputes brought before the various boards of contract appeals.

The TINA requires federal government prime contractors and subcontractors to submit and certify to the government the data related to the basis of estimated contract costs. The objective is to provide the government with all necessary and relevant information to be able to negotiate a fair and reasonable price for a contract. The TINA requires that such information be "current, accurate, and complete" at the time such an agreement is reached by the negotiating parties.[7]

The TINA requires contractors to disclose factual data that prudent buyers and sellers would reasonably expect to significantly affect the contract price negotiation. Some typical data that are disclosed under TINA include the following:

- historical costs, such as material costs, labor hours expanded, labor rates paid, or labor union settlements;
- "make-or-buy" program decisions;
- subcontractor and vendor quotations;
- learning curve projections; and
- other business base projections.

Although the TINA requires disclosure of these types of information to the government, the contractor is not required to rely on these data in developing its proposal. A contractor is not constrained in exercising its best judgment in developing the estimated cost of a contract. The key to compliance with TINA is disclosure of relevant factual data. If current, accurate, and complete cost or pricing data have been disclosed, then it is assumed that the government or prime contractor negotiators have the necessary information to reach an informed agreement and a fair and reasonable contract price.

In order to ensure that government contractors are providing data in compliance with TINA, contractors are required to certify that such disclosures are accurate (i.e., current, accurate, and complete) for contracts or modifications to existing contracts with a value greater than certain dollar thresholds. Exceptions to disclosure and certification are provided in the following cases:

- the contract price is based on adequate price competition;
- an established catalog or market price exists, and the item is sold in substantial quantities to the general public;
- the prices are set by law or regulation; or
- it is an exceptional case. Such cases must be approved after agency head determinations.

Of course, the government negotiator must likewise spend considerable time analyzing and using such information in negotiating the best deal for the government. Accordingly, after the final "handshake," but before signing the certification, the contractor generally performs a final review to be sure that all of the cost and pricing data that may affect the final, agreed-to price have been disclosed.

If the certified cost or pricing data are not current, accurate, or complete on the effective date of the certificate, the government is entitled to a downward adjustment to the contract price. Such a situation is known as "defective pricing" under TINA. In addition to an adjustment to the contract price (if warranted), the contractor may be subject to further investigation for fraud, and, in cases where fraud is determined, criminal penalties may be imposed.

TINA Documentation Requirements

Common sense would dictate that any businessperson would document the results of a business negotiation. For government negotiators, the regulations require extensive and specific documentation. The FAR requires government contracting officers to establish and document written prenegotiation objectives prior to entering negotiations in accordance with FAR 15.406-1:

- a record of significant events in the acquisition;
- a list of attendees at the briefing;
- the current acquisition situation;
- the previous price history;
- a synopsis of offer submitted or received;
- the analytical methods used to establish price objectives;
- the delivery objectives;
- the negotiation plan; and
- signature blocks for the signature(s) of the approving official(s).

For a completed contract negotiation, the government contracting officer shall use a Price Negotiation Memorandum (PNM), in accordance with FAR 15.406-3. Understanding the many federal regulations that are a part of the negotiation process is a major step toward improving the resulting agreements for the buying and selling of products and services for the American public, although having such knowledge is not in itself enough to ensure negotiations reach a fair and reasonable price.

Value-Based Pricing

Value-based pricing (VBP) is the opposite of CBP. VBP is all about determining the value of a product or service from the customer's or buyer's perspective. Clearly, the determination of value varies dramatically in certain products or services. For example, the pricing of works of art is certainly not based upon the cost of clay, paint, and/or canvas, plus a reasonable profit or fee structure.

From a seller's perspective, VBP allows the supplier to research the marketplace and assess the intrinsic and extrinsic value that a product or service may be deemed to possess by one or more buyers. Thus, VBP is a blend of art and science, where traditional buying and selling using cost-based methods do not apply. VBP is like the best value pricing strategy on steroids. VBP provides the seller with the maximum potential opportunity for the highest possible profit and maximum price paid by a buyer. If you are a seller, then VBP is a beautiful thing!

Activity-Based Pricing

Activity-based pricing (ABP) is basically a modified version of CBP. ABP seeks to determine a fair and reasonable price based upon the costs estimated and/or actuals for the accomplishment of activities or processes, plus an appropriate profit/fee. ABP seeks to continuously improve business' activities and processes via internal and external benchmarking, thus reducing costs and increasing profit/fee margins for sellers. Likewise, the ABP method can benefit buyers, as sellers may be able to accelerate price reductions as a result of their continual focus on business activity and process improvement.

ABP has evolved over the past decade as a result of research into activity-based cost and performance (ABC&P), which is a methodology to identify and measure the costs and evaluate the performance of an organization's business processes. ABC&P provides insights into areas of and causes for poor performance, and it helps target efforts on improvement opportunities. Understanding the cost of activities and products helps organizations focus on high-payback areas and target investments for improvement of performance. The real key of ABC&P is to develop performance measures for each activity, then evaluate the actual performance results versus the plan.

Table 6-5 contains the typical ABC&P model and principal components.

Table 6-5 Activity-Based Cost and Performance (ABC&P) Principal Components

ABC&P Component	Definition	Examples
Resources	The elements (e.g., labor, materials, and facilities) used to perform work	• facilities • supplies • hardware and software
Resource driver	A measure of the consumption of a resource, used to determine the portion of the total resource cost assigned to each activity that uses the resource	• number of hours to perform the activity • number of square feet occupied • percent of time spent
Activity	One step within a process that uses resources to perform work; it occurs over time and has recognizable results	• test equipment • teach training classes • enter data
Activity driver	A measure of the frequency of activity performance and the effort required to achieve the end result	• number of classes required • number of forms processed • number of lines of data
Products	Any object that you wish to gain financial and nonfinancial information about through cost and performance measurement	• repaired ship • trained soldier • processed travel voucher • Army base
Cost driver	An indicator of why an activity is performed and what causes the cost of performing the activity to change	• proposed work package for a ship • yield rate of the activity • characteristic of a product
Performance measure	An indicator of the work performed and the results achieved in an activity; a measure of how well an activity meets the needs of its customers	• cycle time • number of errors • customer satisfaction • inventory fill rates

Source: Douglas W. Webster and Karen B. Burk, *Activity Based Costing and Performance* (Fairfax, VA: American Management Systems, 1994).

Table 6-6 Checklist of Key Pricing Best Practices to Improve Performance Results

Buyers and sellers should:

- Understand why price is important to all parties involved in performance-based acquisition.
- Be able to effectively apply and/or evaluate LPTA pricing.
- Be able to effectively apply and/or evaluate best-value pricing.
- Be able to effectively conduct trade-off decision making when evaluating price.
- Realize the evolution of best-value pricing.
- Use a contract type that fairly allocates risk.
- Train all team members to properly use pricing strategies and pricing methods.
- Ensure adequate cost estimating and accounting systems and practices.
- Understand and comply with all applicable U.S. government contracting laws, regulations, and policies.

Sellers should:

- Use best-value pricing strategy to the maximum extent practicable.
- Create value-added differentiators.
- Use the value-based pricing method when appropriate.
- Hire, train, and retain the best contract negotiators.
- Understand the buyer's source selection process and key source selection criteria.
- Not agree/sign a bad deal.
- Ensure a reasonable profit is obtainable.

SUMMARY

In retrospect, this chapter has examined the following aspects of price:

- The two most common pricing strategies
  1. Lowest-price-technically-acceptable
  2. Best value
- The three major methods for determining price:
  1. Cost-based pricing
  2. Value-based pricing
  3. Activity-based pricing

In Chapter 7, we will discuss the world of fixed-price and cost-reimbursement pricing arrangements: what they are, when to use them, how they work, and what are some proven best practices.

QUESTIONS TO CONSIDER

1. How often does your organization purchase products and/or services using the LPTA contract pricing strategy?

2. How often does your organization purchase products and/or services using the best- value contract pricing strategy?

3. What contract pricing method does your organization typically use when selling products and/or services?

4. What are the advantages and disadvantages of the cost-based pricing method?

ENDNOTES

[1] Darryl L. Walker, "Is Your Estimating System Asking for Trouble?" *Contract Management Magazine*, May 2004.

[2] Ibid.

[3] Jeffrey A. Lubeck, "Beyond an 'Adequate' Accounting System," *Contract Management Magazine*, May 2004.

[4] Ibid.

[5] Walker, "Asking for Trouble?"

[6] Ibid.

[7] Ibid.

CHAPTER 7

FIXED-PRICE AND COST- REIMBURSEMENT PRICING ARRANGEMENTS

Introduction

Business professionals who manage contracts must be aware of the many types of contract pricing arrangements available in order to choose the best type for each situation. Over time, three general pricing arrangement categories have evolved: fixed-price (FP), cost-reimbursement (CR), and time-and-materials (T&M). These categories and the contract types within each category are described in this chapter and the next, along with information on determining contract price and using pricing arrangements to balance the risk between contracting parties. In today's complex business world, a solid understanding of contract pricing options is essential for meeting business objectives.

Assessing Requirements to Determine Costs

Contract cost is determined by the contract requirements, which fall into two main categories: technical and administrative.

Technical Requirements

The solicitation specifications and statement of work contain technical requirements. These documents describe what the buyer wants to buy–the products that must be delivered and the services that must be rendered by the seller. The seller must consume resources–labor, capital, and money–to provide products and services to the buyer.

Administrative Requirements

Contract clauses describe other terms and conditions that will require the seller to consume resources, although the terms and conditions relate only indirectly to the technical requirements. The following clause excerpt provides such an example:

Company-Furnished Property

> . . . orders from ABC Company shall be held at the Seller's risk and shall be kept insured by the Seller at the Seller's expense while in Seller's custody and control in an amount equal to the replacement cost thereof, with loss payable to ABC Company.

SEVEN

The insurance requirement will cost money, but it is only indirectly related to the technical requirements of the project. Contracts contain many such administrative requirements.

CONTRACT PRICING

Contract pricing begins with determining the cost of performing the contract. To determine contract cost, a business professional who manages contracts must thoroughly analyze a prospective buyer's solicitation and develop a work breakdown structure based on the technical and administrative performance requirements. Next, he or she decides how the work will be implemented—that is, the order in which it will be performed and the methods and procedures that will be used to accomplish it. Based on these plans, the business professional estimates performance costs so that a price can be proposed. After the company has agreed on a contract price, it will be obligated to complete the work at that price unless a different arrangement can be negotiated.

To estimate performance costs, the following questions must be answered: What resources (labor, capital, money) will be needed to do the work? In what quantities will they be needed? When will they be needed? How much will those resources cost in the marketplace?

Estimating techniques do not necessarily require developing detailed answers to those questions. Parametric estimates, for instance, are used at a very high level and do not involve the type of analysis implied by the four questions. Nevertheless, some level of response to those questions is implicit in every cost estimate.

Uncertainty and Risk in Contract Pricing

The business professional's cost estimate will be a judgment, that is, a prediction about the future, rather than a fact. When the project manager says, "I estimate that the contract will cost US$500,000 to complete," that statement really means, "I predict that when I have completed the project according to the specifications, statement of work, and other contract terms and conditions, I will have consumed US$500,000 worth of labor, capital, and money."

The problem with this prediction, as with all predictions, is that no one will know whether it is true until all the events have occurred. Predictions are based largely on history; they assume that cause-

and-effect relationships in the future will be similar to those in the past. However, people frequently have an incorrect or incomplete understanding of the past. In addition, they may carry out even the best-laid plans imperfectly because of error or unexpected events. All these factors can cause the future to materialize differently than predicted.

Thus, the business professional's estimate may be incorrect. If it is too high, the company's proposal may not be competitive. If it is too low, the contract price may not be high enough to cover the project costs, and the company will suffer a financial loss. However sound the cost estimate, the contract price must be negotiated. Every negotiated price is a compromise between the extremes of an optimistic and a pessimistic prediction about future costs. The range between these two extremes is called the range of possible costs. The compromise results from negotiation between a risk-avoiding buyer and a risk-avoiding seller.

The risk-avoiding buyer wants to minimize the risk of agreeing to a higher price than necessary to cover the seller's costs plus a reasonable profit. Thus, the buyer tends to push the price toward the more optimistic end of the range of possible costs. The risk-avoiding seller wants to avoid the risk of agreeing to a price that may not cover its actual performance costs or allow a reasonable profit. Thus, the seller tends to push the price toward the more pessimistic end of the range of possible costs. The consequence of uncertainty about the future is risk, or the possibility of injury. A seller who undertakes a contractual obligation to complete a project for a fixed price but has estimated too low will suffer financial loss, unless it can shift the excess costs to the buyer or avoid them altogether. The effort made to avoid the injury will be proportional to its magnitude and related to its cause and direction.

Cost Overrun vs. Cost Growth

In both cost overruns and cost growth, actual costs exceed estimated costs, but in each case, they do so for different reasons. *Cost overruns* occur when the work has not changed, but it costs more than anticipated. This circumstance may occur for any number of reasons, including misfortune, mismanagement, faulty estimating, or poor planning, project design, or execution. *Cost growth* occurs when the parties change the work, adding to the cost of the project.

This circumstance may occur because of changes in the buyer's objectives or in marketable technology.

Although the causes are different, the result may be the same—actual costs exceed estimated costs. Usually, the parties will acknowledge cost growth and make appropriate adjustments to the contract price to compensate the seller for cost increases that arise from project changes. However, for cost overruns, neither party may be willing to take responsibility.

Effects of Cost Risk on Contract Performance

The initial injury from a cost overrun will befall the seller, because the seller is performing the work and incurring the costs. If the injury is small, the seller may choose to do nothing and pay the extra costs out of profit. If the injury is large, the seller will try to discover the source and nature of the overrun. The more serious the cost overrun, the more desperate the seller will be to find a remedy. The first step is to determine who is at fault. If the seller is responsible, it has no recourse but to suffer the loss, unless it can find ways to cut project costs to compensate for the overrun. Cutting costs can be accomplished by not doing things or by doing things less expensively than planned. If the seller takes either approach, the buyer will have a legitimate concern that the quality of goods or services will suffer.

Alternatively, the seller may argue with the buyer's interpretation of the contract's terms and conditions, seeking to avoid costly obligations. The seller may assert that various buyer requirements are "extras" or may claim that actions of the buyer were contrary to the terms of the contract, thus entitling the seller to more money. If the overrun is serious enough to threaten its survival, the seller may be unable or unwilling to continue to perform and may default. Frequently the buyer is the cause of cost overruns. This circumstance can occur when the buyer wheedles extra work from an overly responsive sales manager or when a project manager accedes to erroneous interpretations of the contract.

Obviously, risk affects behavior. Accordingly, when the parties to a contract recognize that the cost uncertainties of performance are great—so great that the attendant risks may result in behaviors that threaten the project's objectives—the parties should adopt pricing arrangements that equitably distribute that risk between them.

Developing Pricing Arrangements

Over the years some standard pricing arrangements have evolved. These arrangements fall into three categories: *fixed-price, cost-reimbursement,* and *time-and-materials* contracts. (The Project Management Institute also designates unit-price contracts as a separate category.) These contract categories have developed as practical responses to cost risk, and they have become fairly standard formal arrangements. Incentives can be added to any of the contract types in these three categories and are discussed in detail later in this chapter. Table 7-1 lists several common contract types in these categories.

These pricing arrangements, however, are manifested in the specific terms and conditions of contracts, that is, in the contract clauses. No standard clauses for their implementation exist. Therefore, the contracting parties must write clauses that describe their specific agreement.

Table 7-1 Contract Categories and Types			
Types of Contracts	**Fixed-Price**	**Cost-Reimbursement or Unit-Price***	**Time-and-Materials**
	• Firm-fixed-price • Fixed-price with economic price adjustment • Fixed-price incentive	• Cost-reimbursement • Cost-plus-a-percentage-of-cost • Cost-plus-fixed-fee • Cost-plus-incentive-fee • Cost-plus-award-fee	• Time-and-materials • Labor-hour
*PMI designates this as a separate category.			

Fixed-Price Category

Fixed-price contracts are the standard business pricing arrangement. The two basic types of fixed-price contracts are firm-fixed-price (FFP) and fixed-price with economic price adjustment (FP/EPA). Firm-fixed-price contracts are further divided into lump-sum and unit-price arrangements.

Firm-Fixed-Price Contracts

The simplest and most common business pricing arrangement is the FFP contract. The seller agrees to supply specified goods or deliverables in a specified quantity or to render a specified service or level of effort (LOE) in return for a specified price, either a lump sum or a unit price. The price is fixed, that is, not subject to change based on the seller's actual cost experience. (However, it may be subject to change if the parties modify the contract.) This pricing arrangement is used for the sale of commercial goods and services.

Some companies include a complex clause in their FFP contracts. Such a clause may read in part as follows:

Prices and Taxes

The price of Products shall be ABC Company's published list prices on the date ABC Company accepts your order less any applicable discount. If ABC Company announces a price increase for Equipment, or Software licensed for a one-time fee, after it accepts your order but before shipment, ABC Company shall invoice you at the increased price only if delivery occurs more than 120 days after the effective date of the price increase. If ABC Company announces a price increase for Services, Rentals, or Software licensed for a periodic fee, the price increase shall apply to billing periods beginning after its effective date.

Note that this clause was written by the seller, not the buyer, and reflects the seller's point of view and concerns. Nevertheless, the pricing arrangement it describes is firm-fixed-price, because the contract price will not be subject to adjustment based on ABC Company's actual performance costs.

Clauses such as "Prices and Taxes" frequently form part of a document known as a universal agreement. Such a document is not a contract; it is a precontract agreement that merely communicates any agreed-to terms and conditions that will apply when an order is placed by the buyer. After an order is accepted by the seller, the company's published or announced list prices become the basis for the contract price according to the terms of the universal agreement. (This agreement is discussed later in this chapter under "Purchase Agreements.")

Firm-fixed-price contracts are appropriate for most commercial transactions when cost uncertainty is within commercially acceptable limits. What those limits may be depends on the industry and the market.

Fixed-Price with Economic Price Adjustment

Fixed-price contracts sometimes include various clauses that provide for adjusting prices based on specified contingencies. The clauses may provide for upward or downward adjustments, or both. Economic price adjustments (EPAs) are usually limited to factors beyond the seller's immediate control, such as market forces.

This pricing arrangement is not *firm*-fixed-price, because the contract provides for a price adjustment based on the seller's actual performance costs. Thus, the seller is protected from the risk of certain labor or material cost increases. The EPA clause can provide for price increases based on the seller's *costs* but not on the seller's decision to increase the *prices* of its products or services. Thus, there can be a significant difference between this clause and the "Prices and Taxes" clause discussed previously.

The shift of risk to the buyer creates greater buyer intrusion into the affairs of the seller. This intrusion typically takes the form of an audit provision at the end of the clause, particularly when the buyer is a government. EPA clauses are appropriate in times of market instability, when great uncertainty exists regarding labor and material costs. The risk of cost fluctuations is more balanced between the parties than would be the case under an FFP contract.

Cost-Reimbursement Category

Cost-reimbursement (CR) contracts usually include an estimate of project cost, a provision for reimbursing the seller's expenses, and a provision for paying a fee as profit. Normally, CR contracts also include a limitation on the buyer's cost liability.

A common perception is that CR contracts are to be avoided. However, if uncertainty about costs is great enough, a buyer may be unable to find a seller willing to accept a fixed price, even with adjustment clauses, or a seller may insist on extraordinary contingencies within that price. In the latter case, the buyer may find the demands unreasonable. Such high levels of cost uncertainty are often found in research and development, large-scale construction, and systems integration projects. In such circumstances, the best solution may be a CR contract—but only if the buyer is confident that the seller has a highly accurate and reliable cost accounting system.

The parties to a CR contract will find themselves confronting some challenging issues, especially concerning the definition, measurement, allocation, and confirmation of costs. First, the parties must agree on a definition for acceptable cost. For instance, the buyer may decide that the cost of air travel should be limited to the price of a coach or business-class ticket and should not include a first-class ticket. The buyer will specify other cost limitations, and the parties will negotiate until they agree on what constitutes a reimbursable cost.

Next, the parties must decide who will measure costs and what accounting rules will be used to do so. For example, several depreciation techniques are in use, some of which would be less advantageous to the buyer than others. Which technique will the buyer consider acceptable? How will labor costs be calculated? Will standard costs be acceptable, or must the seller determine and invoice actual costs? What methods of allocating overhead will be acceptable to the buyer? How will the buyer know that the seller's reimbursement invoices are accurate? Will the buyer have the right to obtain an independent audit? If the buyer is also a competitor of the seller, should the seller be willing to open its books to the buyer? If these issues remain unsettled, the buyer is accepting the risk of having to reimburse costs it may later find to be unreasonable. This issue is the central problem with CR contracting, and it has never been resolved entirely.

Clearly, the CR contract presents the parties with difficulties they would not face under a fixed-price contract. The parties must define costs and establish acceptable procedures for cost measurement and allocation, the buyer takes on greater cost risk and must incur greater administrative costs to protect its interests, and the seller faces greater intrusion by the buyer into its affairs. Nevertheless, many contracting parties have found a CR contract to be a better arrangement than a fixed-price contract for undertakings with high cost uncertainty.

Types of CR contracts include *cost, cost-sharing, cost-plus-a-percentage-of-cost (CPPC)*, and *cost-plus-fixed-fee (CPFF)*.

Cost Contracts

The cost contract is the simplest type of CR contract. Governments commonly use this type when contracting with universities and nonprofit organizations for research projects. The contract provides for reimbursing contractually allowable costs, with no allowance given for profit.

Cost-Sharing Contracts

The cost-sharing contract provides for only partial reimbursement of the seller's costs. The parties share the cost liability, with no allowance for profit. The cost-sharing contract is appropriate when the seller will enjoy some benefit from the results of the project and that benefit is sufficient to encourage the seller to undertake the work for only a portion of its costs and without fee.

Cost-Plus-a-Percentage-of-Cost Contracts

The cost-plus-a-percentage-of-cost (CPPC) contract provides for the seller to receive reimbursement for its costs and a profit component, called a *fee*, equal to some predetermined percentage of its actual costs. Thus, as costs go up, so does profit. This arrangement is a poor one from the buyer's standpoint; it provides no incentive to control costs, because the fee gets bigger as the costs go up. This type of contract was used extensively by the U.S. government during World War I but has since been made illegal for U.S. government contracts, for good reason. It is still occasionally used for construction projects and some service contracts in the private sector.

The rationale for this pricing arrangement was probably "the bigger the job, the bigger the fee," that is, as the job grows, so should the fee. This arrangement is similar to a professional fee, such as an attorney's fee, which grows as the professional puts more time into the project. This arrangement may have developed as a response to the cost-growth phenomenon in projects that were initially ill-defined. As a seller proceeded with the work, the buyer's needs became better defined and grew, until the seller felt that the fees initially agreed to were not enough for the expanded scope of work.

Cost-Plus-Fixed-Fee Contracts

Cost-plus-fixed-fee (CPFF) is the most common type of CR contract. As with the others, the seller is reimbursed for its costs, but the contract also provides for payment of a fixed fee that does not change in response to the seller's actual cost experience. The seller is paid the fixed fee on successful completion of the contract, whether its actual costs were higher or lower than the estimated costs.

If the seller completes the work for less than the estimated cost, it receives the entire fixed fee. If the seller incurs the estimated cost without completing the work, and if the buyer decides not to pay for the overrun costs necessary for completion, the seller receives a portion of the fixed fee that is equal to the percentage of work completed. If the buyer decides to pay overrun costs, the seller must complete the work without any increase in the fixed fee. The only adjustment to the fee would be a result of cost growth, when the buyer requires the seller to do more work than initially specified.

This type of contract is on the opposite end of the spectrum from the FFP contract, because cost risk rests entirely on the shoulders of the buyer. Under a CR contract, a buyer might have to reimburse the seller for the entire estimated cost and part of the fee but have nothing to show for it but bits and pieces of the work.

CLASSIFICATION OF CONTRACT INCENTIVES

The fundamental purpose of contract incentives is to motivate desired performance in one or more specific areas. Contract incentives are generally classified as either objectively based and evaluated or subjectively based and evaluated. Further, both classifications of contract incentives are typically categorized as either positive incentives (rewards–get more money) or negative incentives (penalties–get less money) or some combination thereof.

Those incentives that use predetermined formula-based methods to calculate the amount of incentive, either positive or negative, in one or more designated areas are objectively based and evaluated. Facts and actual events are used as a basis for determination–individual judgment and opinions are not considered in an evaluation of performance.

Objectively based and evaluated contract incentives commonly include the following designated performance areas:
- Cost performance
- Schedule or delivery performance
- Quality performance

Subjectively based and evaluated contract incentives are those incentives that use individual judgment, opinions, and informed impressions as the basis for determining the amount of incentive, either positive or negative, in one or more designated areas.

These incentives can and often do contain some objective aspects or factors. However, subjective contract incentives are ultimately determined by one or more individuals making a decision based on their experience, knowledge, and the available information—a total judgment.

Subjectively based and evaluated contract incentives typically include the following:
- Award fees
- Award term
- Other special incentives

Table 7-2 summarizes the link between rewards and penalties and contract incentives as described in the following paragraphs.

Objective Incentives

Incentives Based on Cost Performance

Cost is the most commonly chosen performance variable. For fixed-price (cost) incentive contracts, the parties negotiate a *target cost* and a *target profit* (which equals the *target price*) and a *sharing formula* for cost overruns and cost underruns. They also negotiate a *ceiling price*, which is the buyer's maximum dollar liability. When performance is complete, they determine the final actual costs and apply the sharing formula to any overrun or underrun. Applying the sharing formula determines the seller's final profit, if any.

Table 7-2 Contract Incentives			
Types of Incentives	Positive (rewards)	No Reward or Penalty	Negative (penalties)
Objective incentives			
Cost performance	Under budget	On budget	Over budget
Schedule or delivery performance	Early delivery	On-time delivery	Late delivery
Quality performance	Exceed requirements	Achieve contract requirements	Do not achieve requirements
Subjective incentives Award fee Award term	Exceed requirements	Achieve award fee plan	Do not achieve requirements

Consider an example in which the parties agree to the following arrangement:

- *Target cost:* US $10,000,000
- *Target profit:* US $850,000
- *Target price:* US $10,850,000
- *Sharing formula:* 70/30 (buyer 70 percent, seller 30 percent)
- *Ceiling price:* US $11,500,000

Assume that the seller completes the work at an actual cost of US$10,050,000, overrunning the target cost by US$50,000. The seller's share of the overrun is 30 percent of US$50,000, which is US$15,000. The target profit will be reduced by that amount (US$850,000 - 15,000 = US$835,000). The seller will then receive the US$10,050,000 cost of performance plus an earned profit of US$835,000. Thus, the price to the buyer will be US$10,885,000, which is US$615,000 below the ceiling price. The US$35,000 increase over the target price of US$10,850,000 represents the buyer's 70 percent share of the cost overrun.

Had the seller overrun the target cost by US$100,000, raising the actual cost to US$10,100,000, the seller's share of the overrun would have been 30 percent or US$30,000. That amount would have reduced the seller's profit to US$820,000.

Basically, at some point before reaching the ceiling price, the sharing arrangement effectively changes to 0/100, with the seller assuming 100 percent of the cost risk. This effect is implicit in fixed-price incentive arrangements because of the ceiling price and is not an explicit element of the formula. The point at which sharing changes to 0/100 is called the point of total assumption (PTA), which represents a cost figure. Indeed, the PTA is often appropriately referred to as the high-cost estimate. Figure 7-1 depicts these relationships and outcomes in graphical form. (Note that the graph describes a first-degree linear equation of the form $Y = A - BX$, with cost as the independent variable X, and profit as the dependent variable Y. B, the coefficient of X, is equal to the seller's share.)

The PTA can be determined by applying the following formula:

$$PTA = \left(\frac{\text{Ceiling Price} - \text{Target Price}}{\text{Buyer Share Ratio}} \right) + \text{Target Cost}$$

In the event of an underrun, the seller would enjoy greater profit. If the final cost is US$9,000,000 (a US$1,000,000 underrun), the seller's share of the underrun is 30 percent, which is US$300,000. Thus, the price to the buyer would include the US$9,000,000 cost and the US$850,000 target profit plus the seller's US$300,000 underrun share (total profit of US$1,150,000). Thus, US$9,000,000 actual cost plus US$1,150,000 actual profit equals US$10,150,000 actual price, reflecting precisely the buyer's 70 percent share of the US$1,000,000 underrun [US$10,850,000 target price - 70 percent of the US$1,000,000 underrun (US$700,000) = US$10,150,000].

Incentives Based on Schedule or Delivery Performance

For many years, construction, aerospace, and numerous service industries have used schedule or delivery performance incentives to motivate sellers to provide either early or on-time delivery of products and services.

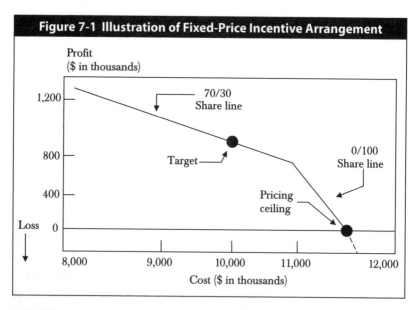

Figure 7-1 Illustration of Fixed-Price Incentive Arrangement

Liquidated damages is a negative incentive (penalty) for late delivery. Typically, a liquidated damages clause stated in the contract terms and conditions designates how much money one party, usually the seller, must pay the other party, usually the buyer, for not meeting the contract schedule. Often the amount of liquidated damages payable is specified as an amount of money for a specific period of time (day, week, month). A key aspect of liquidated damages is that the penalty is to be based on the amount of damages incurred or compensable in nature, not an excessive or punitive amount.

A proven best practice for buyers is to require negative incentives (or penalties) for late delivery and late schedule performance. Likewise, a proven best practice for sellers is to limit their liability on liquidated damages by agreeing to a cap or maximum amount and seeking positive incentives (or rewards) for early delivery and early schedule performance.

Incentives Based on Quality Performance

Quality performance incentives is one of the most common topics in government and commercial contracting. Surveys in both government and industry have revealed widespread service contracting problems, including deficient statements of work, poor contract administration, performance delays, and quality shortcomings.

When a contract is based on performance, all aspects of the contract are structured around the purpose of the work to be performed rather than the manner in which it is to be done. The buyer seeks to elicit the best performance the seller has to offer, at a reasonable price or cost, by stating its objectives and giving sellers both latitude in determining how to achieve them and incentives for achieving them. In source selection, for example, the buyer might publish a draft solicitation for comment, use quality-related evaluation factors, or both. The statement of work will provide performance standards rather than spelling out what the seller is to do. The contract normally contains a plan for quality assurance surveillance. And the contract typically includes positive and negative performance incentives.

Few people disagree with the concept that buyers, who collectively spend billions of dollars on services annually, should look to the performance-based approach, focusing more on results and less on detailed requirements. However, implementing performance-based contracting (using cost, schedule, and/or quality performance variables) is far easier said than done. The sound use of performance incentives is key to the success of the performance-based contracting approach.

Problems with Applying Objective Incentives

The objective-incentive schemes described have some merit, but they also involve some serious practical problems. First, they assume a level of buyer and seller competence that may not exist. Second, they assume effects that may not occur. Third, they create serious challenges for contract administration.

To negotiate objective incentives intelligently, the parties must have some knowledge of the range of possible costs for a project. They also must have some knowledge of the likely causes and probabilities of different cost outcomes. If both parties do not have sufficient information on these issues, they will not be able to structure an effective incentive formula.

It is important that the parties share their information. If one party has superior knowledge that it does not share with the other, it will be able to skew the formula in its favor during negotiation. If that happens, the whole point of the arrangement, which is to equitably balance the risks of performance, will be lost. The buyer is usually at a disadvantage with respect to the seller in this regard.

An objective incentive assumes that the seller can effect a performance outcome along the entire range of the independent variable. However, such may not be true. For instance, the seller may actually exercise control along only a short sector of the range of possible costs. Some possible cost outcomes may be entirely outside the seller's control because of factors such as market performance. In reality, the seller's project manager may have little control over important factors that may determine the cost outcome, such as overhead costs. In addition, short-term companywide factors, especially those involving overhead, may, on some contracts, make incurring additional cost rather than earning additional profit more advantageous for the seller.

In addition, objective cost incentives are complicated and costly to administer, with all the cost definition, measurement, allocation, and confirmation problems of CR contracts. The parties must be particularly careful to segregate the target cost effects of cost growth from those of cost overruns; otherwise, they may lose money for the wrong reasons. As a practical matter, segregating such costs is often quite difficult. When using other performance incentives, the parties may find themselves disputing the causes of various performance outcomes. The seller may argue that schedule delays are a result of actions of the buyer. Quality problems, such as poor reliability, may have been caused by improper buyer operation rather than seller performance. The causes of performance failures may be difficult to determine.

One reason for using such contracts is to reduce the deleterious effects of risk on the behavior of the parties. Thus, if a pricing arrangement increases the likelihood of trouble, it should not be used. The decision to apply objective incentives should be made only after careful analysis.

15 Actions to Improve Your Use of Contract Incentives

These best practices should be followed when using incentive contracts:

- Think creatively. Creativity is a critical aspect in the success of performance-based incentive contracting.
- Avoid rewarding sellers for simply meeting contract requirements.
- Recognize that developing clear, concise, objectively measurable performance incentives will be a challenge, and plan accordingly.
- Create a proper balance of objective incentives—cost, schedule, and quality performance.
- Ensure that performance incentives focus the seller's efforts on the buyer's desired objectives.
- Make all forms of performance incentives challenging yet attainable.
- Ensure that incentives motivate quality control and that the results of the seller's quality control efforts can be measured.
- Consider tying on-time delivery to cost and or quality performance criteria.
- Recognize that not everything can be measured objectively. Consider using a combination of objectively measured standards and subjectively determined incentives.
- Encourage open communication and ongoing involvement with potential sellers in developing the performance-based SOW and the incentive plan, both before and after issuing the formal request for proposals.
- Consider including socioeconomic incentives (non-SOW-related) in the incentive plan.

- Use clear, objective formulas for determining performance incentives.
- Use a combination of positive and negative incentives.
- Include incentives for discounts based on early payments.
- Ensure that all incentives, both positive and negative, have limits.

Subjective Incentives

Award-Fee Plans

In an award-fee plan, the parties negotiate an estimated cost, just as for CPFF contracts. Then they negotiate an agreement on the amount of money to be included in an award-fee pool. Finally, they agree on a set of criteria and procedures to be applied by the buyer in determining how well the seller has performed and how much fee the seller has earned. In some cases, the parties also negotiate a base fee, which is a fixed fee that the seller will earn no matter how its performance is evaluated.

The contract performance period is then divided into equal award-fee periods. A part of the award-fee pool is allocated to each period proportionate to the percentage of the work scheduled to be completed. All this information is included in the award-fee plan, which becomes part of the contract. In some cases, the contract allows the buyer to change the award-fee plan unilaterally before the start of a new award-fee period.

During each award-fee period, the buyer observes and documents the seller's performance achievements or failures. At the end of each period, the buyer evaluates the seller's performance according to the award-fee plan and decides how much fee to award from the portion allocated to that period. Under some contracts, the seller has an opportunity to present its own evaluation of its performance and a specific request for award fee. The buyer then informs the seller how much of the available award fee it has earned and how its performance could be improved during ensuing award-fee periods. This arrangement invariably involves subjectivity on the part of the buyer; precisely how much depends on how the award-fee plan is written.

Pros and Cons of the Award-Fee Arrangement

The cost-plus-award-fee (CPAF) contract is a cost-reimbursement contract, with all its requirements for cost definition, measurement, allocation, and confirmation. For the buyer, the CPAF contract requires the additional administrative investment associated with observing, documenting, and evaluating seller performance. However, this disadvantage may sometimes be overemphasized, because the buyer should already be performing many of these activities under a CR contract.

The disadvantages for the buyer are offset by the extraordinary power it obtains from the ability to make subjective determinations about how much fee the seller has earned. The buyer may have difficulty establishing objective criteria for satisfactory service performance. The power of subjective fee determination tends to make sellers extraordinarily responsive to the buyer's demands. However, the buyer must be careful, because that very responsiveness can be the cause of cost overruns and unintended cost growth.

The buyer's advantages are almost entirely disadvantages from the viewpoint of the seller, because the seller will have placed itself within the power of the buyer to an exceptional degree. Subjectivity can approach arbitrariness or even cross the line. The seller may find itself dealing with a buyer that is impossible to please or that believes that the seller cannot earn all of the award fee because no one can achieve "perfect" performance.

Other Special Incentives

There is a growing recognition by buyers and sellers worldwide, in both the public and private sectors, that contract incentives can be expanded and that they are indeed valuable tools to motivate the desired performance. Increasingly, when outsourcing, buyers are motivating sellers to subcontract with local companies, often with special rewards for subcontracting with designated small businesses. Likewise, many sellers are providing buyers with special incentives for early payment, such as product or services discounts or additional specified services at no change.

INCENTIVE CONTRACTS

Cost-Plus-Incentive-Fee Contracts

Cost-plus-incentive-fee (CPIF) contracts allow overrun or underrun sharing of cost through a predetermined formula for fee adjustments that apply to incentives for cost category contracts. Within the basic concept of the buyer's paying all costs for a cost contract, the limits for a CPIF contract become those of maximum and minimum fees. The necessary elements for a CPIF contract are maximum fee, minimum fee, target cost, target fee, and share ratio(s).

Fixed-Price-Incentive Contracts

In a fixed-price-incentive (FPI) contract, seller profit is linked to another aspect of performance—cost, schedule, quality, or a combination of all three. The objective is to give the seller a monetary incentive to optimize cost performance.

Fixed-price-incentive contracts may be useful for initial production of complex new products or systems, although the parties may have difficulty agreeing on labor and material costs for such projects because of a lack of production experience. However, the cost uncertainty may not be great enough to warrant use of a CR contract.

Cost-Plus-Award-Fee Contracts

Cost-plus-award-fee contracts include subjective incentives, in which the profit a seller earns depends on how well the seller satisfies a buyer's subjective desires. This type of contract has been used for a long time in both government and commercial contracts worldwide. The U.S. Army Corps of Engineers developed an evaluated fee contract for use in construction during the early 1930s, based on its contracting experience during World War I. The U.S. National Aeronautics and Space Administration has used CPAF contracts to procure services since the 1950s. Other U.S. government agencies have also used these contracts extensively, including the Department of Energy and the Department of Defense. A small but growing number of commercial companies now use award fees to motivate their suppliers to achieve exceptional performance.

Cost-plus-award-fee contracts are used primarily to procure services, particularly those that involve an ongoing, long-term relationship between buyer and seller, such as maintenance and systems engineering support. Objective criteria for determining the acceptability of the performance of such services are inherently difficult to establish. The award fee arrangement is particularly well suited to such circumstances, at least from the buyer's point of view. However, this type of contract also is used to procure architecture and engineering, research and development, hardware and software systems design and development, construction, and many other services.

Base Fees

As stated earlier, a base fee on a CPAF contract is a fixed fee established by the buying activity upon contract award. A base fee is incrementally paid to the contractor regardless of its performance on the contract, as long as the contract is not terminated. On government cost-reimbursement type contracts, that actual payment of a base fee typically accompanies a contractor's monthly reimbursement (by the government) for "best efforts" of actual contractor expenses. Simply knowing what a base fee is and how it is paid is good, but knowing how to determine a base fee amount is better!

In the following discussion, I have identified three common concepts to determine an appropriate amount of base fee (which may be used) for CPAF contracts. These concepts have been used by various government buying activities to determine an appropriate amount of base fee for CPAF contracts.

1. **Marginal performance level (MPL) concept:** Inherent in this concept is the idea that the base fee is established with a particular quality or level of performance in mind. Base fees are established by taking into consideration the various profit analysis factors, but in an amount commensurate with that level or quality of performance categorized as minimum acceptable. The MPL concept has been used by NASA and other government buying activities for nearly 30 years to determine the amount of base fee. This concept contains no present limits to the amounts of base fee.

2. **Unallowable cost offset (UCO) concept:** For many years the Defense Federal Acquisition Regulation Supplement (DFARS) stated, "The base fee shall not exceed three percent of the estimated cost of the contract exclusive of the fee." The DFARS

did not provide the rationale for why this limit was required on DoD contracts; however, through research I have concluded that several financial aspects caused the development of this UCO concept. One of the most significant financial aspects, considered vital to the establishment of the UCO concept, was and is the business strategy of all contractors to offset unallowable costs that they incur on government cost-reimbursement types of contracts. Typically, aerospace contractors have had two to three percent of their contract costs deemed unallowable as a result of government cost accounting standards and audits. Thus, many contractors will not agree to enter into a cost-reimbursement type of contract unless they are assured a minimum fee of two to three percent of the estimated cost. The government under the UCO concept would provide contractors a minimum base fee guarantee up to three percent to offset contractor unallowable costs, thereby reducing the possibility of a contractor financial-loss situation.

3. **Zero base fee (ZBF) concept:** Over the past 20 years, many government buying activities have established and used the ZBF concept or policy. The ZBF concept is based upon the assumption that by eliminating base fee, the total fee pool (consisting solely of an award fee) would provide a greater incentive for contractors to achieve superior performance. A ZBF policy was used for many years by the Air Force Systems Command (AFSC), now Air Force Material Command (AFMC), buying activities.

When examining these concepts to determine the amount of base fee, it is obvious that the MPL concept provides the contractor with the largest possible base fee, while the ZBF concept provides none. Therefore, the UCO concept is often considered to be a fair and reasonable compromise to determine a base-fee amount.

Award Fees

For years, major defense buying activities have instructed their buying offices to use objective methods to arrive at either the size of the award-fee pool or the amount of the award-fee determination on CPAF contracts. In many instances, this was manifested in the use of weighted guidelines or an alternate structured approach to arrive at either the size of the award-fee pool or the amount of an award-fee determination on a CPAF contract, which is not appropriate because it is a misapplication of the DoD profit policy. Equally important, the use of totally objective methods to arrive at the award-fee pool or award-fee determination is a contradiction of the concepts that underlie and support the use of a CPAF contract. Flexibility is needed to arrive at both an award-fee pool and award-fee determination that suit the circumstances of a particular procurement.

While there is a need for flexibility in the determination of an award fee, there is also a need for consistency in the process. Consistency and flexibility are not exclusive of each other. Award-fee ratings must be clearly related to the available award-fee pool. Consistency does not mean using an unalterably structured approach. Rather, it means clearly defining the subjective/objective elements of the flexible approach one is using. Defining your philosophy in the determination of award fee is beneficial to both the contractor and the government.

The description of how you will create and administer an award fee is the essence of communications. While there should be flexibility in the application of the philosophy, the philosophy itself should be consistently applied throughout a buying activity. The consistent application of an award-fee determination will improve communications and have an impact on the entire contracting cycle from the request for proposal to the completion of the contract effort.

Award Fee—Lessons Learned

1. **Use award fees on FFP contracts.** Seldom has an award fee been used on a multimillion-dollar contract in conjunction with a firm-fixed-price-type contract. In addition, when an award fee is combined with a type of contract other than CPAF, the profit or fee already part of the contract serves as the equivalent to the base fee. Thus, FFP contracts do not contain a typical base fee, as commonly used on CPAF-type contracts.

2. **Select only a few highly skilled performance monitors.** Some successful organizations managing the government administration of award-fee contracts have selected only a few highly skilled performance monitors in each functional area to provide input to the government's Award Review Board (ARB). Typically, large complex contracts have many people involved in evaluating the contractor's performance. Several

organizations have found that sometimes *fewer highly skilled* performance monitors, who are well educated and trained in their functional area and their specific performance monitoring responsibilities, are *better!*

3. **Create a highly empowered ARB.** Creating highly empowered members of the ARB to evaluate, tailor, and summarize performance monitors' findings has proven very successful. Even with the best performance monitors, it is possible (even likely) to have a variety of opinions when it comes to subjectively evaluating a contractor's performance, no matter how much you objectively structure the evaluation process. The fee-determining official (FDO) needs a clear and concise recommendation from the ARB concerning the contractor's performance versus the award-fee plan. Highly empowering the ARB allows the ARB members to separate the chaff from the wheat and provides the ARB with the flexibility to examine the whole effort from a system perspective, rather than merely reporting functional inputs.

Award Fee—Best Practices

1. **Update the award-fee plan.** Do not be caught with 50 percent of the award fee allocated in the award-fee plan to field performance when you have not fielded the equipment.

2. **Do not be afraid to vary the award fee by period.** Do not be trapped by your previous contractor's performance evaluations. Give the contractor the amount of award fee that the contractor deserves, whether they like it or not!

3. **Develop effective performance evaluation standards.** Award-fee evaluations should not vary dramatically based solely upon evaluator personalities. Performance standards must be established and clearly communicated to the contractor by all government performance monitors.

4. **Award fees must communicate a message.** The FDO must use the award-fee process to clearly communicate to a contractor his or her view of their performance and where improvement is required.

5. **Use rollover of unearned award fees only when appropriate.** Do not allow contractors to be able to receive award fees that were unearned (i.e., not paid in previous award-fee periods) unless the contractor was able to in some appropriate way make up for their previous shortcomings in performance.

6. **Do not be afraid to revise award-fee evaluation criteria.** Many organizations have determined that their criteria needed to reflect a different emphasis, so they changed the criteria. They were not hesitant to change the criteria so that they better met their needs and their desired outcomes. Do not be afraid to change any aspect of the award-fee plan if it better motivates the contractor to achieve superior results.

7. **Use Defense Contract Management Agency (DCMA) contract administration support.** DCMA is organized to support its customers, government/military buying offices. Through the FAR delegation process, DCMA can serve as a valuable asset for evaluating contractor performance.

8. **Write it down!** Sooner or later your memory will fail you. It is imperative to keep detailed written records. Be specific in your examples to include the impact of what you are documenting. Put your written records where you can find them.

9. **Communicate!** Frequent and specific communication with the contractor and other government organizations is a must at all levels. There should be no surprises when there is open communication. An award fee should be a part of daily management of the program.

10. **Only pay incentives and award fees for superior performance.** Do not pay contractors award fees as a means to increase their base fee for merely meeting minimal contract requirements.

Buyer's and Seller's Risk

Figure 7-2 depicts the range of contract types and their corresponding risk to buyer and seller.

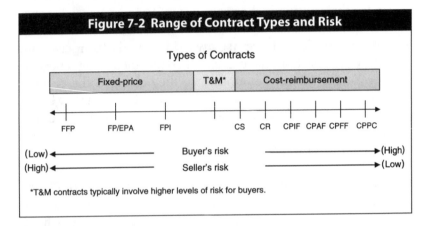

Figure 7-2 Range of Contract Types and Risk

Choosing the Contract Type

Table 7-3 shows the advantages, disadvantages, and suitability of the various contract types.

	Table 7-3 Advantages, Disadvantages, and Suitability of Various Contract Types		
Type	**Essential Elements and Advantages**	**Disadvantages**	**Suitability**
Firm-fixed-price (FFP)	Reasonably definite design or performance specifications available. Fair and reasonable price can be established at outset. Conditions for use include the following: • Adequate competition • Prior purchase experience of the same, or similar, supplies or services under competitive conditions • Valid cost or pricing data • Realistic estimates of proposed cost • Possible uncertainties in performance can be identified and priced • Sellers willing to accept contract at a level that causes them to take all financial risks • Any other reasonable basis for pricing can be used to establish fair and reasonable price	Price not subject to adjustment regardless of seller performance costs. Places 100% of financial risk on seller. Places least amount of administrative burden on contract manager. Preferred over all other contract types. Used with advertised or negotiated procurements.	Commercial products and commercial services for which reasonable prices can be established.

Table 7-3 Advantages, Disadvantages, and Suitability of Various Contract Types			
Type	**Essential Elements and Advantages**	**Disadvantages**	**Suitability**
Fixed-price with economic price adjustment (FP/EPA)	Unstable market or labor conditions during performance period and contingencies that would otherwise be included in contract price can be identified and made the subject of a separate price adjustment clause. Contingencies must be specifically defined in contract. Provides for upward adjustment (with ceiling) in contract price. May provide for downward adjustment of price if escalated element has potential of falling below contract limits. Three general types of EPAs, based on established prices, actual costs of labor or material, and cost indexes of labor or material.	Price can be adjusted on action of an industry-wide contingency that is beyond seller's control. Reduces seller's fixed-price risk. FP/EPA is preferred over any CR-type contract. If contingency manifests, contract administration burden increases. Used with negotiated procurements and, in limited applications, with formal advertising when determined to be feasible. Contract manager must determine if FP/EPA is necessary either to protect seller and buyer against significant fluctuations in labor or material costs or to provide for contract price adjustment in case of changes in seller's established prices.	Commercial products and services for which reasonable prices can be established at time of award.

Table 7-3 Advantages, Disadvantages, and Suitability of Various Contract Types

Type	Essential Elements and Advantages	Disadvantages	Suitability
Fixed-price-incentive (FPI)	Cost uncertainties exist, but there is potential for cost reduction or performance improvement by giving seller a degree of cost responsibility and a positive profit incentive. Profit is earned or lost based on relationship that contract's final negotiated cost bears to total target cost. Contract must contain target cost, target profit, ceiling price, and profit-sharing formula. Two forms of FPI: firm target (FPIF) and successive targets (FPIS). • FPIF: Firm target cost, target profit, and profit-sharing formula negotiated into basic contract; profit adjusted at contract completion. • FPIS: Initial cost and profit targets negotiated into contract, but final cost target (firm) cannot be negotiated until performance. Contains production point(s) at which either a firm target and final profit formula, or a FFP contract, can be negotiated. Elements that can be incentives: costs, performance, delivery, quality.	Requires adequate seller accounting system. Buyer must determine that FPI is least costly and award of any other type would be impractical. Buyer and seller administrative effort is more extensive than under other fixed-price contract types. Used only with competitive negotiated contracts. Billing prices must be established for interim payment.	Development and production of high-volume, multiyear contracts.
Cost-Reimbursement Contracts (Greatest Risk for Buyer)			
Cost	Appropriate for research and development work, particularly with nonprofit educational institutions or other nonprofit organizations, and for facilities contracts. Allowable costs of contract performance are reimbursed, but no fee is paid.	Application limited due to no fee and by the fact that the buyer is not willing to reimburse seller fully if there is a commercial benefit for the seller. Only nonprofit institutions and organizations are willing (usually) to perform research for which there is no fee (or other tangible benefits).	Research and development; facilities.
Cost-sharing (CS)	Used when buyer and seller agree to share costs in a research or development project having potential mutual benefits. Because of commercial benefits accruing to the seller, no fee is paid. Seller agrees to absorb a portion of the costs of performance in expectation of compensating benefits to seller's firm or organization. Such benefits might include an enhancement of the seller's capability and expertise or an improvement of its competitive position in the commercial market.	Care must be taken in negotiating cost-share rate so that the cost ratio is proportional to the potential benefit (that is, the party receiving the greatest potential benefit bears the greatest share of the costs).	Research and development that has potential benefits to both the buyer and the seller.

Table 7-3 Advantages, Disadvantages, and Suitability of Various Contract Types			
Type	**Essential Elements and Advantages**	**Disadvantages**	**Suitability**
Cost-plus-incentive-fee (CPIF)	Development has a high probability that is feasible and positive profit incentives for seller management can be negotiated. Performance incentives must be clearly spelled out and objectively measurable. Fee range should be negotiated to give the seller an incentive over various ranges of cost performance. Fee is adjusted by a formula negotiated into the contract in accordance with the relationship that total cost bears to target cost. Contract must contain target cost, target fee, minimum and maximum fees, fee adjustment formula. Fee adjustment is made at completion of contract.	Difficult to negotiate range between the maximum and minimum fees so as to provide an incentive over entire range. Performance must be objectively measurable. Costly to administer. Seller must have an adequate accounting system. Used only with negotiated contracts. Appropriate buyer surveillance needed during performance to ensure effective methods and efficient cost controls are used.	Major systems development and other development programs in which it is determined that CPIF is desirable and administratively practical.
Cost-plus-Award-Fee (CPAF)	Contract completion is feasible, incentives are desired, but performance is not susceptible to finite measurement. Provides for subjective evaluation of seller performance. Seller is evaluated at stated time(s) during performance period. Contract must contain clear and unambiguous evaluation criteria to determine award fee. Award fee is earned for excellence in performance, quality, timeliness, ingenuity, and cost-effectiveness and can be earned in whole or in part. Two separate fee pools can be established in contract: base fee and award fee. Award fee earned by seller is determined by the buyer and is often based on recommendations of an award fee evaluation board.	Buyer's determination of amount of award fee earned by the seller is not subject to disputes clause. CPAF cannot be used to avoid either CPIF or CPFF if either is feasible. Should not be used if the amount of money, period of performance, or expected benefits are insufficient to warrant additional administrative efforts. Very costly to administer. Seller must have an adequate accounting system. Used only with negotiated contracts.	Level-of-effort services that can only be subjectively measured, and contracts for which work would have been accomplished under another contract type if performance objectives could have been expressed as definite milestones, targets, and goals that could have been measured.

Table 7-3 Advantages, Disadvantages, and Suitability of Various Contract Types			
Type	**Essential Elements and Advantages**	**Disadvantages**	**Suitability**

Cost-Plus-Fixed-Fee (CPFF)	Level of effort is unknown, and seller's performance cannot be subjectively evaluated.
	   Provides for payment of a fixed fee. Seller receives fixed fee regardless of the actual costs incurred during performance.
	   Can be constructed in two ways:
	• Completion form: Clearly defined task with a definite goal and specific end product. Buyer can order more work without an increase in fee if the contract estimated cost is increased.
	• Term form: Scope of work described in general terms.
	
	Seller obligated only for a specific level of effort for stated period of time.
	   Completion form is preferred over term form.
	   Fee is expressed as percentage of estimated cost at time contract is awarded.
		Seller has minimum incentive to control costs.
		   Costly to administer. Seller must have an adequate accounting system.
		   Seller assumes no financial risk.
			Completion form: Advanced development or technical services contracts.
			
			Term form: Research and exploratory development. Used when the level of effort required is known and there is an inability to measure risk.

Other Pricing Methods

In addition to the variety of pricing arrangements already discussed, buyers and sellers use other kinds of agreements to deal with uncertainty and reduce the administrative costs of contracting. These include purchase agreements, memorandums of understanding, and letters of intent.

Purchase Agreements

When two parties expect to deal with one another repeatedly for the purchase and sale of goods and services, they may decide to enter into a long-term purchase agreement. (A universal agreement is an example of such an arrangement.) Rather than negotiating a new contract for every transaction, the parties agree to the terms and conditions that will apply to any transaction between them of a specified type. This arrangement reduces the time required to form a contract and eliminates uncertainty about purchase terms and conditions.

The agreement itself is not a contract, and neither party undertakes an obligation to the other by signing such an agreement. However, if the buyer decides to buy products or services covered by the agreement, it can issue an order that, if accepted by the seller, will become a contract. The contract will then include, by previous consent, the terms and conditions of the purchase agreement. Usually, purchase agreements are written by the seller, who reserves the right to modify or terminate the agreement at will.

Memorandums of Understanding and Letters of Intent

Memorandums of understanding (MOUs) and letters of intent (LOIs) are precontract agreements that establish the intent of a party to buy products or services from or sell products or services to another party. Buyers commonly provide LOIs to sellers to encourage them to begin work—and incur cost—before awarding a contract. Although not contracts, MOUs and LOIs are sometimes assumed to be contracts because they are written documents signed by one or more parties. Therefore, MOUs and LOIs should be used with caution. Many companies strongly discourage using MOUs and LOIs because of the problems that have developed as a result of the perception that an MOU or LOI was a contract.

SUMMARY

Contract pricing arrangements are important tools to transfer financial risk between contracting parties. Although most companies use simple firm-fixed-price contracts and, occasionally, cost-reimbursement contracts, more complex arrangements are available that may be more appropriate and effective. Use of contract incentives by buyers—to motivate sellers to accelerate delivery and improve performance—is increasing worldwide. Business professionals who manage contracts must understand the various contract pricing arrangements to select the most appropriate type for each situation. In Chapter 8, we will discuss the use of time-and-material (T&M) and labor- hour (LH) pricing arrangements in great detail.

Questions to Consider

1. Does your buying organization select the right pricing arrangement for their purchases?

2. What are the biggest challenges for sellers on cost-reimbursement type contracts?

3. Does your organization properly staff for contract administration when selecting a multiple-type contract pricing arrangement?

Endnote

1   Gregory A. Garrett, *World-Class Contracting*, 4th ed. (Chicago: CCH, 2007).

CHAPTER 8

TIME-AND-MATERIALS AND LABOR-HOUR PRICING ARRANGEMENTS*

By Catherine Poole, Paul Cataldo, and Shaw Cohe

INTRODUCTION

Time-and-materials is a type of pricing arrangement in which the buyer agrees to pay the contractor for (1) its time spent (based on preestablished fixed hourly labor rates) and (2) materials purchased in support of the buyer's requirements.

A variation of the time-and-materials (T&M) contract, the labor-hour (LH) contract differs only in that the contractor does not supply materials. Time-and-materials and labor-hour are two of the many contract "types" referred to in Federal Acquisition Regulation (FAR).

As discussed in Chapter 7, the various contract types are grouped into two broad categories: fixed-price and cost-reimbursement. T&M and LH contracts are considered hybrid types of contractual pricing arrangements that contain aspects of both categories. They resemble cost-type arrangements in that they share many of the risk characteristics of a cost-type contract, and they also resemble fixed-price arrangements because direct labor is acquired at specified fixed hourly rates. T&M contracts provide for the payment of direct labor hours at specified fully burdened fixed hourly rates and actual cost for materials.

T&M and LH are the least preferred contract types. They are the only contract types described in FAR Part 16 that require the contracting officer to execute a determination and findings to justify their use. In this chapter, we will discuss many of the common questions about T&M and LH contracts and the most recent government policies and regulations regarding their appropriate use.

Why are T&M and LH the least preferred contract types?

Because some believe T&M and LH contracts offer little or no positive incentive to cost control, labor efficiency, or delivery of a completed product or service. The General Services Board of Contract Appeals provided the following summary comments:

> This type of contract places relatively little cost or performance risk on the contractor. In contrast to a fixed-price contract, such a contract requires only that the contractor use its best efforts to provide the goods or services at the stated price. The contractor

is entitled to be paid for its costs of performance, up to the contract ceiling, whether it succeeds in fully performing the contract requirements or not.[1]

With these contract types, the contractor is not "on the hook" to deliver a final product. It generally is required to deliver the agreed amount of effort up to a specified ceiling price, using its "best efforts." With T&M and LH, there is the risk of expending a lot of contractor effort with nothing substantial to show for it. We've seen this happen when agencies use T&M or LH contracts as a replacement for effectively defining requirements. All too often, we have seen agencies view this as an either/or proposition: I will either define my requirements well, or I will pursue a T&M contract and figure it out as I go along. Perhaps the key is not the contract type but whether it is appropriately and effectively applied.

T&M and LH contracts are often the subject of negative attention for their perceived use as staffing alternatives. In such cases, the requirements are often poorly defined—deliberately so—so that agencies can quickly get "bodies" in the office to keep the work moving. The concern is that these contracts are frequently used to bypass federal hiring rules.

Is there a place for T&M contracts?

Absolutely. Despite the "least preferred" tag, there are many situations in which T&M and LH contracts are appropriate. The key—as with all contract types—is to manage them well. In fact, the choice of contract type is situational, and in the words of one of our senior consultants, "There is no worse type than a firm-fixed-price in situations where a T&M or cost type should be used." His observation is that the comparisons seem to be set up with assumptions about a well-managed firm-fixed-price (FFP) contract versus a not-well-managed T&M contract.

> My experience is that there is nothing worse for the government than a badly managed FFP services contract...and most of them are, because the government has trouble keeping commitments. We've all heard the old saws about the two types of government-furnished material—late and defective...and similar issues arise in services with data, access to personnel, security clearances, and other aspects of contract performance.

Not to be hard on the government, as there are many good reasons for this, but the result is that the contract is always off the hook, and the government many times doesn't have visibility into cost.

Whether or not the government is able to perform well enough to keep the contractor on the hook should also be a determining factor for contract type.

If properly managed, the T&M is like a cost-type contract but has the beneficial feature for the government of "capped" or fixed overhead and general and administrative (G&A) costs, which can be a very good thing in certain financial environments. The T&M also allows for flexibility where necessary, which also avoids expensive claims and/or terminations for convenience and/or needless and expensive recompetes in some situations.

As conveyed by the FAR, the use of T&M and LH contract types is appropriate when it is not possible at the time of contract or order award to accurately estimate the extent or duration of the work or to anticipate costs with a reasonable degree of confidence. The FAR guidance for application is similar to the circumstances under which T&M is used in the commercial sector, as this response to an informal survey conducted by the National Contract Management Association (NCMA) of Fortune 500 companies indicates:

> We believe it is appropriate to use a T&M contract when the expertise to resolve an issue/problem and the time required to troubleshoot and resolve the issue cannot be determined in advance on a fixed-price basis. T&M contracts are also appropriate when the task to be performed is not well defined.[2]

Originally used for repair jobs when the extent of the service required could not be known until well into performance, the application of T&M contracts has evolved to include a wide range of professional services. More flexible and expedient than other contract types, T&M arrangements are providing government agencies access to consulting, technical services, program management, software development, and facilities maintenance services, among many others.

What is the incentive for a contractor to perform in a T&M or LH contract?

The better the performance on this requirement, the more likely that the contractor will be considered for follow-on work or future requirements. This applies to any type of contract, including T&M and LH contracts. Past performance ratings and references also provide positive incentives for contractors to do well on any type of contract.

Frequently in the management of T&M contracts, performance monitoring consists of reviewing daily, weekly, or monthly burn rates. To better monitor progress it could just as easily be set up to track actual hours expended against estimated hours for specific projects that can be set up at the outset or at any time throughout the contract, thereby providing insight into real progress on the effort as opposed to just the passage of time.

And here is an interesting idea: Why not set up a T&M incentive contract to give contractors some award fee for unused estimate hours? This would eliminate the current inherent incentive for "featherbedding" to realize all the revenue up to the ceiling price.

How prevalent are T&M and LH contracting?

Too prevalent, according to some. The truth, however, is that we don't know the real numbers. Our analysis of data in the Federal Procurement Data System – Next Generation (FPDS-NG) revealed some interesting statistics. In fiscal year (FY) 2005, only 5.18 percent of contract obligations were made via T&M or LH contracts. The vast majority– 59 percent–of contracts were some variation of a fixed-price (fixed-price, fixed-price-award-fee, etc.), while 31 percent were some variation of cost-type contracts (cost-sharing, cost-plus-award-fee, etc.) A full 4 percent of contracts, however, were not coded with their contract type. Of course, 5.18 percent of 2005 spending means that $20 billion was awarded through T&M or LH contracts.

A study reflecting FY 2005 data reports more prevalent T&M usage, at least among the survey's 100 corporate respondents. Accounting firm Grant Thornton LLP's 12th Annual Government Contractor Industry Survey reported revenue from T&M contracts growing from 18 percent in the 10th annual survey, to 22 percent last year, and to 33 percent in this year's survey.[3]

What are the key changes made by the new rules?

The new rules effective February 12, 2007, make some long-awaited changes to T&M and LH contracting. The most notable is that T&M and LH contracts can now be used for commercial services (FAR Part 12, Acquisition of Commercial Items). The procedures for commercial services differ slightly from those for noncommercial services, and we detail those differences herein. We provide an "at a glance" summary of the similarities and differences between commercial and noncommercial services in Table 8-2.

Also notable is new FAR coverage that addresses how subcontract labor should be addressed in T&M and LH contracts. The FAR previously was silent on this issue. Now it addresses the applicability of the labor rates and prescribes how the rates should be applied when any performance will be done by workers who are not directly employed by the contractor.

The remainder of our discussion is divided into three sections:
- Guidance applicable to all T&M and LH contracts
- Guidance applicable only to commercial services
- Guidance applicable to noncommercial services

We address the new requirements in combination with other frequently asked questions to present a comprehensive picture of the requirements surrounding T&M and LH contracting.

ALL T&M AND LH CONTRACTS

What are the primary requirements when using a T&M or LH contract?

There are three primary regulatory requirements related to the use of T&M or LH contracts, as follows:
- the contracting officer must conclude that *no other contract type is suitable* to the requirement before executing a T&M or LH contract;
- the contract must include a ceiling price that the contractor exceeds at its own risk; and
- the contract (including base plus option years) should not exceed three years, unless approved by the head of the contracting activity (HCA) prior to the execution of the base period.

What are the performance obligations of contractors under a T&M or LH contract?

Under a T&M or LH contract, a contractor is agreeing to use its "best efforts" to perform the work specified in the contract schedule and all obligations under the contract within the ceiling price in the contract.

Why are contracts limited to three years (unless approved by the HCA)?

As noted in the discussion accompanying the Federal Register publication of the final rule, this is to "help ensure T&M contracts are only used when no other type of contract is suitable, to maximize the use of fixed-price commercial contracts consistent with the statute, and to avoid protracted use of non-commercial time-and-materials contracts after experience provides a basis for firmer pricing." This requirement now appears in FAR 16.601(d)(1)(ii).

Is a justification required prior to award of a T&M or LH contract?

Yes, this has not changed. A determination and findings (D&F) document is required any time a contracting officer intends to award a T&M or LH contract— whether for commercial or non-commercial services, and will even be required when placing T&M orders under indefinite-delivery contracts for commercial items in certain circumstances (explained further in the "Commercial Services" section).

A D&F must present sufficient facts and rationale to justify that no other contract type is suitable for the requirement. FAR 16.601(c) provides that this contract type "may only be used when it is not possible at the time of placing the contract to estimate accurately the extent or duration of the work or to anticipate costs with any reasonable degree of confidence." The D&F must provide the facts and rationale to support this conclusion.

What has changed is that there are more "burdensome" requirements for the D&F for commercial services, as acknowledged by the Civilian Agency Acquisition Council and Defense Acquisition Regulations Council, which formulated the rules. The reason? Additional requirements are needed, said the councils, "to encourage the preference for the use of fixed-price contracts for commercial items.[4]

Is there a threshold over which a D&F is required?

No. The statute requires a D&F for T&M and LH contracts regardless of the dollar amount.

Who must approve the D&F?

In most cases, the D&F can be signed by the contracting officer, per FAR 16.601(d)(1), before execution of the base period and any option periods.

If the base period plus option periods exceeds three years, however, the D&F must be approved by the head of the contracting activity, per FAR 16.601(d)(1)(ii). The rationale for this approval is to "avoid protracted use of noncommercial time-and-materials contracts after experience provides a basis for firmer pricing."[5]

How will a contracting officer make the determination that no other contract type is suitable for the requirement?

Of course, the contracting officer must apply business judgment to the situation at hand. The objective to keep in mind is that fixed-price contracts are preferred, so the contracting officer should examine each requirement received to assess whether it is feasible for the work to be priced into a single fixed-price or several fixed-price line items. In many cases, this is possible with some careful planning and creative thinking about the objectives and expected outcomes of the work: What is the government trying to accomplish with this contract? What deliverable(s) does the government want from this contract?

In other cases, the contracting officer may reasonably conclude that T&M and LH contracts are the only choice, given the situation. An example might be an emergency plumbing repair, in which the exact nature of the repair cannot be identified until the contractor can assess the situation, and there is not ample time to craft the requirement and solicit a fixed-price quote or proposal. Rather, swift action to fix the problem is the critical driver.

Of course, FAR Part 10 requires that agencies conduct market research "appropriate to the circumstances" before developing requirements or soliciting offers. The recent FAR change added language to 10.002(b)(1)(iii) to provide that market research should include an examination of customary practices, to include the "contract type, considering the nature and risk associated with the requirement."

The bottom line is that this decision requires sound business judgment based on the facts of the situation. It is reasonable to award a T&M or LH contract in many cases, but don't rely on them simply because of their ease of establishment.

What is priced in a T&M or LH contract?

In a labor-hour contract, labor is priced at a fixed rate per hour for workers meeting specific qualification criteria. T&M contracts are priced the same way and also allow for the reimbursement of costs for materials necessary in the performance of the contract. As a simple example, a contract's pricing schedule might read as shown below in Table 8-1.

The fixed hourly rates are loaded rates, meaning that they include wages, overhead, G&A expenses, and profit.

Table 8-1 Sample Contract Pricing Schedule				
Level	Minimum Years' Experience	Education	Description of Duties	Hourly Rate
Business Consultant 1	2	Bachelor's degree	Supporting role. Works under supervision.	$90.00
Business Consultant 2	4	Bachelor's degree	Supports tasks for one or multiple clients. May lead a specific task in support of a particular client.	$140.00
Business Consultant 3	8	Bachelor's degree	Manages tasks or contracts for a single client and is responsible for performance. Performs work in a variety of operational areas or in a single consulting area.	$185.00
Business Consultant 4	12	Master's degree	Serves as a senior advisor to client's executive management. Serves as the project lead and the primary client point of contact.	$230.00
Business Consultant 5	16	Master's degree	Same as Business Consultant 4 but is recognized as an industry expert.	$310.00

To whom do the hourly rates apply?

The new rules make this question easier to answer. As noted in the discussion that accompanied the publication of the final rule, the prior FAR language had caused significant confusion because it did not adequately describe the application of labor.

As long as the labor meets the qualifications specified in the contract for the hourly rates, the hourly rates can apply to: (1) employees of the contractor; (2) subcontractor employees who meet the qualifications applicable to a labor rate; and (3) employees of an affiliate.

However, the specific application is dependent on (1) whether the contract is for commercial versus noncommercial services, and (2) if noncommercial, whether it was based on adequate price competition. We address the specifics in their respective sections below.

What should we consider when evaluating the cost of services based on fixed hourly rates?

It is important to consider that the cost of services based on hourly rates is dependent on three separate factors: labor categories, the corresponding labor rates, and the number of hours proposed to fulfill the task. To illustrate, suppose you have one contractor that offers a "business consultant" at $35 an hour. Another firm offers a "business consultant" at $100 an hour. On the surface, it would appear that the $35 expert is the best value at the lowest overall price. Not necessarily. Suppose it would take the $35 expert 100 hours ($3,500) to perform a task because he doesn't have the knowledge he needs to perform efficiently. In contrast, suppose the $100 expert knows the answer and can perform the task in 10 hours ($1,000). The best value at the lowest overall cost in that case would be the $100 expert. In our consulting, we have reviewed a number of projects that were overstaffed numerically with many excess hours of low-cost labor that was not only more expensive in total than contracting for more expert personnel, but also the labor that was contracted for was unable to successfully perform and resulted in total project failure due to the lack of expertise on the job.

What's crucial is matching the labor category to the work to be performed– getting the right person for the job. Whenever a high-level person does low-level work, or a less experienced person is put on too complex a task, the government will wind up paying more than it should.

The challenge is that there are no universally accepted definitions for labor categories. For example, a senior engineer in one company may not be considered a senior engineer at another, and what the government thinks is a senior engineer may be something else entirely.

The bottom line is that reviewing a list of hourly rates is not enough and can be counterproductive to mission success. Through discussions, the contractor must clearly understand the government's requirement and the government must be familiar with the contractor's staffing approach.

What about establishing a separate contract line item for each labor category?

We have observed this in practice, but we wouldn't recommend it. The FAR requires only that a ceiling price be established for the contract, not for each line item or labor category. By establishing a ceiling price for each labor category, the government is putting unnecessary, and perhaps counterproductive, constraints on itself and on the contractor—more constraints, in fact, than would be in place on a (preferred) fixed-price contract or order.

For example, to support the top line price of a firm-fixed-price contract, a labor profile would have been developed, demonstrating the build-up of labor categories and estimated hours of each. However, after contract award, the focus would be on getting the job done within the total fixed price, with the contractor having the flexibility to modify the labor profile as needed to meet the requirements in the most efficient and effective way.

To establish a ceiling price or fixed price per labor category is, at best, creating a false sense of control, and can be counterproductive to the flexibility that is normally inherent and necessary in a T&M engagement, in which the requirements are relatively uncertain. If the requirements were more certain, a fixed-price contract would have been awarded instead. Think of it this way: Does it make sense to "hard-wire" the labor categories rather than allowing the contractor in the more "uncertain" situation the flexibility to trade off between the labor categories within the total "not to exceed" price to complete the work in the most efficient and effective manner?

Some contracting officers might argue for the labor line item approach, thinking that it would prevent "grade creep," in which contractors might assign more expensive labor to the task to capture the revenue faster. However, a reputable contractor should and will focus on the overall objectives of the task. In the course of our experience, we've seen many situations in which bringing on a more expensive labor category expert at the right time has saved many hours and the associated dollars by completing a task quickly and effectively that the lesser category individual would have struggled with for many more relatively unproductive hours. We've also seen the opposite, where higher category individuals are dysfunctionally used for mundane tasks such as briefing chart production because that's the category that has labor hours available at that point in the contract.

We believe a best practice is to establish contract line items (CLIN) to recognize an effort or "work," with informational subline items to identify all the labor rates that can be billed against up to the total estimated price of the CLIN and trade-offs among the labor categories allowed within the not-to-exceed price. There are many processes that can be used to track progress against the work to provide much more effective stewardship than hard-wiring labor categories on an effort uncertain enough to require an T&M or LH contract.

What are "materials" in a time-and-materials contract?

"Materials" are newly defined to include:
- Direct materials (including supplies transferred between divisions, subsidiaries, or affiliates under a common control)
- Subcontractor for supplies and ancillary services (for which there is not a labor category specified in the contract)
- Other direct costs (including incidental services for which there is not a labor category specified in the contract)
- Applicable indirect costs

As noted in the discussion that accompanied the rule, the prior FAR language had caused significant confusion because it did not adequately describe what is included in "labor" or "materials."

How are materials paid?

It depends on whether the materials are a product of the contractor and whether they fit the definition of a commercial item:
- When the contractor furnishes its own materials that fit the definition of commercial item (as defined in FAR 2.101), the government will pay the contractor's established *catalog* or *market price* (versus paying the "cost" of those materials).
- Noncommercial materials–including ancillary services–are reimbursed at the contractor's actual cost of purchasing the

materials, subject to the provisions of FAR Subpart 31.2, in effect on the date of the contract.

Other indirect costs (often called ODCs) are reimbursed based on the contractor's actual cost. (Note, however, that for commercial T&M and LH contracts, payment is made for only the ODCs specified in the contract.)

What about material handling costs?

Per FAR 16.601(c)(3), when included as part of material costs, material handling costs shall include only costs clearly excluded from the labor-hour rate. In other words, material handling costs should not already be included in the overhead or G&A rates that are included in the loaded labor rates. Material handling costs may include all appropriate indirect costs allocated to direct materials in accordance with the contractor's usual accounting procedures consistent with FAR Part 31.

What about indirect costs?

The payment for indirect costs differs depending on whether the contract is for a commercial or noncommercial service. We address this question in the corresponding sections below.

Can the government pay profit or fee on materials?

No, not to the prime contractor (except for commercial items or as otherwise provided for in the FAR 31.205-26, Material Costs). The FAR rule clarifies that the "recovery of profit or fee is accomplished as part of the labor-hour portion of the T&M/LH contract."

Can the ceiling price be increased?

Yes, a contract's ceiling price can be increased if the contracting officer documents the contract file to justify the (1) reason for and (2) amount of any subsequent change in the ceiling price (per FAR 16.601(d)(2)). For a commercial services T&M or LH contract, the contracting officer must also determine and document in the file that "it is in the best interest of the procuring agency to change the ceiling price," per FAR 12.207(b)(ii)(C).

Can the government examine contractors' records to verify cost?

Yes. The government—for both commercial and noncommercial T&M and LH contracts—has the right to examine contractors' records to verify claimed costs. For commercial contracts, this is addressed in clause 52.212-4(i)(4), Alternate 1; for noncommercial contracts, this is addressed in 52.215-2.

Can the contractor be required to reperform the services under a T&M/LH contract if they are not acceptable?

Yes. At any time during contract performance, but not later than six months (or such other time as may be specified in the contract) after acceptance of the services or materials last delivered under the T&M or LH contract, the FAR provides that the government "may require the Contractor to replace or correct services or materials that at time of delivery failed to meet contract requirements." In such cases, the government pays the hourly rate less profit for reperformance. (For noncommercial items, this is addressed in FAR 52.246-6, Inspection – Time-and-Material and Labor-Hour; for commercial items, it is addressed in 52.212-4, Contracts Terms and Conditions – Commercial Items.)

This is, to many, an ironic requirement, given that T&M and LH contracts are "best efforts" contracts. Practically speaking, this is most likely to be enforceable if performance requirements are well defined in the contract.

In addition, the government may at any time require the contractor to remedy at its own expense any failure by the contractor to comply with the requirements of the contract, if the failure is due to:

■ fraud, lack of good faith, or willful misconduct on the part of the contractor's managerial personnel; or

■ the conduct of one or more of the contractor's employees selected or retained by the contractor after any of the contractor's managerial personnel has reasonable grounds to believe that the employee is habitually careless or unqualified.

Table 8-2 Summary of Requirements for Commercial vs. Noncommercial Time-and-Materials and Labor-Hour Contracts		
	Commercial	**Noncommercial**
Authorized use	Only authorized when no other contract type is suitable.	
Standard of performance	The contractor agrees to use its best efforts to perform the work specified in the schedule and all obligations under the contract within such ceiling price.	
Competitive procedures	Must be awarded using the competitive procedures of: • FAR 6.102; • FAR 19.5 (set-aside procedures); or • FAR Part 13 (competitive procedures).	Can be awarded using any of the procedures authorized by the FAR.
Sole source allowable?	No	Yes. Can be sole source under FAR 6.3
Contract length	Limited to three years, unless approved by the head of the contracting activity via D&F.	
Determination and findings (D&F) required?	Yes. D&F must indicate that no other contract type is suitable and must be signed by the contracting officer before the execution of the base period or any option periods.	
Other D&F inclusions	D&F must: • Describe market research. • State why it is not possible to accurately estimate the extent of the work, duration of work, or anticipated costs. • Establish that the requirement has been structured to maximize fixed-price (FP) contracts for future acquisitions. • Describe actions planned to maximize the use of FP contracts on future acquisitions.	N/A
Requirements for indefinite-delivery contracts	T&M contract must be structured to allow FP orders, to maximum extent practicable. If contract only authorizes T&M/LH orders, the D&F must be approved one level above contracting officer. If contract authorizes T&M/LH and FP orders, each T&M/LH order must have a separate D&F.	N/A

Table 8-2 Summary of Requirements for Commercial vs. Noncommercial Time-and-Materials and Labor-Hour Contracts

	Commercial	Noncommercial
Definition of hourly rates	Fixed labor rates (which include wages, overhead, G&A, and profit) for labor categories specified in the contract. Each labor category has corresponding qualifications.	
Hourly rate application —separate rates required?	Separate rates are *not* required for prime contractor, subcontractor, and affiliate labor. The offeror must specify whether the fixed hourly rate for each labor category applies to labor performed by the offeror; subcontractors; and/or division, subsidiaries, or affiliates of the offeror under a common control (Provision 52.216-31).	If there is not adequate price competition, separate rates are required for prime contractor labor, each subcontractor, and each affiliate (Provision 52.216-30). If adequate price competition, separate rates are *not* required (Provision 52.216-29). *Note:* For Department of Defense, separate rates are required, regardless of the extent of competition (Provision 52.216-29, with alternate paragraph (c) in 252.216-7002).
Consent to subcontract	No consent requirement	Consent rules of FAR 52.244-2 apply; the government is not required to reimburse subcontract costs incurred prior to obtaining required consent for subcontractors.
Definition of materials	Direct materials (including supplies transferred between divisions, subsidiaries, and affiliates); subcontractors for supplies and incidental services that do no have a labor category specified in the contract; other direct costs (travel, computer usage charges, etc.); and indirect costs.	
Payments for materials	Contractor material that meets the definition of a commercial item at FAR 2.101 is paid at the contractor's established catalog or market price. Noncommercial material and commercial material that the prime contractor does not have an established catalog or market price for is paid at contractor's actual costs, with no profit allowed.	
Payments for other direct costs (ODCs)	To be reimbursable, the categories of reimbursable ODCs (such as travel and computer usage) must be listed in the contract. ODCs are paid at the contractor's actual costs.	Reimbursed based on established accounting practices. ODCs are paid at the contractor's actual costs.
Payment for indirect costs	Fixed amount is negotiated at the time of contract award and paid on a pro rata basis. The fixed amount is the total amount paid on the contract.	Contractor's actual costs

Table 8-2 Summary of Requirements for Commercial vs. Noncommercial Time-and-Materials and Labor-Hour Contracts		
	Commercial	**Noncommercial**
Payment clauses	52.212-4, Alternate 1	52.232-7, Payments under Time-and-Materials and Labor-Hour Contracts 52.216-7, Allowable Cost and Payment (only applicable to the portion of the contract that provides for reimbursement of materials at actual cost and related indirect costs)
Prompt payment act	All	Applies to services only (does not apply to reimbursement for materials)
Withholding from billings	No withholding provision	Contracting officer may require contractor to withhold 5 percent of the contract value, up to $50,000, if necessary to protect the government's interest, per FAR 52.232.7.
Rebates, refunds, and discounts	FAR 52.212-4 requires contractors to reduce the costs of materials for any rebates, refunds, or discounts that are identifiable to the contract.	FAR 52.232-7 requires contractors to credit the government for cash and trade discounts, rebates, scrap, commission, and other amounts that have "accrued to the benefit of the contractor."

Changes in ceiling price	Contracting officer must execute a determination that change in ceiling price is in the best interest of the agency (FAR 12.207(b)(1)(ii)(C)).
	  Determination must be documented in contract file (FAR 16.601(d)(2)).
		Contracting officer required to justify the reasons for and amount of change (FAR 16.601(d)(2)).
		  Justification must be documented in contract file (FAR 16.601(d)(2)).

Payment basis for reperformance of nonconforming services	Hourly rate less profit. Profit is assumed to be 10 percent if not otherwise prescribed in the contract.	Hourly rate less profit.
Oversight and government access to records	Contracting officer has access to records to verify that (1) employees meet the qualifications for labor categories at which they were billed; (2) employees (including subcontractors billed at hourly rates) worked the hours billed; and (3) materials were reimbursed at actual cost.	Contracting officer has right to examine and audit "records and other evidence" to verify claimed costs, per FAR 52.215-2.

COMMERCIAL SERVICES

What prevented the use of T&M for commercial services, and why is it now authorized?

Prior to this rule, all commercial services were required by FAR 12.207 to be either fixed-price or fixed-price with economic price adjustment. The FAR prohibited all other contract types. This meant the government was unable to buy commercial services on an hourly rate basis even though it was standard practice in commercial transactions.

This FAR change implements a provision in the Services Acquisition Reform Act of 2003, which amended Section 8002(d) of the Federal Acquisition Streamlining Act of 1994 (FASA) to expressly authorize T&M and LH contracts for commercial services under specified conditions.

Does this mean that the definition of commercial items has changed?

Yes, the definition of "commercial item" in FAR 2.101 has been changed to delete the following provision, which had excluded services "sold based on hourly rates" from the definition: "This does not include services that are sold based on hourly rates without an established catalog or market price for a specific service performed or a specific outcome to be achieved."

The services still must be a type that are offered and sold:
■ competitively in substantial quantities in the commercial marketplace;
■ based on established catalog or market prices for specific tasks performed or specific outcomes to be achieved; and
■ under standard commercial terms and conditions.

What types of commercial services are now authorized to be acquired on a T&M or LH basis?

Any commercial service is available for acquisition on a T&M or LH basis, as long as the circumstances warrant the use of these contract types.

As background, this is actually a departure from the original intent of FASA, which limited T&M and LH contracts to commercial services in support of a commercial item, and "any other category of commercial services that is designated by the administrator of the Office of Federal Procurement Policy (OFPP)." However, after much research and review, the OFPP ultimately did not create a definitive list of services, but instead indicated that "any service" is available for acquisition on a T&M or LH basis because "services under any general categorization of service…are commonly sold to the general public on a T&M and LH basis under certain conditions," and "use of T&M and LH contracts under these conditions may be in the government's best interest." In short, OFPP concluded that the "identification of effective boundaries for the use of T&M and LH contracts is a function of the specific circumstances surrounding the acquisition rather than the specific type of service being sold."

OFPP had three main findings:
1. Commercial services are commonly sold on a T&M and LH basis in the marketplace when requirements are not sufficiently well understood to complete a well-defined scope of work and when risk can be managed by maintaining surveillance of costs and contractor performance.
2. These same services are also commonly sold on a fixed-price basis.
3. A few types of services are sold predominantly on a T&M and LH basis– specifically, emergency repair services, which by their nature, are difficult to capture in a well-defined scope of work.[6]

OFPP ultimately concluded that it was not the type of service that drove companies engaged in commercial business-to-business transactions to use T&M or LH contracts, but rather whether the scope of work is defined well enough to allow for fixed-price terms.

Can a T&M or LH commercial service award be sole source?

No. Sole source is not authorized for T&M or LH commercial services, and if procedures "other than full and open competition" are used, the agency must receive offers from at least two responsible offerors to proceed.

As detailed in FAR 12.207, the contract (or order) must be awarded using one of the following procedures:

- Competitive procedures
    - Full and open competitive procedures (described in FAR 6.102), including ordering under the General Services Administration's multiple award schedules (federal supply schedules)
    - The small business set-aside procedures in FAR Subpart 19.5
    - The simplified acquisition procedures in FAR Part 13
- Procedures for "other than full and open competition" (FAR Subpart 6.3)
    - Provided that offers satisfying the government's requirement are received from *two or more* responsible offerors
- "Fair opportunity" procedures (FAR 16.505)
    - If placing an order under a multiple-award task order contract

Can commercial service orders against T&M indefinite-delivery, indefinite-quantity (IDIQ) contracts be issued on a fixed-price basis?

Yes, and there is now a strong preference for orders against T&M and LH contracts to be issued on a fixed-price basis as opposed to a T&M or LH basis. The new rules indicate that, for commercial services, when establishing an indefinite-delivery contract with services priced on a T&M or LH basis, contracting officers "shall, to the maximum extent practicable" structure the contract to allow for the issuance of orders on a T&M or LH basis and must justify this decision in writing. In this case, the D&F executed for the base contract "shall also explain why providing for an alternative firm-fixed-price or fixed-price with economic price adjustment pricing structure is not practicable." Per FAR 12.207(c)(3), this D&F requires an approval one level above the contracting officer.

What if we need to place the order on a T&M basis?

If the contract has been structured to allow the issuance of orders on a fixed-price basis, and you have a need to place an order on a T&M or LH basis, the order will require a separate D&F document justifying why the order must be placed on a T&M/LH basis.

Fixed-price orders against such contracts do not require a D&F, nor do T&M or LH orders issued against an IDIQ contract that was not established to accept fixed-price orders.

How can orders be issued on a fixed-price basis under a T&M or LH contract?

It isn't difficult. A T&M IDIQ contract establishes fixed labor rates for a variety of labor categories expected to be employed by the contractor in performance of future task orders, the size and exact requirements of which are often "to be determined." When the agency identifies a requirement (an order) to be placed under (or perhaps completed under) an IDIQ contract, the contracting officer can solicit a fixed price that is based on (built up from) the fixed labor rates detailed in the contract. The fixed price would be based on an appropriate combination of the contract's labor rates, labor categories, materials, and other direct costs needed to perform the government's requirement.

Of course, requesting a fixed price for an order means that the government must be able to effectively define its requirements, so that the contractor can reasonably propose a fixed price for delivering on those requirements.

Another approach can be illustrated via an equipment repair example. Prior to performance it is not possible to estimate accurately the extent or duration of work necessary, so a T&M order would be issued with a ceiling price. But does all the work need to be done on a T&M basis? If, after diagnosing the problem, the contractor knows what parts will be required and through past experience the number of hours required, why should the government assume the entire performance risk? A possible approach would be to issue an order with both a T&M line item and a fixed-price line item. The time required to troubleshoot and prepare an estimate would be T&M, whereas the actual repair would be a fixed price.

We note that it is important that the indefinite-quantity contract has been structured so that it contains all the required clauses for each contract type. For commercial services, include both the terms and conditions at 52.212-4 and 52.212.-4 Alternate 1. (For noncommercial services, review the "Provision and Clause Matrix" in Part 52 to make sure the required clauses, such as those for payment and changes, are all included.)

Back to the D&F, what are the more "burdensome" requirements when acquiring commercial services?

In addition to the requirements previously mentioned, FAR 12.207(b)(2) requires that the D&F for the use of a T&M or LH contract for commercial services must:

- describe the market research conducted;
- establish why it is not possible to accurately estimate the extent or duration of the work or anticipated costs with any reasonable degree of certainty;
- establish that the requirement has been structured to maximize the use of fixed-price contracts on future acquisitions for the same or similar requirements; and
- describe actions planned to maximize the use of fixed price on future acquisitions.

A representative D&F template is shown below (Form 8-1).

Form 8-1

SAMPLE

DETERMINATION AND FINDINGS

Authority to Use a [specify Time-and-Materials or Labor-Hours]
[specify contract or task order] for Commercial Services in
Accordance with FAR 12.207(b)(1)(ii) and 16.601(d)

Findings

The [specify contracting office] within the [specify agency] proposes to contract for [describe the supplies and/or services being procured and identify program/project, if applicable].

The estimated amount of the [specify contract or task order] is $_____.

[Explain why no other type of contract is suitable for procuring the supplies or services of the kind or quantity required without using the proposed type of contract.]

[Describe the market research conducted.]

[Explain why it is not possible to accurately estimate the extent or duration of the work or anticipated costs.]

[Establish that the requirement has been structured to maximize fixed-price contracts for future acquisitions.]

[Describe actions planned to maximize the use of fixed-price contracts on future acquisitions.]

Determination

On the basis of the above findings, I hereby determine that no contract type other than a [specify time-and-materials or labor-hour] is suitable for this acquisition.

Signatures:

Contracting Officer
(prior to the execution of the base period and any option periods) (if contract authorizes T&M/LH/FP orders, each T&M/LH order must have separate D&F)

(specify title one level above contracting officer)
(indefinite-delivery contract that only authorizes T&M/LH orders)

Head of the Contracting Activity
(prior to the execution of base period when base period plus any option periods exceeds three years)

How can we structure the requirement to maximize the use of fixed-price contracts on future acquisitions?

The FAR cites several examples, including:

■ Limiting the value of the T&M/LH contract or order
■ Limiting the length of the T&M/LH contract or order
■ Establishing fixed prices for portions of the requirement

The key is to look for opportunities to apply what is learned from one contract to the definition of requirements and structure of future contracts, toward ultimately performing more contracts on a fixed-price, less risky, basis.

Under a commercial T&M/LH order, how are the labor rates applied?

For commercial requirements, offerors must specify their fixed hourly rates, then for each, specify whether the rate applies to labor performed by the offeror (contractor), a subcontractor, and/or a division, subsidiary, or affiliate of the offeror (contractor).

Separate rates for the prime contractor, subcontractor, and affiliate labor are permitted, but are not required. The result may be a single rate for each labor category, or separate rates within each labor category applicable to contractor versus subcontractor or affiliate labor, as illustrated in the examples below:

Example: Single rate for each category:
■ Engineer (contractor and all subcontractors): $30/hour
■ Senior Engineer (contractor and all subcontractors): $45/hour

Example: Separate rates for contractor and subcontractor:
■ Engineer (prime contractor): $30/hour
■ Engineer (subcontractor): $35/hour
■ Senior Engineer (prime contractor): $45/hour
■ Senior Engineer (subcontractor A): $50/hour

These options are communicated to prospective offerors via a new provision at FAR 52.216-31 (see box below.)

52.216-31 Time-and-Materials/Labor-Hour Proposal Requirements – Commercial Item Acquisition (February 2007)

The government contemplates award of a time-and-materials or labor-hour type of contract resulting from the solicitation.

The offeror must specify fixed hourly rates in its offer that include wages, overhead, general and administrative expenses, and profit. The offeror must specify whether the fixed hourly rate for each labor category applies to labor performed by:
• the offeror;
• subcontractors; and/or
• divisions, subsidiaries, or affiliates of the offeror under a common control.

(End of provision)

All labor hours that qualify under the labor-hour requirements of the contract are to be paid at the labor-hour rate(s) specified in the contract. Any labor that doesn't qualify under a labor category specified in the contract will be reimbursed as "materials" at actual costs (including subcontracts for ancillary or incidental services).

Is there any requirement for consent to subcontract on T&M/LH commercial contracts?

No. There is no requirement for the subcontractor to request government approval prior to choosing a subcontractor.

What ODCs will be reimbursed on a commercial service T&M/LH contract?

For commercial services contracts, only those in categories pre-specified in the contract will be reimbursed.

FAR 52.212-4, Alternate I (used on commercial item T&M and LH contracts) indicates that "unless listed below, other direct and indirect costs will not be reimbursed." In the contract award, the contracting officer will establish the types of ODCs that will be reimbursed at actual costs. The type of ODCs that will be needed to perform an order may need to be established on an order-by-order basis.

What about indirect costs?

On a commercial service T&M contract, the government will reimburse the contractor for indirect costs on a pro rata basis over the period of contract performance at a fixed price that is negotiated at the time of contract award. The fixed amount is the total amount that is paid on the contract for indirect costs. As with ODCs, the fixed amount for indirect costs may need to be established on an order-by-order basis.

Does the Prompt Payment Act apply to T&M and LH commercial contracts?

Yes. The clause at 52.212-4, Contract Terms and Conditions – Commercial Items, provides that all payments will be made in accordance with the Prompt Payment Act.

Will the government have access to contractor records?

Contracts for commercial items are subject to the access to records provision contained in FAR 52.212-4, Alternate I, which allows the government to:

- Verify that contractor employees meet qualification requirements the labor categories invoiced
- Inspect timekeeping procedures and time card records, including hours worked and distribution of labor between jobs and contracts
- Substantiate amounts paid for material and subcontracts reimbursed at cost

Can incentives be used with a commercial T&M or LH contract?

Yes. While the FAR was previously silent on this issue, FAR 12.207(d) now indicates that T&M and LH contracts "may be used in conjunction with an award fee and performance or delivery incentives when the award fee or incentive is based solely on factors other than cost."

How are contractors paid if they must reperform nonconforming services?

On all T&M contracts, contractors are paid an hourly rate less profit for time spent reperforming nonconforming services. For commercial item contracts, profit is assumed to be 10 percent if not otherwise indicated in the contract. This is detailed in Alternate I to clause 52.212-4, which is required for T&M and LH contracts for commercial items.

NONCOMMERCIAL SERVICES

The following questions address the rules applicable to T&M and LH contracts for noncommercial services.

Under a noncommercial T&M or LH order, how are the labor rates applied?

It depends on two things: (1) whether the contract was based on adequate price competition, and (2) whether your agency has made a certain approach mandatory.

If the contract is based on adequate price competition, the offeror may elect to propose for any labor category:

- separate labor rates for its own employees, each subcontractor, and any affiliate;
- a blended rate that applies to its own employees, all subcontractors and affiliates; or
- any combination of separate and blended rates.

If the contract is not based on adequate price competition, the offeror must propose separate labor rates for its own employees, each subcontractor, and any affiliates.

Example: Separate rates for contractor, subcontractors, and affiliate:

Engineer
    Prime Contractor: $30/hour
    Subcontractor: $32/hour
    Contractor Affiliate B: $35/hour

Senior Engineer
    Prime Contractor: $45/hour
    Subcontractor A: $50/hour
    Contractor Affiliate: $51/hour

Example: Blended rate for each category:

Engineer (contractor and all subcontractors): $30/hour
Senior Engineer (contractor and all subcontractors): $45/hour

This requirement is communicated to prospective offerors via two new provisions:

- FAR 52.216-29, Time-and-Materials/Labor-Hour Proposal Requirements – Non-Commercial Item Acquisition with Adequate Price Competition
- FAR 52.216-30, Time-and-Materials/Labor-Hour Proposal Requirements – Non-Commercial Item Acquisition without Adequate Price Competition

The new rule allows agencies to make mandatory one of the three approaches. Agency procedures may also require the identification of all subcontractors, divisions, subsidiaries, or affiliates included in a blended labor rate.

Have any agencies made one of the approaches mandatory?

Yes, the Department of Defense (DoD) has. A Defense FAR Supplement (DFARS) final rule published on September 6, 2007 requires the offeror to propose separate labor rates for its own employees, each subcontractor, and any affiliate. The DoD's rationale for eliminating the flexibility includes:

- the relatively large dollar value of many DoD noncommercial T&M and LH contracts;
- the significant oversight and legislative initiatives that have focused on DoD in recent years; and
- the preponderance of DoD noncommercial T&M and LH contracts performed by traditional DoD contractors and subcontractors, who already have the necessary mechanisms in place to establish separate fixed hourly rates for each performing entity without significant administrative burden.[7]

These changes are incorporated in DFARS Section 216.601. The provision at 252.216-7002 prescribes an alternate paragraph (c) to the FAR provision at 52.216-29, as follows:

> (c) The offeror must establish fixed hourly rates using separate rates for each category of labor to be performed by each subcontractor and for each category of labor to be performed by the offeror, and for each category of labor to be transferred between divisions, subsidiaries, or affiliates of the offeror under a common control.

What competitive procedures can be used for a T&M or LH noncommercial service award?

There are no specific restrictions applicable to noncommercial T&M and LH contracts; any competitive procedures in the FAR can apply.

Can T&M and LH noncommercial awards be sole source?

Yes. There is no prohibition on awarding noncommercial T&M or LH requirements on a sole-source basis.

What ODCs will be reimbursed on a noncommercial service T&M or LH contract?

For noncommercial services contracts, ODCs are paid at the contractor's actual costs. Unlike T&M/LH contracts for commercial services, there is no need to prespecify the categories for the ODCs in the contract.

What about indirect costs?

Indirect costs are reimbursable at the contractor's actual costs. Unlike T&M and LH contracts for commercial services, indirect costs are not required to be preestablished in the contract.

Does the Prompt Payment Act apply to T&M and LH noncommercial contracts?

Yes, but only to the services portion of the contract. It does not apply to the reimbursement of materials.

The recent rule changes amended FAR 52.232-7(i) to include application of the Prompt Payment Act for interim payments under T&M and LH contracts for services. The Prompt Payment Act has applied to fixed-price contracts for services for many years; recently, Congress amended the Prompt Payment Act to include cost-reimbursement contracts for services. Because the Prompt Payment Act is applicable to both fixed-price and cost-reimbursement contracts for services, the rule-formulating councils concluded it also should be applicable to T&M and LH contracts for services. In the discussion accompanying the final rule, the councils explained, however, that they lacked authority to extend the act to interim payments for supplies.

How do all these new regulations apply to existing contracts?

As indicated in FAR 1.108(d), Unless otherwise specified:
1. FAR changes apply to solicitations issued on or after the effective date of the change;
2. contracting officers may, at their discretion, include the FAR changes in solicitations issued before the effective date, provided award of the resulting contract(s) occurs on or after the effective date; and
3. contracting officers may, at their discretion, include the changes in any existing contract with appropriate consideration.

How do the new rules impact orders under existing General Services Administration (GSA) federal supply schedule contracts?

GSA has not yet publicly addressed how the new rules will affect federal supply schedule contracts with hourly labor rate pricing. We understand that the GSA is planning to issue an Acquisition Letter in the near future to address this.

SUMMARY

The new FAR rules will be welcomed by many government contracting officers, as they clarify many issues that were heretofore unclear, and they add new flexibilities for applying these contract types to a broad array of commercially available services, where appropriate.

While T&M and LH contracts are the least preferred contract types, there are situations for which they are appropriate, including for the purchase of commercial services when market research reveals that it would be the most appropriate contract type for the situation. The key is to use them when no other contract type is legitimately suitable for the requirement and only for as long as it takes to apply lessons learned to the development of fixed-price requirements in the future.

In the next chapter, we will discuss price analysis: tools, techniques, and best practices.

QUESTIONS TO CONSIDER

1. How effectively does your organization implement T&M contracts?

2. When do you typically use T&M or LH contracts?

3. What proven best practices has your organization documented regarding the creation and use of T&M and LH contracts?

ENDNOTES

* Adapted from the Acquisition Solutions, Inc. Acquisition Advisory, April 2007, with the permission of Acquisition Solutions, Inc

1 *CACI, Inc. – Federal v. General Services Administration,* General Services Administration Board of Contract Appeals (GSBCA 15588) (December 13, 2002), http:// www.gsbca.gsa/appeals/w1558813.txt.

2 "Use of T&M and LH Contracts for Procurement of Commercial Services under Part 12 of the FAR" (position paper, National Contract Management Association).

3 Grant Thornton LLP, "12th Annual Government Contractor Industry Survey 2006," http://www.gt.com/staticfiles/GTCom/images/ecommimages/GovConHighlightsFinal.pdf.

4 Ibid.

5 Ibid.

6 "Final Rule: FAR Case 2003-027, Additional Commercial Contract Types," *Federal Register* 71, no. 238 (December 12, 2006), http://a257.g.akamaitech. net/7/257/2422/01jan20061800/edocket.access.gpo.gov/2006/pdf/06-9602.pdf.

7 Ibid.

CHAPTER 9

PRICE ANALYSIS: TOOLS, TECHNIQUES, AND BEST PRACTICES

Introduction

Price analysis is the process of examining and evaluating a proposed price to determine if it is fair and reasonable without evaluating its separate cost elements and proposed profit. Price analysis always involves some form of comparison with other prices. Adequate price competition is normally considered one of the best bases for price analysis.

In this chapter, we will discuss how price analysis may involve a number of comparisons. The comparison process is typically described using five steps:
1. Select prices for comparison:
   a. Competitive proposal prices
   b. Catalog prices
   c. Historical prices
   d. Price estimates based on parametric analysis
   e. Independent company estimates
2. Identify factors that affect comparability (including terms and conditions).
3. Determine the effect of identified factors.
4. Adjust prices selected for comparison.
5. Compare adjusted prices.

Select Prices for Comparison

Types of comparisons used typically vary with the estimated dollar value of the contract. Evidence of price reasonableness might include previous prices paid for same or similar items purchased competitively and/or knowledge of the supply or service gained from published price catalogs, newspapers, and other sources of market information. If you believe the quoted price is unreasonable, it will be necessary to solicit additional quotes.

Competitive Proposal Prices

Price competition is generally considered to be one of the best bases for price analysis. Competitive prices are offers received from sellers under conditions of adequate price competition. Adequate price competition exists when two or more responsible sellers, competing independently, submit price offers that satisfy the expressed requirement, and if the award will be made to a responsible seller whose proposal offers either the greatest value or the lowest evaluated price and you have not found that the price of the otherwise successful seller is unreasonable.

When comparing competitive offers, never use an offer from a seller that you have determined is nonresponsible. Never use a nonresponsive bid. Also, never use a price from a proposal that is technically outside the competitive range. Although price competition is considered to be one of the best bases for price analysis, you should normally place less reliance on competition when you find the solicitation was made under conditions that unreasonably denied one or more known and qualified sellers an opportunity to compete. In assessing reasonableness, you need to make sure that the offers are comparable.

Catalog Prices

Catalog prices are prices taken from a catalog, price list, schedule, or other verifiable and established record that is regularly maintained by a manufacturer or vendor and is published or otherwise available for customer inspection.

Historical Prices

Historical prices are prior prices paid by the buyer for the same or similar end items. Important items to think about when considering historical price analysis is whether the product and/or service has been purchased before (by your office or another office within the company); what the historical price was and can it be obtained; and was that historical price fair and reasonable (make sure the circumstances are the same or similar).

Price Estimates Based on Parametric Analysis

Parametric analyses—often referred to as *pricing yardsticks*—are also known as *cost estimating relationships (CER)*. They are formulas for estimating prices based on the relationship of past prices with one or more product's physical or performance characteristics (i.e., dollars per pound, dollars per horsepower, or dollars per square foot). Important items to think about when considering a yardstick for price analysis is whether the yardstick has been widely accepted in the marketplace (do both buyers and sellers agree on the validity and reasonableness of the values obtained by a particular yardstick); whether the yardstick has been properly developed (the developer of the yardstick should be able to produce data and calculations used in developing their estimate); and the accuracy of the yardstick (some yardsticks provide rough estimates and not precise prices).

Independent Company Estimates

Independent company estimates are those made by the buyer itself. The most common estimate is the material requisition, where a blind estimate is made on the approximate price of the item. A value analysis estimate is another type of buyer estimate. This analysis takes into account the apparent value of one proposed item over another; while the prices may not be comparable, the value of the item to the company may be.

Individuals familiar with the product and/or service and its use should perform these estimates independent of the requisition and solicitation process. They should determine what the product must do and what the total costs are related to purchasing the product and/or service, identify other ways in which the function can be performed, and document the total costs related to purchasing an alternative produce and/or service.

IDENTIFYING FACTORS THAT AFFECT COMPARABILITY

When comparing prices you must attempt to account for any factors that affect comparability. The following factors affect many price analysis comparisons:
■ market conditions;
■ quantity or size;
■ geographic location;
■ extent of competition;
■ technology; and
■ terms and conditions of the deal.

Market Conditions

The passage of time usually is accompanied by changes in supply, demand, technology, product designs, pricing strategies, laws and regulations that affect supplier costs, and other such factors. Generally select the most recent prices available. The greater the time difference, the greater the likelihood and impact of differences in market conditions. However, do not select a price for comparison merely because it is the most recent; look instead for prices that were established under similar market conditions.

Quantity or Size

Variations in quantity can have a significant impact on unit price. Economies of scale do not always apply. For example, increases in order size beyond a certain point may tax a seller's capacity and result in higher prices.

Geographic Location

Geography can have a range of effects on comparability. In major urban centers, you will be able to rely on data from within that geographic region; in more remote, less urban areas, you often must get data from beyond the immediate area. When you must compare prices across geographic boundaries, take the following steps to enhance comparability:

1. Check the extent of competition.
2. Determine the extent to which variations in the price of labor must be neutralized.
3. Check the freight requirements and accompanying costs.
4. Identify geographic anomalies or trends. For example, many items are more expensive in one region than in another.

Extent of Competition

When comparing one price with another, assess the competitive environment shaping the prices. For example, you can compare last year's competitive price with a current offer for the same item. However, if last year's procurement was made without competition (e.g., based on urgency), you may not have a good price with which to compare the current offer.

Technology

Prices from declining industries can rise because the technologies don't keep pace with rising costs. However, technological advances have been made so fast that a comparison of prices separated by a single year must account for these advances. Engineering or design changes must also be taken into account. This means you must identify the new or modified features and estimate their effect on price.

Terms and Conditions

Collectively, clauses form the terms and conditions (Ts and Cs) of the contract, and they define the rights and responsibilities of the parties to the contractual agreement. If called upon to enforce the contract in arbitration or a lawsuit, the arbitrator or court will look to these Ts and Cs in resolving the dispute.

A *term* is simply a part of the contract that addresses a specific subject. In most contracts, terms address payment, delivery, product quality, warranty of goods or services, termination of the agreement, resolution of disputes, and other subjects. Terms are described in clauses. The "Governing Law" clause is a contract term.

A *condition* is a phrase that either activates or suspends a term. A condition that activates a term is called a *condition precedent;* one that suspends a term is called a *condition subsequent.* Understanding the effect of conditions is critical to properly documenting and administering a contract. For example, the following sentence might appear in a "Specifications and Inspections" clause:

> Buyer may charge Seller for the cost of an above-normal level of inspection if rejection of the shipment based on the Buyer's normal inspection level endangers production schedules and if the inspected products are necessary to meet production schedules.

In other words, if the buyer rejects the seller's products based on a normal level of inspection, and if that causes those products to be unavailable for production, and if the products in question are necessary to meet a production schedule that will be endangered because of their availability, then the seller must pay the buyer the cost of performing inspections made at above-normal levels in order to meet that production schedule.

When experience teaches that certain clauses should always be included in contracts of a given type, those clauses may be preprinted in standard form. Such preprinted clauses are often called *standard terms and conditions,* which are useful when a business regularly enters many contracts and wants to reduce the administrative costs of its purchasing or sales operation. Standard Ts and Cs eliminate the need to hire an attorney to write a new contract every time a firm wants to buy or sell something.

In addition to reducing the administrative costs of contracting, standard Ts and Cs also reduce the risk of contract ambiguity.

Contract managers, project managers, buyers, and sellers can become familiar with standard clauses and their proper interpretation, which will greatly reduce the potential for misunderstandings and disputes.

Certain clauses appear in virtually every kind of contract. Take, for example the following clause:

> ABC Company is not liable for failing to fulfill its obligations due to acts of God, civil or military authority, war, strikes, fire, failure of its suppliers to meet commitments, or other causes beyond its reasonable control.

Clauses of this type are often called *force majeure*, a French term for "major or irresistible force." They appear in nearly all large contracts. Another commonly used clause requires suppliers to:

> ...comply with all federal, state, and local laws, regulations, rules, and orders. Any provision which is required to be a part of this Agreement by virtue of any such law, regulation, rule, or order is incorporated by reference.

Of course, neither party is familiar with all such provisions, but the idea is to relieve the buyer of any responsibility for the indiscretions of the seller.

Other clauses may give the buyer the right to purchase additional quantities of goods or extend the performance of services at agreed-on prices. Indemnification clauses often require one party to protect the other from certain types of losses, liabilities, judgments, and so forth. The indemnified party is given security of financial reimbursement by the indemnifying party for any loss described in the clause.

A common misunderstanding is that price is separate and distinct from the Ts and Cs, but that is not so. Nearly all Ts and Cs affect price, either increasing or decreasing costs or liabilities to the parties. In world-class companies, senior management ensures that all business managers involved with contracts are aware of and fully understand the cost, risk, and value of Ts and Cs and how they affect price.

Some common Ts and Cs are described in the following paragraphs.

Acceptance

Acceptance means agreement to the terms offered. Acceptance must be communicated, and it must be the mirror image of the offer. If the terms change, it is a *counteroffer* that then must be accepted. The Uniform Commercial Code (UCC) changes this mirror image rule by stating that definite and reasonable expression of the acceptance that is sent within a reasonable time operates as an acceptance even though it states terms additional to or different from those offered.

> *Civil law:* Many jurisdictions lack a mirror image rule. Rather, the acceptance must merely be to the significant terms of the offer.

Consideration

For a common law contract to be enforceable, the parties must exchange something of value *(consideration)*. Consideration can be something of monetary value, or it can be promising to do something not required by law or promising to refrain from doing something permitted by law.

> *Civil law:* There is no concept of consideration.

Contract Privity

One key concept of contract law is contract privity, which is the legal connection or relationship that exists between the contracting parties.[1] Such privity must exist between the plaintiff and defendant with respect to a matter being contested. A major exception to this principle that only the contracting parties can sue each other was created with the enactment of warranty statutes. For example, any person who is in the buyer's family or household may now sue for the breach of a seller's warranty.

Statute of Frauds

The *statute of frauds* is named for an old English statute designed to alleviate fraudulent claims. It provides that any contract that cannot be fully performed in less than a year and any contract for more than US$500 must be in writing to be enforceable.

Civil law: Few jurisdictions require that a sales contract be in writing. However, almost all civil law countries require that a sales contract involving real estate be in writing.

Waiver

A *waiver* is the voluntary and unilateral relinquishment by some act or conduct of a person of a right that he or she has. In common law countries, any contractual right of a party can be waived explicitly or implicitly by the party benefiting from the right. Similarly, any contractual obligation can be waived explicitly or implicitly by the party to whom the obligation is owed.

Civil law: Like the United States, every sovereign jurisdiction has specific areas sensitive to public policy based on the culture and economy of a nation. Frequently, in areas that touch on public policy, there are statutory rights that cannot be waived in a contract. Each jurisdiction must be examined to determine what, if any, nonwaivable rights the trading partner may have.

Forbearance

Forbearance is an intentional failure of a party to enforce a contract requirement, usually done for an act of immediate or future consideration from the other party. Sometimes forbearance is referred to as a *nonwaiver* or as a *one-time waiver*, but not a relinquishment of rights.

Specific Performance vs. Damages

Most contractual disputes are remedied with *damages* (money) to make the aggrieved (wronged) party "whole." In certain limited circumstances, a party may be forced to actually perform the contract, known as *specific performance.*

Liquidated and Compensatory vs. Punitive Damages

After determining that a party has been wronged and is entitled to damages, a determination must be made regarding the appropriate amount of damages. Using the evidence presented by the parties and rules of laws, the court will find an exact amount due (*compensatory damages*). In certain situations, parties may agree in advance that if a party is wronged in a specific way, then a specific amount of damages will be due the other party, thereby liquidating the damages in advance. Thus, if the parties include a *liquidated damages* clause in their contract, the court will determine only whether a party was in fact wronged and entitled to damages. Both common law and civil law allow the parties to the contract to agree on future damages. Note, however, that in common law, liquidated run-in damages must have reasonable relation to the probable actual damages; they cannot be a mere penalty. *Punitive damages,* unlike compensatory damages, are those damages awarded to the plaintiff over and above what will barely compensate for his or her loss. Punitive damages are based on actively different public policy consideration, that of punishing the defendant or of setting an example for similar wrongdoers.

Warranties

The UCC is the source of the now well-known "warranty of merchantability" and the "warranty of fitness for a particular purpose." The UCC states specifically how these warranties can and cannot be waived. These warranties are incorporated into European Union uniform laws and are rapidly being adopted around the world.

Signature

One significant change in the UCC is how it defines *signature.* Under common law, signature of the party to be charged meant the handwritten signature of the party's name. Under the UCC, signature means any affixation of the party's name or symbol to the document by hand, type, or other means, by the party to be charged. Such significance can include initials, letterhead, logos, stamps, or preprinted forms.

Comity

Comity is the concept of deferring to the law of another jurisdiction that has a greater connection (nexus) to the case. Comity exists in both common and civil law jurisdictions and manifests itself in several ways. Initially, when an action is brought, a court may transfer the case to a more convenient forum (for instance, where all the witnesses live). Then, while a case is tried, a court may apply the law of another forum that is more closely connected to the case. Finally, if another court has already rendered a final decision on the same case, the court will defer to the decision of the other court.

Choice-of-Law Rules

To determine whether comity demands application of the law of another jurisdiction, courts have sets of rules that, given the facts of the case and the residency of the parties, determine which jurisdiction has the greatest connection to the case. Courts in the United States may apply the law of a different state or a different country, if appropriate. For example, a New York court may apply the law of Virginia or the law of France.

Choice-of-Law Clauses

Caution should be exercised when using choice-of-law clauses. Some examples follow:

> This contract shall be governed by U.S. law.

Contract law in the United States is state law. No U.S. contract law exists. Even the UCC is state law. Without choosing a state, the contract does not effectively choose the governing law.

> This contract shall be governed by the law of the state of New York.

The law of the state of New York includes its choice-of-law rules. Therefore, this clause does not guarantee that New York law will be applied.

> This contract shall be governed by the law of the state of New York, without regard to its choice-of-law rules.

DETERMINING THE EFFECT OF IDENTIFIED FACTORS

Once you have identified the factors that may affect comparability, you must determine the effect on each specific comparison with the offered price. Questions to keep in mind are:
- What factors affect this specific comparison?
- How do these factors affect the comparison?
- Does this comparison, even with its limitations, contribute to the price analysis?

ADJUSTING THE PRICES SELECTED FOR COMPARISON

If you have a price analysis comparison base that does not require adjustment, use it. If you must make an adjustment, try to make the adjustment as objectively as possible. Remember, in order to establish price comparability you must:

- Identify and document price-related differences, taking into account the factors affecting comparability.
- Factor out price-related differences.

Restoring comparability by establishing a common basis for comparison requires that you assign a monetary value to each identified difference. The cost of terms and conditions peculiar to certain contracts is hard to estimate, so exercise discretion. The challenge is to use the available information and to estimate the price that should be paid. If you cannot objectively adjust the prices for the factor involved, you may need to make a subjective adjustment such as when estimating the effect on price of unique contract terms and conditions.

COMPARING ADJUSTED PRICES

After adjusting prices for comparison, determine what weight to give each price comparison. Then establish a should-pay price. If the should-pay price departs significantly from the apparent successful offer, analyze and document any differences.

SUMMARY

This chapter has provided a brief discussion of the importance of price analysis and some of the proven best practices. Remember, the key to conducting contract negotiations is to stay focused on building a strong relationship with the other party and creating a mutually successful deal. In Chapter 10, we will review the concept of total ownership cost and its application in the U.S. Department of Defense.

QUESTIONS TO CONSIDER

1. How well does your organization conduct price negotiations?

2. How often is your organization actually able to negotiate and obtain agreement on all of the key terms and conditions included in your negotiation plan?

3. Which price analysis techniques does your organization typically use?

4. How well does your organization build strong business relationships while conducting contract negotiations?

ENDNOTES

[1] For example, when a buyer contracts with a seller and the seller contracts with a third party to perform part of the project work, the seller is called the *prime contractor* and the third party is a *subcontractor*. Under ordinary circumstances, privity of contract exists between the buyer and the prime contractor and between the prime contractor and the subcontractor, but not between the buyer and the subcontractor. This principle holds true even though the subcontractor and the buyer have contact with one another on a day-to-day basis during contract performance

CHAPTER  10

TOTAL OWNERSHIP COST IN THE DEPARTMENT OF DEFENSE*

Introduction

Is the Department of Defense (DoD) headed down the right path to get total ownership cost under control? There are, no doubt, weapon systems that the DoD procures without regard for the total ownership cost (TOC), as the capability needed is so critical that the government would pay nearly anything to have it…at least for a while. For example, the SR-71 Blackbird was an extremely effective reconnaissance aircraft, but the Air Force was happy to retire the last of the fleet due primarily to the cost to operate the system, purported to be as high as $200,000 per hour in TOC terms. Eventually, the excessive TOC burden of even the most capable weapon system becomes unbearable.

Many useful approaches have been advanced over the past several years to get our collective arms around total ownership cost, or TOC. The various techniques may be employed, as appropriate, over the total life cycle of a warfighting system. Yet, the DoD has not reached the point where it can declare victory. For whatever reason, DoD leadership has not mandated employment of some of its most potent tools to get TOC under control.

This chapter will identify several tools that are of use in controlling TOC, provide cost as an independent variable and reduction of total ownership cost examples, and point out where the DoD needs to refocus its efforts to achieve better results.

TOC—What Is It?

There are two commonly used definitions of total ownership cost. The first is very broad, written from a top-level DoD or service perspective.

> DoD TOC is the sum of all financial resources necessary to organize, equip, train, sustain, and operate military forces sufficient to meet national goals in compliance with all laws, all policies applicable to DoD, all standards in effect for readiness, safety, and quality of life, and all other official measures of performance for DoD and its components. DoD TOC is comprised of costs to research, develop, acquire, own, operate, and dispose of weapon and support systems, other equipment and real property; the costs

TEN

to recruit, train, retain, separate and otherwise support military and civilian personnel; and all other costs of business operations of the DoD.[1]

The second definition is deliberately written from the vantage point of the program manager of the warfighting system and is a subset of the definition above.

Defense Systems TOC is defined as life cycle cost (LCC). LCC (per DoD 5000.4M) includes not only acquisition program direct costs, but also the indirect costs attributable to the acquisition program (i.e., costs that would not occur if the program did not exist). For example, indirect costs would include the infrastructure that plans, manages, and executes a program over its full life and common support items and systems. The responsibility of program managers in support of reducing DoD TOC is the continuous reduction of LCC for their systems.[2]

As Dr. Gansler said in his 1998 memorandum, from which the above definition was extracted, the program manager's job, in trying to reduce TOC, is a very difficult one, and program managers should seek help wherever they can to reduce ownership costs. This article examines TOC from the perspective of the program manager of the warfighting system.

Pursuit of TOC reduction at the level of the warfighting system may be separated into two major approaches that are connected, end-to-end, along a life-cycle time line. During the developmental phases, the effort or process is called cost as an independent variable (CAIV). For systems in the field or fleet, the process or goal becomes reduction of total ownership cost (R-TOC). Figure 10-1 is a typical depiction of the CAIV/R-TOC relationship.

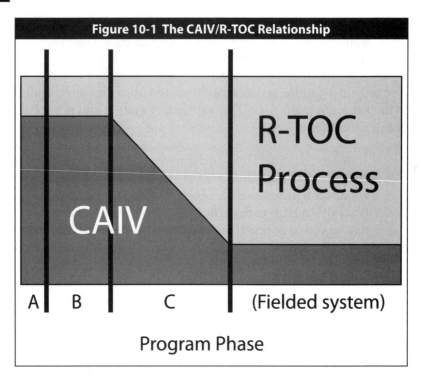

Figure 10-1 The CAIV/R-TOC Relationship

The first approach, cost as an independent variable, addresses total ownership cost during the warfighting system's developmental phases, beginning with the concept refinement. The focus of CAIV is to establish cost targets based on affordability and requirements and then to manage to those targets, thereby controlling TOC. CAIV includes consideration of costs for development, production, operations and support, and disposal. An example of the CAIV process would be to set specific cost and reliability targets for each subsystem or component of a weapon system in development, such that the warfighting system will be able to achieve the required operational availability at the specified cost.

During concept refinement, a mix of performance requirements and cost constraints would lead to a trade-off analysis wherein a team led by the sponsor or warfighter and populated by the stake-holders (sponsor, users, maintainers, developers) would critically assess the various possible solutions and arrive at the solution set that best meets the users' required capabilities within cost constraints. This activity is called an *analysis of alternatives* within the Joint Capabilities Integration and Development System (JCIDS) directives; the Army Training and Doctrine Command (TRADOC) has used a very instructive name for the team itself: an "integrated concept team."[3, 4]

Employing CAIV early in the developmental process offers, potentially, the greatest opportunity for TOC reduction at the lowest possible investment cost. As an example, the TOC impacts of using two different power plants presents an opportunity to use the CAIV evaluation technique to estimate the TOC impact and make a best-value decision. For illustrative purposes, consider a standard internal combustion engine at a cost of $7,500 versus a hybrid-electric power plant costing $19,000. The impact to the acquisition cost is evident, but that excludes the cost savings associated with fuel consumption over the life of the system. If the system's operational mode indicates an average usage of 15,000 miles per year and an economic useful life (EUL) of 20 years, the total miles expected is 300,000. If the standard engine in our comparison is estimated at 10 miles per gallon and the hybrid engine is estimated at 25 miles per gallon, the estimated fuel saved by the hybrid-powered system would be 18,000 gallons. At a current estimate of $1.25 per gallon and using constant dollars, the operations and support (O&S) impact is $22,500 per system. From a TOC perspective, the hybrid engine is $11,000 less expensive than the standard engine, and there are other reductions in fuel supply assets and attendant personnel that apply.[5]

THE BEST EFFECT—UP FRONT AND EARLY

Capability Documents

Key performance parameters (KPPs) are identified within the weapon system's capabilities documents and represent those minimum attributes or characteristics considered most essential for an effective military capability. Depending on the nature of the weapon system, the KPPs may be validated by the Joint Requirements Oversight Council, the Functional Capabilities Board, or the DoD Component. Key performance parameters that appear in the Capability Development Document (CDD) or Capability Production Document (CPD) are then inserted verbatim into the acquisition program baseline (APB). These KPPs typically represent minimum or threshold performance requirements that are not considered for trade-off during CAIV analyses.

KPPs bring DoD and service leadership to a crossroads. If CAIV is critical within DoD, then a forceful way to express its importance is to designate TOC limits as a KPP. The GAO, in a February 2003 report entitled, "Best Practices: Setting Requirements Differently Could Reduce Weapon Systems' Total Ownership Costs" (GAO-03-57), has recommended the use of TOC KPPs as a way to mirror commercial best practice.[6] Yet the Office of the Secretary of Defense does not require making life-cycle cost or total ownership cost a key performance parameter. To be more precise, CJCSI 3170.01C, by its definition of KPP, appears to allow LCC to be a KPP but does not require it.[7] It should be noted that the use of KPPs establishes constraints to possible solution sets and other risks. Therefore, KPPs should be kept to a minimum.

A PROMISING EXAMPLE OF THE USE OF KPPS

The Joint Strike Fighter (JSF) provides an example of KPPs that address total ownership cost. JSF has six KPPs; three of the six address supportability/affordability.[8] First, mission reliability directly impacts O&S cost for parts replacement and the associated expenditure of maintenance man-hours. Second, logistics footprint influences both program acquisition cost and O&S cost; the smaller the footprint, the smaller the acquisition cost and the less expensive to transport and maintain. Third, sortie generation rate depends on maintenance man-hours per operating hour and heavily influences design for maintainability. These three Joint Strike Fighter KPPs have brought about the use of autonomics, which includes on-board diagnostics/prognostics and improves the cost effectiveness of maintenance. These three KPPs all impact affordability and could be at least partially redefined in terms of average procurement unit cost (APUC) and O&S costs.

THE NEXT BEST TOC OPPORTUNITY—EARLY IN SUSTAINMENT

If TOC is not fully integrated into a system's design during the developmental phases, an opportunity is missed, but all is not lost. This is where R-TOC kicks in. The reality is that programs never get LCC 100 percent right during the development phases. R-TOC provides the process "toolbox" for working on cost improvements once the warfighting system is in production and/or sustainment.

R-TOC focuses on the reduction of APUC and weapon system sustainment cost (i.e., O&S costs). R-TOC is employed as the warfighting system is produced and placed in service and cost drivers are identified and isolated. Examples of R-TOC would be a value engineering change proposal (VECP) to reduce the cost of manufacturing a component by improving the process yield (the percentage of manufactured items that are defect-free) or a VECP to reduce the O&S cost by improving the reliability of an expensive subsystem or component. Often R-TOC initiatives result in secondary benefits that enhance performance (i.e., improved reliability and operational availability); however, the forcing function is generally the reduction of O&S costs, the largest constituent of TOC for most systems.

Operations and Support Costs

The O&S phase includes most sustainment costs and administration during the weapon system's operation in the field or fleet (e.g., repair parts or the labor cost associated with an engine repair). It includes uniformed personnel and civilian labor costs. Operations and maintenance (O&M) appropriations pay a large part of O&S costs (including civilian personnel but not military personnel). O&M funds also pay for disposal costs.[9]

Operating and support costs may be dramatically reduced by identifying O&S cost drivers (i.e., those components that, through Pareto analysis, are recognized as major contributors to the cost of operation) and correcting them (often, but not always, through redesign). The most efficient time to accomplish this is during the pre-acquisition and development phases, while the system is only a paper design and may be changed relatively inexpensively. However, cost drivers that are discovered during the production and sustainment phases also may lead to redesign or other actions that can save or avoid significant expenditures. DoD pilot programs exhibit many useful examples of R-TOC, such as Abrams Tank engine (PROSE), the SH-60 Affordable Readiness Initiatives, Aviation Support Equipment reliability improvement initiatives, the EA-6B Inertial Navigation System, and SLAM-ER Data Link Pod.[10]

A HIGH-PAYOFF EXAMPLE OF THE USE OF R-TOC

The Aegis system provides an example of a very successful R-TOC effort that began in the mid-1980s and today is still paying off like a "gilt-edged bond." Each ship requires microwave-producing equipment that includes a device called a crossed-field amplifier (CFA). Early in Aegis deployment, the CFA proved to be a cost driver with relatively expensive failures attributable to an arcing condition between the cathode and anode in the microwave tube. This arcing caused the CFA to fail at about 6,000 hours mean time before failure (MTBF). A change to anode metallurgy, along with other minor changes, reduced arcing and increased MTBF to between 40,000 and 45,000 hours, which drastically reduced the frequency of corrective maintenance, maintenance man-hours, and stockage level requirements, while simultaneously improving the reliability and availability of the microwave system.

This dramatic improvement was the result of a team effort among the Aegis Program Office, Communications and Power Industries (CPI, the vendor that provided the CFA, was formerly part of Varian), Crane Naval Surface Warfare Center (the Navy In-Service Engineering Agent for Aegis microwave tubes), the Navy MANTECH Office, and Raytheon (the prime contractor, located in Sudbury, Massachusetts). This TOC reduction affects 27 Aegis cruisers (each of which has 76 CFAs) and 40 Aegis destroyers (equipped with 38 CFAs). In 2002 dollars, the annual cost avoidance averages about $1.9 million per Aegis cruiser and $950,000 per Aegis destroyer. Eventually, TOC reduction will benefit an additional 22 Aegis destroyers that are yet to be completed and deployed, each of which will have 32 CFAs.

TOOLS, TECHNIQUES, AND CONCEPTS SUPPORTING EFFICIENT TOC SOLUTIONS

As a system progresses from early concept, through prototyping and production, and finally reaches the sustainment phase, the opportunities to significantly reduce TOC diminish. Clearly, TOC reduction efforts are most effective early in the developmental cycle where changes are least expensive, easiest to implement, and have the widest effect. Looking from the perspective of the warfighter, the possible effect of a balance between capabilities and affordability is that *more warfighting assets may be available to the warfighter*. To that end, TOC stakeholders have a vested interest in influencing the system design and development, especially early in the process, to yield a suitable, effective, and *affordable* solution. The challenge is how to accomplish this goal.

One answer to this challenge has been postulated earlier—make TOC goals part of the system key performance parameters. One of the only methods of keeping the TOC goals from being in the "trade-space" for CAIV or other trade-off analyses is to designate those goals as KPPs. As with other KPPs, a TOC KPP would be considered a mandatory threshold, and the use of other tools and techniques would then serve to reinforce the importance of TOC. As KPPs are also part of the APB, TOC would receive attention from decision makers at every level, throughout the developmental process.

CAIV and Other Trade-off Analyses

With a firm understanding of those performance characteristics (hopefully including TOC) that the warfighter deems critical to the system effectiveness and suitability via the KPP, CAIV analysis techniques can be used to effect TOC reduction on subsystems, features, and capabilities in the "trade-space" (i.e., items not identified as KPPs). These analyses serve the materiel developer in balancing system capabilities, technologies, schedules, and costs within the parameters set by the sponsor. Proper identification of performance parameters and closer connectivity between materiel developer and sponsor will help ensure that the developed system is effective, suitable, and affordable.

Integrated Product Teams (IPTs)

Cost-performance IPTs (CPIPTs) play a key role in trade-off analyses that impact TOC, and other IPTs can, and should, participate in reducing costs as well. By their nature, IPTs solve problems and make recommendations based on their research of a particular program aspect in accordance with their charter. If each IPT charter includes the goal of reducing TOC within its area of concentration, significant opportunities for TOC reduction could be captured.

In addition to cost trade-offs that occur in the CPIPT, other trade-off analyses may reduce system TOC. For example, a high-maintenance, low-availability, cutting-edge system that is not a KPP requirement might be traded off or deferred to a future block upgrade, allowing the technology to mature, reliability to improve, and life-cycle cost to be reduced. Schedule trade-offs, while often considered negative, may allow software engineers to more fully test and integrate a critical software function, eliminating frustrating downtime and costly diagnostics. Both of these trade-offs would likely result in reduced TOC.

It is important to recognize that cost-performance trade-offs may reduce TOC, but they may do so at the price of reduced performance. In that regard, the warfighters–the real users of the systems–must be involved in the process to ensure that the solution set is acceptable, balancing warfighting capability and O&S cost, which is typically borne by the warfighter.

Ownership Cost Databases

We currently are limited in our understanding of life-cycle costs for our legacy systems, due to the lack of reliable information databases. Without that knowledge, we are limited in estimating the impact of TOC reduction efforts on those life-cycle costs. Asking a program office how much they will save through an R-TOC effort is rather like asking a person the distance of the path he *didn't* take and comparing it to the one he did. Someone else certainly has traveled the other path, but there is simply no record of it. Establishing reliability, maintainability, sustainability (RMS) cost databases may seem an expensive initiative, but the knowledge gained from capturing sustainment costs would help focus R-TOC efforts and influence the design of future systems, bringing about a better balance of capabilities and affordability.

Contractor and Government R-TOC Incentives

The profit incentive present in the commercial marketplace provides the DoD with a powerful tool for reducing TOC. Contract incentives (e.g., reliability improvements, increase in MTBF, and reduced maintenance cycle time), value engineering change proposals (VECPs), shared savings from cost reduction initiatives, and other incentives motivate the contractor to perform in a manner that enhances its profit and reduces the TOC of the weapon system –a true "win-win" situation. In the sustainment phase, improvements are possible and there are many good examples from the TOC pilots.[11] However, the "home runs" in TOC reduction are more likely to occur prior to production, rather than afterward.

Source selection criteria shape how contractors compete for development, production, and contractor logistics support (CLS) contracts and, therefore, TOC elements in the source selection plan impact in a positive way the proposals that contractors submit. In the case of public-private competition or partnerships for logistics support contracts, the same concept applies: The winning bidder must present the most advantageous proposal, and the source selection criteria define those parameters. Selecting key TOC elements as source selection criteria ensures that the competing entities focus on methods of achieving TOC efficiencies to gain advantage over other bidders.

TOC incentives for government sponsors[12] and materiel developers have been less effective than desired.[13] While TOC is obviously important to the combat developer and user community, it seems that more emphasis has been placed on emerging warfighting capabilities and modernization efforts than on TOC performance in the early stages of development–stakeholders are more interested in what the weapon system will do than in what it will cost to do it. After introduction to the field or fleet, typically, TOC has become an issue and R-TOC efforts are initiated in response, precisely at the point in development where such efforts are becoming more costly and less effective.

Following suit, the materiel developer communities focus on those APB elements, including KPPs, specified by the sponsor in the capability documents. With little TOC emphasis passed from the sponsor in the defining capability documents, materiel developers have the incentive to manage to the *acquisition cost*, program schedule, and specified performance. The reason materiel developers are focused on the acquisition cost is that, typically, the program and budget elements they manage are RDT&E and procurement funding, which relate primarily to the acquisition cycle; but these accounts only represent about 25 to 30 percent of TOC. Except for TOC-related KPPs, TOC elements inevitably drop into the "trade-space" for managing to the acquisition cost, program schedule, and performance identified by the combat developer. This often suboptimizes TOC by trading off features/functions (resulting in higher O&S costs) in favor of lower acquisition cost, even though O&S costs consume about 70 to 75 percent of TOC.

Reduction in Total Ownership Cost

Although R-TOC initiatives are more effective and less costly when performed early in the development cycle, TOC reduction still can be beneficial throughout the system's life cycle. Confirming through cost-benefit analyses that R-TOC initiatives will reduce cost, these initiatives will also likely result in increasing capability for the warfighter. More funding available in the acquisition phase or in the O&S phase either provides more assets directly (acquisition phase) or buys increased readiness rates (O&S phase). Therefore, R-TOC initiatives can increase military effectiveness when evaluated on their own merits and not coupled with other interests such as increased system capability.

Summary

1. Up-front planning can result in major TOC savings—but JCIDS offers little emphasis on CAIV and R-TOC at the front end of the process (i.e., in the concept refinement and technology development phases). Current guidance permits TOC to be designated a KPP, but this is not required.

2. Serious consideration must be given to elevating TOC to KPP status. This will go a long way to avoid trading off TOC during the developmental process. The JSF certainly offers an example of creativity in treating TOC as KPP.

3. There are many success stories, many documented in TOC pilot programs, that might be beneficial to other acquisition programs, especially legacy systems. R-TOC success hinges on finding the cost drivers and addressing them with innovative R-TOC solutions. Limited funding hinders aggressive action to redesign components that are cost drivers.

4. Tools and processes are generally available, with the exception of complete and integrated cost databases. Without complete, easily retrievable cost data, it is difficult to identify cost drivers and recognize components or warfighting systems that need redesign to reduce TOC.

5. The real question is: Does DoD leadership have the will to demand that TOC be addressed seriously?

The final chapter of this book will address the practical value and use of Earned Value Management Systems.

Endnotes

* The contents of this chapter are taken from a paper, "Reduction of Total Ownership Cost," prepared for the Naval Postgraduate School and Naval Sea Systems Command as one of the Acquisition Research Sponsored Report Series, September

2003. It is available for download at http://www.nps.navy.mil/gsbpp/acqn. The research presented in this material was supported by the Acquisition Chair of the Graduate School of Business and Public Policy at the Naval Postgraduate School. Copies of the Acquisition-Sponsored Research Reports may be printed from our Web site at www.nps.navy.mil/gsbpp/acqn/publications.

1   Jacques S. Gansler, "Definition of Total Ownership Cost (TOC), Life Cycle Cost, and the Responsibilities of Program Managers," memorandum, 13 November 1998, Office of the Secretary of Defense.

2   Ibid.

3   Office of the Joint Chiefs of Staff, "Joint Capabilities Integration and Development System." Chairman of the Joint Chiefs of Staff Instruction 3170.01C, 24 June 2003.

4   U.S. Army Training and Doctrine Command Pamphlet 71-9, Requirements Determination, March 1996 (Obsolete). Guidance on Use of Integrated Concept Teams Currently Specified in AR 70-1, Army Acquisition Policy, 31 December 2003.

5   This example is calculated in constant dollars to provide an accurate cost comparison; this is a practice typically used in DoD cost estimation. For budgetary purposes, constant dollars would have to be inflated in future years to take into account that the dollars used in future years are incrementally less valuable than the dollars used in earlier years, i.e., the time value of money.

6   U.S. General Accounting Office, "Best Practices: Setting Requirements Differently Could Reduce Weapon Systems' Total Ownership Costs." Report to the Subcommittee on Readiness and Management Support, Committee on Armed Services, U.S. Senate. GAO-03-57, February 2003.

7   Office of the Joint Chiefs of Staff, "Joint Capabilities Integration and Development System." Chairman of the Joint Chiefs of Staff Instruction 3170.01C, 24 June 2003, pages A-10 and A-11.

8   Jack Hudson (Major General, USAF), "JSF Program Update," briefing, October 2003. Program Executive Officer, Joint Strike Fighter.

9   Department of Defense, "Operation of the Defense Acquisition System," DoD Instruction 5000.2, 12 May 2003.

10   Institute for Defense Analysis (IDA), "Reduction of Total Ownership Cost" Web site, http://rtoc.ida.org/rtoc/rtoc.html

11   Ibid.

12   The term, "sponsor," is consistent with CJCSI 3170.01C. Sponsor supercedes the term, "combat developer," which may still be used in some DoD communities.

13   U.S. General Accounting Office, "Best Practices: Setting Requirements Differently."

CHAPTER  11

A GUIDE TO EARNED VALUE MANAGEMENT SYSTEMS

Introduction

This guide provides information pertaining to project planning, scheduling, and the earned value management systems (EVMS) required by the U.S. Department of Defense (DoD) Instruction 5000.2 and the *Defense Acquisition Guidebook*. It should be useful to project managers, program managers, functional managers, project control managers, contract managers, and others involved in project management.

Earned Value Management

Earned value management (EVM) is now a hot topic in the U.S. Department of Defense and the defense industry for a couple of reasons. First, the Office of Management and Budget (OMB) is working to add the requirement for EVM to the *Federal Acquisition Regulation*. Second, the DoD has recently made some relatively significant changes to its policy on this key project management process, which has been used in the defense acquisition process for more than 35 years.

EVM is a widely accepted industry best practice for project management, which is used across the DoD, federal government, and the commercial sector. A common operational definition of EVM is "the use of an integrated management system that coordinates work scope, schedule, and cost goals and objectively measures progress toward these goals." The term EVM replaces the old term used since the 1960s, cost/schedule control systems criteria (C/SCSC).

On March 7, 2005, the defense acquisition executive signed a memorandum approving revisions to the department's EVM policy. The policy has been modified to provide consistency in application across DoD programs and to better manage the programs through improvements in DoD and industry practices.

New Application Thresholds for EVM

EVM compliance is required on cost or incentive contracts, subcontracts, intragovernment work agreements, and other agreements valued at or greater than $20 million. An EVM system that has been formally validated and accepted by the cognizant contracting officer is required on cost or incentive contracts, subcontracts, intragovernment work agreements, and other agreements valued at or greater than $50 million.

Contract Implementation of EVM

The changes to the DoD's EVM policy are required to be implemented on applicable contracts that are awarded based on solicitations or requests for proposal valued at or greater than $20 million and issued on or after April 6, 2005, using Defense Federal Acquisition Regulation Supplement (DFARS) clauses 252.242-7005 and 252.252-7006.

The revised policy is being incorporated into DoD Instruction 5000.2 and the *Defense Acquisition Guidebook*. The changes have been incorporated into the *Earned Value Management Implementation Guide* (EVMIG), the principal reference for detailed implementation guidance, which is available on the Defense Contract Management Agency (DCMA) Web site at http://guidebook.dcma.mil/79/guidebook_process.htm.

Understanding the Earned Value Management System

To understand EVM you must become familiar with the ten basic project management building blocks: (1) organizing, (2) authorizing, (3) scheduling, (4) budgeting, (5) cost accumulation, (6) performance measurement, (7) variance analysis, (8) change management, (9) internal audit, and (10) performance formulae, analysis, DoD reviews, and reports.

Organizing Work

Organizing the work is the initial task of project management. The operations organization is made up of those individuals responsible for the various tasks required by the contract statement of work (SOW) or performance work statement (PWS).

Work Breakdown Structure

The work breakdown structure (WBS) provides the framework for the organization of the contract effort. It is an indentured listing of all of the products (e.g., hardware, software, services, and data) to be furnished by the contractor. It is used as the basis for all contract planning, scheduling, and budgeting; cost accumulation; and performance reporting throughout the entire period of project performance.

Integrated Project Team

The integrated project team (IPT) structure reflects the organization required to support the project. The project manager is responsible for ensuring the cost, schedule, and technical management of the project. The project manager draws upon the functional groups to accomplish the work through the assignment of responsibility to appropriate managers.

Responsibility Assignment Matrix

The responsibility assignment matrix (RAM) ties the work that is required by the WBS elements to the organization responsible for accomplishing the assigned tasks. The intersection of the WBS with the IPT structure identifies the control account. The RAM includes the organization and the individual responsible for the work, which is then tracked to a control account.

Authorizing Work

All work within a project should be described and authorized through the contractor's work authorization system. Work authorization ensures that performing organizations are specifically informed regarding their work scope, schedule for performance, budget, and charge number(s) for the work assigned to them. Work authorization is a formal process that can consist of various levels. Each level of authorization is agreed upon by the parties involved so that there is no question as to what is required. The document involved in work authorization should be maintained in a current status throughout the life cycle of the contract as revisions take place.

Customer Authorization

Customer authorization is comprised of:
- The Basic contract
- Contract change notices
- Engineering change notices

Internal Authorization

Internal authorization is comprised of these steps:
- Upon receipt of a contract (or change notice), the contracts management team provides the project manager authorization

to perform the contract work in the form of a project authorization notice (PAN) or equivalent document.

■ The project manager prepares a document authorizing the assigned functional manager to perform work. This authorization is a contract between the functional manager and the project manager.

Figure 11-1 shows the typical contractor work authorization flow.

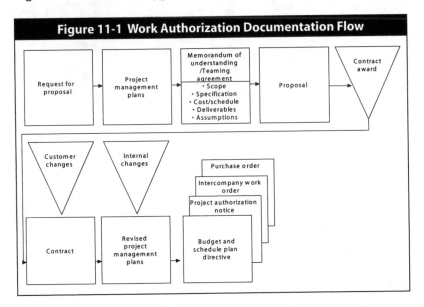

Figure 11-1 Work Authorization Documentation Flow

SCHEDULING WORK

The subjects of scheduling and budgeting are interrelated and iterative. In order to develop a time-phased budget plan, the schedule must be prepared first. Scheduling is the process of integrating activities and resources into a meaningful arrangement, depicting the timing of the critical activities that will satisfy the customer's requirements.

Project Scheduling

Project scheduling is a logical time-phasing of the activities that are necessary to accomplish the entire project scope. It is the most important tool for cost and schedule:

■ Planning
■ Tracking
■ Analysis of variances
■ Reporting of project performance

Each activity in the network is characterized by scope, logical relationships, duration, and resources.

Figure 11-2 shows the steps required to build a project schedule.

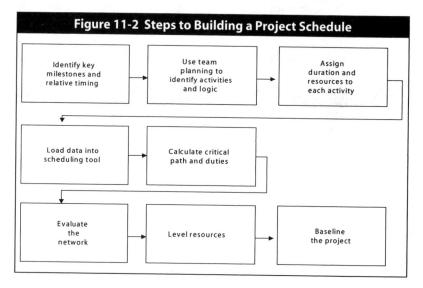

Figure 11-2 Steps to Building a Project Schedule

Scheduling Definitions

- **Milestone:** An event of particular significance that has no duration.
- **Activity:** Something that occurs over time; work that must be accomplished, also referred to as a *task*.
- **Sequential:** Activities that are performed in sequence, or one right after the other.
- **Concurrent/parallel:** Two or more activities that are performed at the same time or that overlap.

Scheduling Terms

- **Finish-to-start:** The predecessor activity must be completed before the successor activity can begin.

- **Start-to-start:** The predecessor activity must begin before the successor activity can begin.

- **Finish-to-finish:** The predecessor activity must end before the successor activity can end.

| Task A | | Task B |

- **Lag:** Any schedule time delay between two tasks. Lags can be positive or negative.
- **Critical path:** The longest continuous sequence of tasks through the network, given the underlying relationships that will affect the project end date.
- **Float:** The difference between the time available (when tasks *can* start/finish) and the time necessary (when tasks *must* start/finish).

Schedule Outputs

There are three basic scheduling outputs:
- Network diagram
- Gantt chart
- Resource histogram

Once the project schedule is complete, the cost/schedule performance baseline is established. Figure 11-3 shows the steps required to establish the baseline and track and analyze performance on the project.

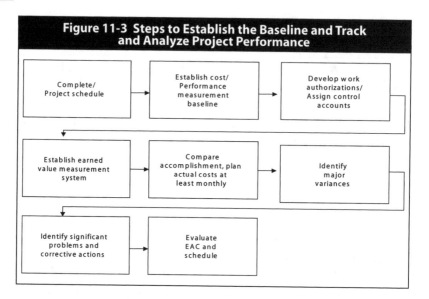

Figure 11-3 Steps to Establish the Baseline and Track and Analyze Project Performance

A diagram of the performance measurement system is shown in Figure 11-4.

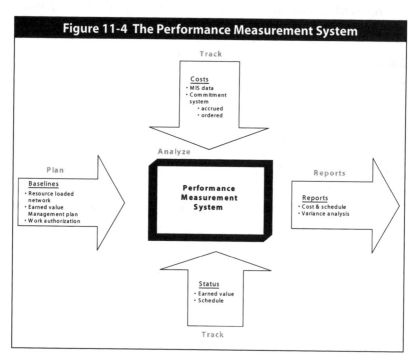

Figure 11-4 The Performance Measurement System

Budgeting Work

Budgeting is the process of distributing budgets to individual work segments. Figure 11-5 gives a top-down overview of the relationships.

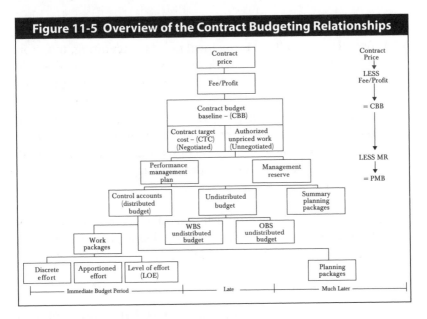

Figure 11-5 Overview of the Contract Budgeting Relationships

Total Allocated Budget

The total allocated budget (TAB) is the sum of all budgets allocated to the contract. It is the same as the contract budget base unless an over target baseline (OTB) has been established. (See "Changes" for an explanation of OTB).

Contract Budget Base

The contract budget base (CBB) is the sum of the contract target cost (CTC) plus the estimated cost of any authorized, unpriced (not yet negotiated) work. It is made up of the performance measurement baseline and management reserve.

Performance Measurement Baseline

The performance measurement baseline (PMB) is the time-phased budget plan against which contract performance is measured. It is composed of the budgets assigned to control accounts and undistributed budget. It equals the TAB minus management reserve.

Management Reserve

The management reserve (MR) is a budget amount that is set aside to provide for unforeseen, within-contract-scope requirements.

Control Account

The control account (CA) is the focal point for planning, monitoring, and controlling project work as it represents the work within a single WBS element and is the responsibility of a single organizational unit. Virtually all aspects of the performance management system come together at the CA level, including budgets, schedules, work assignments, cost collection, progress assessment, problem identification, corrective actions, and estimate at completion (EAC) development. Day-to-day management is performed at the CA level.

The level selected for the establishment of a CA must be carefully considered to ensure that work is properly defined into manageable units with responsibilities clearly delineated.

Undistributed Budget

The undistributed budget (UB) is the budget that is applicable to a specific contract effort but has not yet been distributed to the WBS elements. Undistributed budget is intended to serve only as a temporary holding account until the budget is properly distributed.

Summary Planning Packages

Summary planning packages are used to plan time-phased budgets for far-term work that cannot practically be planned in full detail.

Work Packages

A work package is a detailed job that is established by the functional manager for accomplishing work within a control account. A work package has these characteristics:

- Represents units of work (activities or tasks) at the levels where the work is performed
- Is clearly distinct from all other work packages and is the responsibility of a single organizational element
- Has scheduled start and completion dates (with interim milestones, if applicable) that are representative of physical task accomplishment

- Has a budget or assigned value expressed in terms of dollars, labor hours, or other measurable units
- Has a duration that is relatively short, unless it is subdivided by discrete milestones to permit objective measurement of work performed
- Has a schedule that is integrated with all other activities occurring on the project
- Has a unique earned value technique, either discrete, apportioned effort, or level of effort (LOE)

Planning Package

If a CA cannot be subdivided into fully detailed work packages, the far-term effort is identified in larger planning packages for budgeting and scheduling purposes. The budget for the planning package is identified according to the work for which it is intended, is time-phased, and should have controls that prevent its use in the performance of other work. Eventually, all work in planning packages will be planned to the appropriate level of detail in work packages.

Cost Accumulation

Cost accumulation is the process of recording and assembling the actual costs for a project. The lowest level of accumulation is the work package, although many large projects accumulate costs at the control account level. These actual costs plus accruals are called the actual cost of work performed (ACWP).

Direct Cost Elements

Within the control account or a work package (depending upon the level of cost accumulation), there are direct cost elements, which consist of direct labor, other direct costs (ODCs), material, and subcontracts.

Direct labor Timekeeping/cost collection for labor costs uses a labor distribution/accumulation system. The management information system (MIS) reports biweekly expenditure data based on labor charges against control accounts or work packages.

Other direct costs ODCs include charges such as:

- Travel and per diem Service centers Purchased services
- Material/subcontracts

Indirect Cost Elements

Indirect cost elements consist of overhead (OH) and fringe and general and administrative (G&A). Within each indirect cost element there are multiple subelements.

Overhead (OH) and fringe Overhead and fringe costs are accumulated in pools for biweekly distribution to projects. Overhead and fringe are allocated to each charge number in each organization based on the individual contractor's overhead and fringe rates.

General and administrative (G&A) These indirect costs are also accumulated in pools for biweekly distribution to project charge numbers.

Performance Measurement

Performance measurement for the functional managers, project control managers, and others consists of evaluating work package status calculated at the work package level. A comparison of the planned value (budgeted cost for work scheduled [BCWS]) to earned value (budgeted cost for work performed [BCWP]) is made to obtain the schedule variance, and a comparison of the BCWP to the actual costs of work performed (ACWP) is made to obtain the cost variance. Performance measurement provides a basis for management decisions by the project manager, the contractor's management, and, in some cases, the customer.

Performance measurement provides:
1. Work progress status
2. Relationship of planned cost and actual cost to actual accomplishment
3. Valid, timely, auditable data
4. A basis for the EAC

Elements required to measure project progress and status are:
1. Work package schedule status
2. BCWS or the planned expenditure
3. BCWP or earned value
4. ACWP or MIS costs and accruals

Control account/work packages:
1. Measurable work and related event status form the basis for determining progress for BCWP calculations.
2. BCWP measurements at summary WBS levels result from accumulating BCWP upward through the control account from the work package levels.
   a. Within each control account, the inclusion of LOE is kept to a minimum to prevent distortion of the total BCWP.
   b. Calculation methods used for measuring work package performance are:
      i. Short work packages (2 months or less) may use the measured effort or formula method (e.g., 0 to 100 percent), where a status can be applied each month.
      ii. Longer work packages (over 2 months) should have milestones assigned. The milestones are then asssessed monthly for the life cycle of the work package.
      iii. In manufacturing, work packages may use the earned standards or equivalent units method to measure performance based on the manufacturing work measurement system output.
      iv. Effort that can be measured in direct proportion to other discrete work may be measured as apportioned effort work packages. Apportioned effort is used primarily in manufacturing.
      v. Sustained efforts are planned using the LOE earned value method. The earned value for LOE work packages is equal to the time-phased plan (BCWS).
   c. The measurement method used depends on an analysis of the work to be performed in the work package. Whichever method is selected for planning (BCWS) must also be used for determining progress (BCWP).

Estimate to Complete (ETC) Preparation to develop an ETC, the control account manager (CAM) must consider and analyze:
1. Cumulative ACWP/ordered commitments
2. Schedule status
3. BCWP to date
4. Remaining control account scope of work
5. Previous ETC
6. Historical data
7. Required resources by type
8. Projected cost and schedule efficiency

Tools Techniques and Best Practices

9. Future actions
10. Approved contract changes

The functional managers or control account managers (CAMs) prepare the ETC as required by the project manager.

■ **EAC preparation**–The ETC is then summarized to all necessary reporting levels, added to the ACWP and commitments, and reported to corporate management and the customer, as appropriate.

■ A bottoms-up EAC should be prepared quarterly for all contracts.

The EAC is the estimated cost at the end of the project. It is composed of the cost of what has been accomplished and the estimated cost of the remaining work. Figure 11-6 illustrates the two primary components of the EAC.

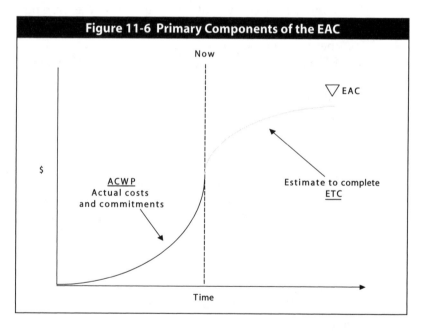

Figure 11-6 Primary Components of the EAC

Figure 11-7 shows the components of the EAC.

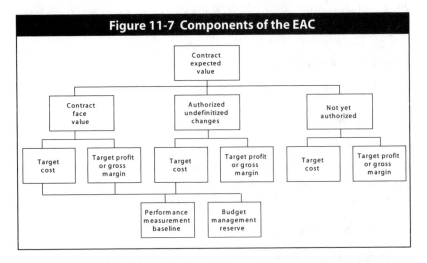

Figure 11-7 Components of the EAC

Revenues at Completion

Revenues at completion are the total revenues anticipated on the contract at the completion of the project. Revenues at completion are composed of the EAC and the EAC profit.

EAC Profit

EAC profit is the profit expected to be achieved at the completion of the project.

Estimate at Completion (EAC)

EAC is the cost of work performed to date plus the estimated cost of all remaining work on the project. The EAC is made up of four components: ACWP, open commitments, estimate to complete (ETC), and hard reserves.

Actual Cost of Work Performed

ACWP is the cost of work performed to date plus accruals, which are costs for goods or services the contractor has received but has not yet paid for.

Ordered Commitments

Ordered commitments are costs for goods or services that have been ordered but for which the work has not yet been performed.

Estimate to Complete

ETC is the estimated cost of the remaining work on the project.

Hard Reserves

Hard reserves are reserves associated with the EAC and are intended to cover the potential cost of risks to be mitigated on the project. The hard reserves are equal to the sum of the mitigation costs plus the sum of the residual risk remaining.

Variance Analysis

If performance measurement produces schedule or cost variances in excess of pre-established thresholds, the cause must be determined. The functional managers or CAM are responsible for the analysis of the control account and understanding trends that indicate potential future problems.

Variance Calculations

There are three types of variances: schedule variances, cost variances, and variances at completion (VACs). They are calculated as follows:

$$SV = BCWP - BCWS$$

$$CV = BCWP - ACWP$$

$$VAC = BAC - EAC$$

Variance Thresholds

Variance analysis is required when one or more of the variances exceeds the threshold established for the project. Variance thresholds are defined by a percentage or a dollar amount, or a combination of the two. The latter method is usually more appropriate because it eliminates very small variances from the analysis requirement. The thresholds are generally established by the seller but may be provided by the customer.

Variance Analysis Operation

- Variance analysis reports (VARs) provide current period, cumulative, and at-completion data. CAMs provide VARs for control accounts that have a schedule variance, cost variance, or VAC that exceeds the established thresholds.
- The CAM completes the VAR by providing a description of the cause of the variance, its impact on the control account and other elements of the project, the corrective action to be taken, and any follow-up on previous actions taken.
- The VAR is submitted through the appropriate project channels for approval.
- The project manager uses the control account VARs to report project status to upper management.
- The project manager has a continuing responsibility to monitor corrective actions.
- Periodic, formal project reviews, scheduling meetings, and staff meetings serve as forums for variance trend analysis and corrective action monitoring.

Changes

When an authorized change is received, all affected work authorization, budget planning, and scheduling documents should be updated in a timely manner to reflect the change.

Revision Types

- **Internal replanning**: This is the replanning that is undertaken within the scope, schedule and budget constraints of the current contract. It is often associated with the use of management reserve.
- **External replanning**: These are contract changes directed and authorized by the customer.
- **Over target replanning**: This is replanning that results in the planning of a new PMB that is above the CBB. It results in a plan to overrun the contract value.

Replanning Rules

Four replanning rules are:
- Retroactive changes to BCWS, BCWP, or ACWP already incurred are strictly prohibited, except to correct accounting errors.
- Closed work packages or control accounts will not be reopened.

- Work scope will not be transferred from one control account to another without the associated budget transfer.
- Work packages that are open (in process) will not be replanned.

Internal Audit/Verification

The functional managers or CAMs are the most significant contributors to the successful operation of the EVMS and to the successful completion of any subsequent audits or customer reviews, if appropriate. Day-to-day management of the project takes place at the control account level. If each control account is not managed competently, project performance will suffer. Because of the emphasis on cost schedule and technical performance, the functional managers must be proficient in all areas of control account management. Audits are performed periodically to ensure that the management system is fully operational.

In addition to auditing the internal system, there is a responsibility to periodically audit our subcontractors to ensure that we receive reliable schedule and performance measurement data.

Performance Formulae, Analysis, DoD Reviews, and Reports

Performance Formulae and Analysis The following legend is applicable to the formulae and charts that follow:

BCWS = Budgeted cost for work scheduled

BCWP = Budgeted cost for work performed

ACWP = Actual cost of work performed

BAC = Budget at completion

ETC = Estimate to complete

EAC = Estimate at completion

Cost Variance

$$CV = BCWP - ACWP$$

Cost Variance %

$$CV\% = \frac{CV}{BCWP} \times 100$$

Cost Performance Index

$$CPI = \frac{BCWP}{ACWP}$$

To Complete Performance Index

$$TCPI = BAC - BCWPcum$$

$$EAC - ACWPcum$$

Schedule Variance

$$SV = BCWP - BCWS$$

Schedule Variance %

$$SV\% = \frac{SV}{BCWP} \times 100$$

Schedule Performance Index

$$SPI = \frac{BCWP}{BCWS}$$

Schedule Variance in Months

$$SV\ months = \frac{SV\ cum}{BCWP\ current\ period}$$

Percent Spent

$$\% \text{ spent} = \frac{\text{ACWP cum}}{\text{BAC*}} \times 100$$

Percent Complete

$$\% \text{ complete} = \frac{\text{BCWP cum}}{\text{BAC*}}$$

*EAC, PMB, CBB, or TAB may also be used.

Statistical Examples

Independent EAC

The basic formulae are:

$$\text{EAC1} = \text{ACWPcum} + (\text{BAC} - \text{BCWPcum})$$

$$\text{EAC2} = \frac{\text{BAC}}{\text{CPIe}}$$

$$\text{EAC3} = [(\text{BAC} - \text{BCWP})/(\text{CPI} \times \text{SPI})] + \text{ACWP}$$

Variance at Completion %

$$\text{VAC\%} = \frac{\text{VAC} \times 100}{\text{BAC}}$$

Budget/Earned Rate

$$\text{E/B Rate} = \frac{\text{BCWP dollars}}{\text{BCWP hours}}$$

Actual Rate

$$\text{Actual Rate} = \frac{\text{ACWP dollars}}{\text{ACWP hours}}$$

Rate Variance

Rate Variance = (B/E Rate - Actual Rate) × Actual Hours

To-Go Rate

$$\text{To-Go Rate} = \frac{\text{ETC dollars}}{\text{ETC hours}}$$

Efficiency Variance

Efficiency Variance = (BCWP hours - ACWP hours) × B/E Rate

Price Variance

PV = (Planned/Earned Price - Actual Price) × Actual Quantity

Usage Variance

UV = (Planned/Earned Quantity - Actual Quantity) × Earned Price

Cost and schedule performance data are often displayed graphically to give the analyst and the manager a picture of the trends. The two most common displays are shown here. Figures 11-8 and 11-9 can be used for a control account, an organization, a WBS element, or the entire project.

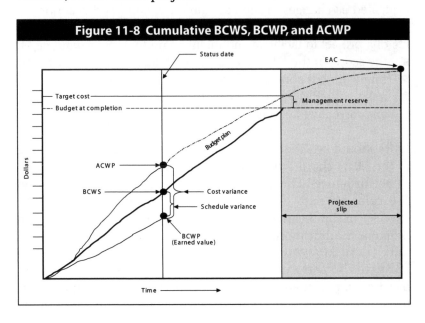

Figure 11-8 Cumulative BCWS, BCWP, and ACWP

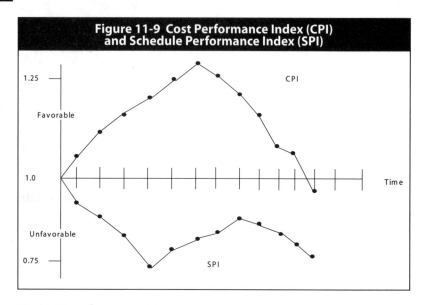

Figure 11-9 Cost Performance Index (CPI) and Schedule Performance Index (SPI)

DoD Performance Reviews and Reports

Integrated Baseline Reviews

An integrated baseline review (IBR) is a joint assessment of the performance measurement baseline (PMB) conducted by the government program manager and the contractor. The IBR is not a one-time event. It is a process, and the plan should be continually evaluated as changes to the baseline are made (modifications, restructuring, etc.). IBRs should be used as necessary throughout the life of a project to facilitate and maintain mutual understanding of:

■ the scope of the PMB consistent with authorizing documents;
■ management control processes;
■ risks in the PMB associated with cost, schedules, and resources; andcorrective actions where necessary.

IBRs should be scheduled as early as practicable, and the timing of the IBRs should take into consideration the contract period of performance. The process should be initiated not later than 180 calendar days (6 months) after: (1) contract award, (2) the exercise of significant contract options, and (3) the incorporation of major modifications.

IBRs are also performed at the discretion of the program manager or within a reasonable time after the occurrence of major events in the life of a program. These events may be completion of the preliminary design review, completion of the critical design review, a significant shift in the content and/or time-phasing of the PMB, or when a major milestone such as the start of the production option of a development contract is reached. Continuous assessment of the PMB will identify when a new IBR should be conducted.

In accordance with an Office of the Under Secretary of Defense for Acquisition, Technology and Logistics (USD AT&L) policy memorandum dated March 7, 2005, program managers are required to conduct IBRs on all cost or incentive contracts that require the implementation of EVM (contracts valued at or greater than $20 million). However, conducting the IBR is not dependent on the contractor's EVMS being formally validated as complying with the EVMS guidelines in ANSI/EIA-748. Subcontractors, intragovernment work agreements, and other agreements should also require IBRs as applicable. The scope of the IBRs should be tailored to the nature of the work effort.

Contract Performance Management Reporting

The contract performance report (CPR) and the integrated master schedule (IMS) apply to all contracts that meet the EVM applicability requirements in USD AT&L policy memorandum dated March 7, 2005. On contracts valued at or greater than $20 million but less than $50 million, it is recommended that CPR and IMS reporting be tailored. See the DoD *Earned Value Management Implementation Guide* (EVMIG) for additional guidance on tailoring reporting.

A common WBS that follows the DoD *Work Breakdown Structure Handbook* (MIL-HDBK-881A) is required for the CPR, IMS, and contractor cost data report (CCDR). Except for high-cost or high-risk elements, the required level of reporting detail should not normally exceed level three of the contract WBS.

Contract Performance Report

The CPR provides contract cost and schedule performance data that are used to identify problems early in the contract and forecast future contract performance. The CPR should be the primary means of documenting the ongoing communication between the contractor and the program manager to report cost and schedule trends to date and to permit assessment of their effect on future performance.

The program manager should obtain a CPR (DD Form 2734) on all cost or incentive contracts, subcontracts, intragovernment work agreements, and other agreements valued at or greater than $20 million. The CPR is not typically required for cost or incentive contracts valued at less than $20 million, contracts less than 12 months in duration, or firm-fixed-price contracts regardless of dollar value. The DoD EVMIG discusses some circumstances where the CPR may be appropriate for contracts in these categories.

Data item description (DID) DI-MGMT-81466A should be used to obtain the CPR. The contracting officer and contractor should negotiate reporting provisions in the contract, including frequency and selection of formats, level of detail, submission dates, variance thresholds and analysis, and the contract WBS to be used. The program manager should tailor the CPR to the minimum data necessary for effective management control, particularly on contracts valued at less than $50 million. See the DoD EVMIG for additional guidance on tailoring CPR reporting.

In exceptional cases, the contractor may determine that the performance measurement budget or existing contract schedule cannot be achieved and no longer represents a reasonable basis for management control. With government approval, the contractor may implement an over target baseline or over target schedule. For cost-reimbursement contracts, the contract budget base excludes changes for cost growth increases except for authorized changes to the contract scope.

Integrated Master Schedule

The integrated master schedule (IMS) is a time-based schedule that contains the networked, detailed tasks necessary to ensure successful program/control execution. The IMS is traceable to the integrated master plan, the contract work breakdown structure, and the statement of work. The IMS is used to verify the attainability of contract objectives, to evaluate progress toward meeting program objectives, and to integrate the program schedule activities with all related components.

The program manager should obtain an IMS on all cost or incentive contracts, subcontracts, intragovernment work agreements, and other agreements valued at or greater than $20 million. The IMS is applicable to development, major modification, and low-rate initial production efforts; it is not typically applied to full-rate production efforts. It is also not normally required for contracts valued at less than $20 million, contracts less than 12 months in duration, or firm-fixed-price contracts regardless of dollar value. The DoD EVMIG discusses some circumstances where the IMS may be appropriate for contracts in these categories.

Contract Funds Status Report

The contract funds status report (CFSR) supplies funding data about defense contracts to program managers for:

- updating and forecasting contract funds requirements;
- planning and decision making on funding changes in contracts;
- developing funds requirements and budget estimates in support of approved programs;
- determining funds in excess of contract needs and available for deobligation;
- obtaining rough estimates of termination costs; and
- determining if sufficient funds are available by fiscal year to execute the contract.

The program manager should obtain a CFSR (DD Form 1586) on contracts over six months in duration. The CFSR has no specific application thresholds; however, the program manager should carefully evaluate application to contracts valued at less than $1.5 million (in then-year dollars).

DID DI-MGMT-81468 should be used to obtain the CFSR. The contracting officer and contractor should negotiate reporting provisions in the contract, including level of detail and reporting frequency. The program manager should require only the minimum data necessary for effective management control. The CFSR should not be applied to firm-fixed-price contracts unless unusual circumstances dictate specific funding visibility.

Contractor Cost Data Reporting

Contractor cost data reporting (CCDR) is the primary means by which the Department of Defense collects data on the costs incurred by DoD contractors in performing DoD programs (Acquisition Category ID and IC). DoD Instruction 5000.2 makes CCDR mandatory. These data enable reasonable program cost estimates and satisfy other analytical requirements. The chair of the Cost

Analysis Improvement Group (CAIG) ensures consistent and appropriate CCDR application throughout the DoD by defining the format for submission of CCDRs and CCDR system policies and by monitoring implementation.

CCDR coverage extends from Milestone B or equivalent to the completion of production in accordance with procedures described in this section. Unless waived by the chair of the CAIG, CCDR reporting is required on all major contracts and subcontracts that support Acquisition Category ID and IC programs, regardless of contract type, when the contracts are valued at more than $50 million (FY2002 constant dollars). CCDR reporting is not required for contracts below $7 million. The CCDR requirements on high-risk or high-technical-interest contracts priced between $7 and $50 million is left to the discretion of the cost working-level integrated product team.

Exclusions. CCDR reporting is not required for procurement of commercial systems or for noncommercial systems bought under competitively awarded, firm-fixed-price contracts, as long as competitive conditions continue to exist.

Software Resources Data Report

The software resources data report (SRDR) is a recent initiative with a primary purpose to improve the ability of the DoD to estimate the costs of software-intensive programs. DoD Instruction 5000.2 requires that data be collected from software development efforts with a projected value greater than $25 million (FY2002 dollars) contained within major automated information systems (Acquisition Category IA) and major defense acquisition programs (Acquisition Category IC and Acquisition Category ID).

Data collected from applicable projects describe the type and size of the software development, and the schedule and labor resources needed for the development. There are three specific data items to be provided:

- The Initial Government Report (DD Form 2630-1) records the government program manager's estimate at completion for the project. This report is due 180 days prior to contract award and is forwarded as part of the cost analysis requirements description.
- The Initial Developer Report (DD Form 2630-2) records the initial estimates by the developer (i.e., contractor or govern-

ment central design activity). This report is due 60 days after contract award.

- The Final Developer Report (DD Form 2630-3) is used to report actual experience. This item is due within 60 days after final delivery.

For particularly small or large software developments, the program manager may choose to shorten or lengthen the submission deadlines accordingly. Also, for projects with multiple releases, the program manager may elect to combine the SRDR reporting of incremental releases within a single contract, and provide SRDR data items for the overall project.

Further information is available in an online SRDR manual. This manual provides additional background and technical details about the data collection. In particular, the manual contains information about the process by which each project defines, collects, and submits the data. The manual also contains sample data items and provides suggested language to include in a request for proposal for this reporting requirement.

SUMMARY

So in retrospect, this chapter has provided a comprehensive discussion of the value, use, and practical application of Earned Value Management Systems. The U.S. Department of Defense learned many years ago that requiring contractors to have an effective management system to proactively plan, schedule, manage, and track performance on large complex programs was vital to success. Over the past 30 years EVMS has evolved as a proven effective project management tool in both the public and private sectors worldwide. Essentially, an EVMS system provides an organization an effective early warning system to ensure both the buyer and seller they are jointly keeping their projects and programs on schedule, on budget, and achieve their mutually agreed to desired results.

BIBLIOGRAPHY

Agrawal, Raj. *Overcoming Software Estimation Challenges.* McLean, VA.: MITRE, May, 22, 2007.

Albert, Neil F. *Cost Estimating: The Starting Point of Earned Value Management.* McLean, VA: MCR LLC, June 2005.

Developing a Work Breakdown Structure. McLean, VA: MCR LLC, June 16, 2005.

Anderson, Mark, and David Nelson. *Developing an Averaged Estimate at Completion (EAC) Utilizing Program Performance Factors and Maturity.* Arlington, VA: Tecolote Research Inc., June 14–17, 2005.

Atkinson, William. "Beyond the Basics" *PM Network Magazine,* May 2003 (Project Management Institute).

Badgerow, Dana B., Gregory A. Garrett, Dominic F. DiClementi, and Barbara M. Weaver. *Managing Contracts for Peak Performance.* Vienna, VA: National Contract Management Association, 1990.

Barkley, Bruce T., and James H. Saylor. *Customer Driven Project Management: A New Paradigm in Total Quality Implementation,* New York: McGraw-Hill, 1993.

Black, Hollis M. *Impact of Cost Risk Analysis on Business Decisions.* Huntsville, AL: Boeing, June 14–17, 2005.

Bonaldo, Guy. "Interview with Business 2.0 Magazine," *Business Intelligence*, February 2003.

Bossidy, Larry, and Ram Charan. *Confronting Reality: Doing What Matters to Get Things Right.* New York: Crown Business, 2004.

Bruce, David L., Marlys Norby, and Victor Ramos, *Guide to the Contract Management Body of Knowledge (CMBOK).* Vienna, VA: National Contract Management Association, 2002.

Bucholz, Mark, Shaw Cohe, and Robert Tomasetti. *Earned Value Management Moving Toward Governmentwide Implementation.* Arlington, VA: Acquisition Directions Advisory, August 2005.

Christensen, David S., and Carl Templin. *An Analysis of Management Reserve Budget on Defense Acquisition Contracts.* Cedar City: Southern Utah University, 2000.

Cleland, David I. *Project Management: Strategic Design and Implementation.* New York: McGraw-Hill, 1994.

Cleland, David I., and William R. King. *Project Management Handbook.* 2nd ed. New York: Van Nostrand Reinhold, 1988.

Coleman, Richard L., Shishu S. Gupta, and Jessica R. Summerville. *Two Timely Short Topics: Independence and Cost Realism.* Chantilly, VA: Northrop Grumman, The Analytical Sciences Corporation, and Intelligence Community Cost Analysis Improvement Group, June 16, 2005.

Coleman, Richard L., and Jessica R. Summerville. *Advanced Cost Risk.* Chantilly, VA: Northrop Grumman, The Analytical Sciences Corporation, June 16, 2005.

Basic Cost Risk. Chantilly, VA: Northrop Grumman, The Analytical Sciences Corporation, June 15, 2005.

Collins, Jim. *Good to Great: Why Some Companies Make the Leap... and Others Don't.* New York: Harper Collins, 2001.

DAU (Defense Acquisition University). *Cost Estimating Methodologies.* Fort Belvoir, VA: April, 2005.

BIBLIOGRAPHY

Fleming, Quentin W. *Earned Value Management (EVM) Light... But Adequate for All Projects*. Tustin, CA: Primavera Systems, Inc., November 2006.

Fleming, Quentin W., and Joel M. Koppelman. "The Earned Value Body of Knowledge." Presented at the 30th Annual Project Management Institute Symposium, Philadelphia, PA, October 10–16, 1999.

Flett, Frank. *Organizing and Planning the Estimate*. McLean, VA: MCR LLC, June 12–14, 2005.

Galorath, Daniel D. *Software Estimation Handbook*. El Segundo, CA: Galorath Inc., n.d.

GAO. *Cost Assessment Guide, GAO-07-11345P*. Washington, DC: July 2007.

Garrett, Gregory A. "Achieving Customer Loyalty," *Contract Management Magazine* (National Contract Management Association), August 2002,

Garrett, Gregory A. *Contract Negotiations: Skills, Tools, and Best Practices*. Chicago: CCH, 2005.

Garrett, Gregory A. *Managing Complex Outsourced Projects* Chicago: CCH, 2004.

Garrett, Gregory A. *Performance-Based Acquisition: Pathways to Excellence*. McLean, VA: NCMA, 2005.

Garrett, Gregory A. *World-Class Contracting: How Winning Companies Build Successful Partnerships in the e-Business Age*.4th ed. Chicago: CCH, 2006.

Garrett, Gregory A., and Ed Bunnik. "Creating a World-Class PM Organization," *PM Network Magazine*, September 2000 (Project Management Institute).

Garrett, Gregory A., and Reginald J. Kipke, *The Capture Management Life-Cycle: Winning More Business*. Chicago: CCH, 2003.

Garrett, Gregory A. and Rene G. Rendon. *Contract Management Organizational Assessment Tools.* McLean, VA: NCMA, 2005.

U.S. Military Program Management: Lessons Learned and Best Practices. McLean, VA: Management Concepts, 2007.

Gates, Bill. *Business @ the Speed of Thought: Using a Digital Nervous System.* New York: Warner Books USA, 1999.

International Society of Parametric Analysts. *Parametric Estimating Handbook.* 4th ed. Vienna, VA: ISPA/SCEA Joint Office, 2007.

Johnson, Jim, et al. "Collaboration: Development and Management–Collaborating on Project Success." *Software Magazine,* Sponsored Supplement, February–March 2001.

Kerzner, Harold. *In Search of Excellence in Project Management.* New York: Van Nostrand Reinhold, 1998.

Kratzert, Keith. *Earned Value Management (EVM): The Federal Aviation Administration (FAA) Program Manager's Flight Plan.* Washington, DC: Federal Aviation Administration, January 2006.

Kumley, Alissa, et al. *Integrating Risk Management and Earned Value Management: A Statistical Analysis of Survey Results.* N.p.: June 14–17, 2005.

Lavdas, Evaggelos. *Identifying the Characteristics of a Good Cost Estimate: A Survey.* Cranfield, Bedfordshire, Eng.: Cranfield University, June 2006.

Lewis, James P. *Mastering Project Management: Applying Advanced Concepts of Systems Thinking, Control and Evaluation, Resource Allocation.* New York: McGraw-Hill, 1998.

Liker, Jeffrey K., and Thomas Y. Choi. "Building Deep Supplier Relationships," *Harvard Business Review,* December 2004, 104–13.

McFarlane, Eileen Luhta. "Developing International Proposals in a Virtual Environment," *Proposal Management,* Spring 2000 (Association of Proposal Management Professionals).

Mickells Bova, Regina. *The Desktop Guide to Basic Contracting Terms.* 4th ed. Vienna, VA: The National Contract Management Association, 1994.

Monroe, Kent B. *Pricing: Making Profitable Decisions.* 2nd ed. New York: McGraw-Hill, 1990.

Moran, Robert T., and John R. Riesenberger. *The Global Challenge: Building the New Worldwide Enterprise.* New York: McGraw-Hill, 1994.

O'Connell, Brian. *B2B.com: Cashing-in on the Business-to-Business E-commerce Bonanza.* Holbrook, MA: Adams Media Corp., 2000.

Ohmae, Kenichi. *The Borderless World: Power and Strategy in the Interlinked Economy.* (New York: Harper Collins, 1991.

Ohmae, Kenichi, ed. *The Evolving Global Economy.* Boston: Harvard Business School (HBS) Press, 1995.

Project Management Institute Standards Committee. *A Guide to the Project Management Body of Knowledge.* Upper Darby, PA: Project Management Institute, 2001.

Remez, Shereen G., and Daryl W. White. *Return on Investment (ROI) and the Value Puzzle.* Washington, DC: Capital Planning and Information Technology Investment Committee, Federal Chief Information Officer Council, April 1999.

Reifer, Donald J. *Poor Man's Guide to Estimating Software Costs.* Torrance, CA: Reifer Consultants Inc., June 2005.

Scapparo, John, NAVAIR *Integration Project Management Brief to U.S. Government Accountability Office.* Pax River, MD: Naval Air Systems Command, April 19, 2007.

Society of Cost Estimating and Analysis (SCEA). *Cost Programmed Review of Fundamentals (CostPROF): Basic Data Analysis Principles— What to Do Once You Get the Data.* Vienna, VA: SCEA, 2003.

Webster's Dictionary, *The New Lexicon of the English Language.* New York: Lexicon Publications, 1989.

Wiley, David. *Software Cost Estimating: Techniques for Estimating in a Software Development Environment.*. Chantilly, VA: Northrop Grumman, The Analytical Sciences Corporation, 2005.

Wright, R., J. Comer, and Justin Morris. *Enhancing Remediation Project Credibility with Defensible and Documented Cost Estimates.* N.p.: n.d.

Younossi, Obaid, Lionel A. Galway, Bernard Fox, and John C. Graser. *Impossible Certainty: Cost Risk Analysis for Air Force Systems.* Arlington, VA: RAND Corp., 2006

Younossi, Obaid, and Mark Arena. RAND Corp. "Toward a Cost Risk Estimating Policy," presentation given at the 38th Annual Department of Defense Cost Analysis Symposium, Williamsburg, VA: February 17, 2005.

Zubrow, Dave. *Earned Value Management (EVM): Basic Concepts.* Pittsburgh, PA: Carnegie Mellon Software Engineering Institute, 2002.

Implementing Earned Value Management (EVM) to Manage Program Risk. Pittsburgh, PA: Carnegie Mellon Software Engineering Institute, 2002.

GLOSSARY

acceptance
(1) The taking and receiving of anything in good part, and as if it were a tacit agreement to a preceding act, which might have been defeated or avoided if such acceptance had not been made. (2) Agreement to the terms offered in a contract. An acceptance must be communicated, and (in common law) it must be the mirror image of the offer.

acquisition cost
The money invested up front to bring in new customers.

acquisition plan
A plan that serves as the basis for initiating the individual contracting actions necessary to acquire a system or support a program.

acquisition strategy
The conceptual framework for conducting systems acquisition. It encompasses the broad concepts and objectives that direct and control the overall development, production, and deployment of a system.

act of God
An inevitable, accidental, or extraordinary event that cannot be foreseen and guarded against, such as lightning, tornadoes, or earthquakes.

actual authority

The power that the principal intentionally confers on the agent or allows the agent to believe he or she possesses.

actual damages

See *compensatory damages*.

affidavit

A written and signed statement sworn to under oath.

agency

A relationship that exists when there is a delegation of authority to perform all acts connected within a particular trade, business, or company. It gives authority to the agent to act in all matters relating to the business of the principal.

agent

An employee (usually a contract manager) empowered to bind his or her organization legally in contract negotiations.

allowable cost

A cost that is reasonable, allocable, and within accepted standards, or otherwise conforms to generally accepted accounting principles, specific limitations or exclusions, or agreed-on terms between contractual parties.

alternative dispute resolution

Any procedure that is used, in lieu of litigation, to resolve issues in controversy, including, but not limited to, settlement negotiations, conciliation, facilitation, mediation, fact-finding, mini-trials, and arbitration.

amortization

Process of spreading the cost of an intangible asset over the expected useful life of the asset.

apparent authority

The power that the principal permits the perceived agent to exercise, although not actually granted.

as is

A contract phrase referring to the condition of property to be sold or leased; generally pertains to a disclaimer of liability; property sold in as-is condition is generally not guaranteed.

assign

To convey or transfer to another, as to assign property, rights, or interests to another.

assignment

The transfer of property by an assignor to an assignee.

audits

The systematic examination of records and documents and/or the securing of other evidence by confirmation, physical inspection, or otherwise, for one or more of the following purposes: determining the propriety or legality of proposed or completed transactions; ascertaining whether all transactions have been recorded and are reflected accurately in accounts; determining the existence of recorded assets and inclusiveness of recorded liabilities; determining the accuracy of financial or statistical statements or reports and the fairness of the facts they represent; determining the degree of compliance with established policies and procedures in terms of financial transactions and business management; and appraising an account system and making recommendations concerning it.

base profit

The money a company is paid by a customer, which exceeds the company's cost.

best value

The best trade-off between competing factors for a particular purchase requirement. The key to successful best-value contracting is consideration of life-cycle costs, including the use of quantitative as well as qualitative techniques to measure price and technical performance trade-offs between various proposals. The best-value concept applies to acquisitions in which price or price-related factors are *not* the primary determinant of who receives the contract award.

bid

An offer in response to an invitation for bids (IFB).

bid development

All of the work activities required to design and price the product and service solution and accurately articulate this in a proposal for a customer.

bid phase

The period of time a seller of goods and/or services uses to develop a bid/proposal, conduct internal bid reviews, and obtain stakeholder approval to submit a bid/proposal.

bilateral contract

A contract formed if an offer states that acceptance requires only for the accepting party to promise to perform. In contrast, a *unilateral contract* is formed if an offer requires actual performance for acceptance.

bond

A written instrument executed by a seller and a second party (the surety or sureties) to ensure fulfillment of the principal's obligations to a third party (the obligee or buyer) identified in the bond. If the principal's obligations are not met, the bond ensures payment, to the extent stipulated, of any loss sustained by the obligee.

breach of contract

(1) The failure, without legal excuse, to perform any promise that forms the whole or part of a contract. (2) The ending of a contract that occurs when one or both of the parties fail to keep their promises; this could lead to arbitration or litigation.

buyer

The party contracting for goods and/or services with one or more sellers.

cancellation

The withdrawal of the requirement to purchase goods and/or services by the buyer.

capture management

The art and science of winning more business.

capture management life cycle
The art and science of winning more business throughout the entire business cycle.

capture project plan
A document or game plan of who needs to do what, when, where, how often, and how much to win business.

change in scope
An amendment to approved program requirements or specifications after negotiation of a basic contract. It may result in an increase or decrease.

change order/purchase order amendment
A written order directing the seller to make changes according to the provisions of the contract documents.

claim
A demand by one party to contract for something from another party, usually but not necessarily for more money or more time. Claims are usually based on an argument that the party making the demand is entitled to an adjustment by virtue of the contract terms or some violation of those terms by the other party. The word does not imply any disagreement between the parties, although claims often lead to disagreements. This book uses the term *dispute* to refer to disagreements that have become intractable.

clause
A statement of one of the rights and/or obligations of the parties to a contract. A contract consists of a series of clauses.

collaboration software
Automated tools that allow for the real-time exchange of visual information using personal computers.

collateral benefit
The degree to which pursuit of an opportunity will improve the existing skill level or develop new skills that will positively affect other or future business opportunities.

compensable delay
A delay for which the buyer is contractually responsible that excuses the seller's failure to perform and is compensable.

compensatory damages
Damages that will compensate the injured party for the loss sustained and nothing more. They are awarded by the court as the measure of actual loss, and not as punishment for outrageous conduct or to deter future transgressions. Compensatory damages are often referred to as "actual damages." See also *incidental* and *punitive damages*.

competitive intelligence
Information on competitors or competitive teams that is specific to an opportunity.

competitive negotiation
A method of contracting involving a request for proposals that states the buyer's requirements and criteria for evaluation; submission of timely proposals by a maximum number of offerors; discussions with those offerors found to be within the competitive range; and award of a contract to the one offeror whose offer, price, and other consideration factors are most advantageous to the buyer.

condition precedent
A condition that activates a term in a contract.

condition subsequent
A condition that suspends a term in a contract.

conflict of interest
Term used in connection with public officials and fiduciaries and their relationships to matters of private interest or gain to them. Ethical problems connected therewith are covered by statutes in most jurisdictions and by federal statutes on the federal level. A conflict of interest arises when an employee's personal or financial interest conflicts or appears to conflict with his or her official responsibility.

consideration

(1) The thing of value (amount of money or acts to be done or not done) that must change hands between the parties to a contract. (2) The inducement to a contract—the cause, motive, price, or impelling influence that induces a contracting party to enter into a contract.

constructive change

An oral or written act or omission by an authorized or unauthorized agent that is of such a nature that it is construed to have the same effect as a written change order.

contingency

The quality of being contingent or casual; an event that may but does not have to occur; a possibility.

contingent contract

A contract that provides for the possibility of its termination when a specified occurrence takes place or does not take place.

contra proferentem

A legal phrase used in connection with the construction of written documents to the effect that an ambiguous provision is construed most strongly against the person who selected the language.

contract

(1) A relationship between two parties, such as a buyer and seller, that is defined by an agreement about their respective rights and responsibilities. (2) A document that describes such an agreement.

contract administration

The process of ensuring compliance with contractual terms and conditions during contract performance up to contract closeout or termination.

contract closeout

The process of verifying that all administrative matters are concluded on a contract that is otherwise physically complete—in other words, the seller has delivered the required supplies or performed the required services, and the buyer has inspected and accepted the supplies or services.

contract fulfillment

The joint buyer/seller actions taken to successfully perform and administer a contractual agreement and meet or exceed all contract obligations, including effective changes management and timely contract closeout.

contract interpretation

The entire process of determining what the parties agreed to in their bargain. The basic objective of contract interpretation is to determine the intent of the parties. Rules calling for interpretation of the documents against the drafter, and imposing a duty to seek clarification on the drafter, allocate risks of contractual ambiguities by resolving disputes in favor of the party least responsible for the ambiguity.

contract management

The art and science of managing a contractual agreement(s) throughout the contracting process.

contract negotiation

The process of unifying different positions into a unanimous joint decision regarding the buying and selling of products and/or services.

contract negotiation process

A three-phased approach composed of planning, negotiating, and documenting a contractual agreement between two or more parties to buy or sell products and/or services.

contract type

A specific pricing arrangement used for the performance of work under a contract.

contractor

The seller or provider of goods and/or services.

controversy

A litigated question. A civil action or suit may not be instigated unless it is based on a "justifiable" dispute. This term is important in that judicial power of the courts extends only to cases and "controversies."

copyright

A royalty-free, nonexclusive, and irrevocable license to reproduce, translate, publish, use, and dispose of written or recorded material, and to authorize others to do so.

cost

The amount of money expended in acquiring a product or obtaining a service, or the total of acquisition costs plus all expenses related to operating and maintaining an item once acquired.

cost accounting standards

Federal standards designed to provide consistency and coherency in defense and other government contract accounting.

cost contract

The simplest type of cost-reimbursement contract. Governments commonly use this type when contracting with universities and nonprofit organizations for research projects. The contract provides for reimbursing contractually allowable costs, with no allowance given for profit.

cost of goods sold (COGS)

Direct costs of producing finished goods for sale.

cost-plus-a-percentage-of-cost (CPPC) contract

A type of cost-reimbursement contract that provides for a reimbursement of the allowable cost of services performed plus an agreed-on percentage of the estimated cost as profit.

cost-plus-award-fee (CPAF) contract

A type of cost-reimbursement contract with special incentive fee provisions used to motivate excellent contract performance in such areas as quality, timeliness, ingenuity, and cost-effectiveness.

cost-plus-fixed-fee (CPFF) contract

A type of cost-reimbursement contract that provides for the payment of a fixed fee to the contractor. It does not vary with actual costs, but may be adjusted if there are any changes in the work or services to be performed under the contract.

cost-plus-incentive-fee (CPIF) contract

A type of cost-reimbursement contract with provision for a fee that is adjusted by a formula in accordance with the relationship between total allowable costs and target costs.

cost proposal

The instrument required of an offeror for the submission or identification of cost or pricing data by which an offeror submits to the buyer a summary of estimated (or incurred) costs, suitable for detailed review and analysis.

cost-reimbursement (CR) contract

A type of contract that usually includes an estimate of project cost, a provision for reimbursing the seller's expenses, and a provision for paying a fee as profit. CR contracts are often used when there is high uncertainty about costs. They normally also include a limitation on the buyer's cost liability.

cost-sharing contract

A cost-reimbursement contract in which the seller receives no fee and is reimbursed only for an agreed-on portion of its allowable costs.

counteroffer

An offer made in response to an original offer that changes the terms of the original.

customer revenue growth

The increased revenues achieved by keeping a customer for an extended period of time.

customer support costs

Costs expended by a company to provide information and advice concerning purchases.

default termination

The termination of a contract, under the standard default clause, because of a buyer's or seller's failure to perform any of the terms of the contract.

defect
> The absence of something necessary for completeness or perfection. A deficiency in something essential to the proper use of a thing. Some structural weakness in a part or component that is responsible for damage.

defect, latent
> A defect that existed at the time of acceptance but would not have been discovered by a reasonable inspection.

defect, patent
> A defect that can be discovered without undue effort. If the defect was actually known to the buyer at the time of acceptance, it is patent, even though it otherwise might not have been discoverable by a reasonable inspection.

definite-quantity contract
> A contractual instrument that provides for a definite quantity of supplies or services to be delivered at some later, unspecified date.

delay, excusable
> A contractual provision designed to protect the seller from sanctions for late performance. To the extent that it has been excusably delayed, the seller is protected from default termination or liquidated damages. Examples of excusable delay are acts of God, acts of the government, fire, flood, quarantines, strikes, epidemics, unusually severe weather, and embargoes. See also *forbearance* and *force majeure clause.*

depreciation
> Amount of expense charged against earnings by a company to write off the cost of a plant or machine over its useful life, giving consideration to wear and tear, obsolescence, and salvage value.

design specification
> (1) A document (including drawings) setting forth the required characteristics of a particular component, part, subsystem, system, or construction item. (2) A purchase description that establishes precise measurements, tolerances, materials, in-process and finished product tests, quality control, inspection requirements, and other specific details of the deliverable.

direct cost
The costs specifically identifiable with a contract requirement, including but not restricted to costs of material and/or labor directly incorporated into an end item.

direct labor
All work that is obviously related and specifically and conveniently traceable to specific products.

direct material
Items, including raw material, purchased parts, and subcontracted items, directly incorporated into an end item, which are identifiable to a contract requirement.

discount rate
Interest rate used in calculating present value.

discounted cash flow (DCF)
Combined present value of cash flow and tangible assets minus present value of liabilities.

discounts, allowances and returns
Price discounts, returned merchandise.

dispute
A disagreement not settled by mutual consent that could be decided by litigation or arbitration. Also see *claim.*

e-business
Technology-enabled business that focuses on seamless integration between each business, the company, and its supply partners.

EBITDA
Earnings before interest, taxes, depreciation and amortization, but after all product/service, sales and overhead (SG&A) costs are accounted for. Sometimes referred to as *operating profit.*

EBITDARM
Acronym for earnings before interest, taxes, depreciation, amortization., rent and management fees.

e-commerce
A subset of e-business, Internet-based electronic transactions.

electronic data interchange (EDI)
Private networks used for simple data transactions, which are typically batch- processed.

elements of a contract
The items that must be present in a contract if the contract is to be binding, including an offer, acceptance (agreement), consideration, execution by competent parties, and legality of purpose.

enterprise resource planning (ERP)
An electronic framework for integrating all organizational functions, evolved from manufacturing resource planning (MRP).

entire contract
A contract that is considered entire on both sides and cannot be made severable.

e-procurement
Technology-enabled buying and selling of goods and services.

estimate at completion (EAC)
The actual direct costs, plus indirect costs allocable to the contract, plus the estimate of costs (direct or indirect) for authorized work remaining.

estoppel
A rule of law that bars, prevents, and precludes a party from alleging or denying certain facts because of a previous allegation or denial or because of its previous conduct or admission.

ethics
Of or relating to moral action, conduct, motive, or character (such as ethical emotion). Also, treating of moral feelings, duties, or conduct; containing precepts of morality; moral. Professionally right or befitting; conforming to professional standards of conduct.

e-tool
An electronic device, program, system, or software application used to facilitate business.

exculpatory clause
The contract language designed to shift responsibility to the other party. A "no damages for delay" clause would be an example of one used by buyers.

excusable delay
See *delay, excusable.*

executed contract
A contract that is formed and performed at the same time. If performed in part, it is partially executed and partially executory.

executed contract (document)
A written document, signed by both parties and mailed or otherwise furnished to each party, that expresses the requirements, terms, and conditions to be met by both parties in the performance of the contract.

executory contract
A contract that has not yet been fully performed.

express
Something put in writing, for example, "express authority."

express warranty
See *warranty, express.*

fair and reasonable
A subjective evaluation of what each party deems as equitable consideration in areas such as terms and conditions, cost or price, assured quality, timeliness of contract performance, and/ or any other areas subject to negotiation.

Federal Acquisition Regulation (FAR)

The government-wide procurement regulation mandated by Congress and issued by the Department of Defense, the General Services Administration, and the National Aeronautics and Space Administration. Effective April 1, 1984, the FAR supersedes both the Defense Acquisition Regulation (DAR) and the Federal Procurement Regulation (FPR). All federal agencies are authorized to issue regulations implementing the FAR.

fee

An agreed-to amount of reimbursement beyond the initial estimate of costs. The term "fee" is used when discussing cost-reimbursement contracts, whereas the term "profit" is used in relation to fixed-price contracts.

firm-fixed-price (FFP) contract

The simplest and most common business pricing arrangement. The seller agrees to supply a quantity of goods or to provide a service for a specified price.

fixed cost

Operating expenses that are incurred to provide facilities and organization that are kept in readiness to do business without regard to actual volumes of production and sales. Examples of fixed costs consist of rent, property tax, and interest expense.

fixed price

A form of pricing that includes a ceiling beyond which the buyer bears no responsibility for payment.

fixed-price incentive (FPI) contract

A type of contract that provides for adjusting profit and establishing the final contract price using a formula based on the relationship of total final negotiated cost to total target cost. The final price is subject to a price ceiling, negotiated at the outset.

fixed-price redeterminable (FPR) contract

A type of fixed-price contract that contains provisions for subsequently negotiated adjustment, in whole or in part, of the initially negotiated base price.

fixed-price with economic price adjustment

A fixed-price contract that permits an element of cost to fluctuate to reflect current market prices.

forbearance

An intentional failure of a party to enforce a contract requirement, usually done for an act of immediate or future consideration from the other party. Sometimes forbearance is referred to as a nonwaiver or as a onetime waiver, but not as a relinquishment of rights.

force majeure clause

Major or irresistible force. Such a contract clause protects the parties in the event that a part of the contract cannot be performed due to causes outside the control of the parties and could not be avoided by exercise of due care. Excusable conditions for nonperformance, such as strikes and acts of God (e.g., typhoons) are contained in this clause.

fraud

An intentional perversion of truth to induce another in reliance upon it to part with something of value belonging to him or her or to surrender a legal right. A false representation of a matter of fact, whether by words or conduct, by false or misleading allegations, or by concealment of that which should have been disclosed, that deceives and is intended to deceive another so that he or she shall act upon it to his or her legal injury. Anything calculated to deceive.

free on board (FOB)

A term used in conjunction with a physical point to determine (a) the responsibility and basis for payment of freight charges and (b) unless otherwise agreed, the point at which title for goods passes to the buyer or consignee. *FOB origin*–The seller places the goods on the conveyance by which they are to be transported. Cost of shipping and risk of loss are borne by the buyer. *FOB destination*–The seller delivers the goods on the seller's conveyance at destination. Cost of shipping and risk of loss are borne by the seller.

functional specification
A purchase description that describes the deliverable in terms of performance characteristics and intended use, including those characteristics that at minimum are necessary to satisfy the intended use.

general and administrative (G&A)
(1) The indirect expenses related to the overall business. Expenses for a company's general and executive offices, executive compensation, staff services, and other miscellaneous support purposes. (2) Any indirect management, financial, or other expense that (a) is not assignable to a program's direct overhead charges for engineering, manufacturing, material, and so on, but (b) is routinely incurred by or allotted to a business unit, and (c) is for the general management and administration of the business as a whole.

General Agreement on Tariffs and Trade (GATT)
A multinational trade agreement signed in 1947 by 23 nations.

generally accepted accounting principles (GAAP)
A term encompassing conventions, rules, and procedures of accounting that are "generally accepted" and have "substantial authoritative support." The GAAP have been developed by agreement on the basis of experience, reason, custom, usage, and to a certain extent, practical necessity, rather than being derived from a formal set of theories.

gross profit margin
Net sales minus cost of goods sold. Also called *gross margin*, *gross profit*, or *gross loss*.

gross profit margin % or ratio
Gross profit margin divided by net sales.

gross sales
Total revenues at invoice value before any discounts or allowances.

horizontal exchange
A marketplace that deals with goods and services that are not specific to one industry.

implied warranty

See *warranty, implied.*

imply

To indirectly convey meaning or intent; to leave the determination of meaning up to the receiver of the communication based on circumstances, general language used, or conduct of those involved.

incidental damages

Any commercially reasonable charges, expenses, or commissions incurred in stopping delivery; in the transportation, care and custody of goods after the buyer's breach; or in connection with the return or resale of the goods or otherwise resulting from the breach.

indefinite-delivery/indefinite-quantity (IDIQ) contract

A type of contract in which the exact date of delivery or the exact quantity, or a combination of both, is not specified at the time the contract is executed; provisions are placed in the contract to later stipulate these elements of the contract.

indemnification clause

A contract clause by which one party engages to secure another against an anticipated loss resulting from an act or forbearance on the part of one of the parties or of some third person.

indemnify

To make good; to compensate; to reimburse a person in case of an anticipated loss.

indirect cost

Any cost not directly identifiable with a specific cost objective but subject to two or more cost objectives.

indirect labor

All work that is not specifically associated with or cannot be practically traced to specific units of output.

intellectual property

The kind of property that results from the fruits of mental labor.

interactive chat
A feature provided by automated tools that allow for users to establish a voice connection between one or more parties and exchange text or graphics via a virtual bulletin board.

Internet
The World Wide Web.

intranet
An organization-specific, internal, secure network.

joint contract
A contract in which the parties bind themselves both individually and as a unit.

liquidated damages
A contract provision providing for the assessment of damages on the seller for its failure to comply with certain performance or delivery requirements of the contract; used when the time of delivery or performance is of such importance that the buyer may reasonably expect to suffer damages if the delivery or performance is delinquent.

mailbox rule
The idea that the acceptance of an offer is effective when deposited in the mail if the envelope is properly addressed.

marketing
Activities that direct the flow of goods and services from the producer to the consumers.

market intelligence
Information on your competitors or competitive teams operating in the marketplace or industry.

market research
The process used to collect and analyze information about an entire market to help determine the most suitable approach to acquiring, distributing, and supporting supplies and services.

memorandum of agreement (MOA)/ memorandum of understanding (MOU)

The documentation of a mutually agreed-to statement of facts, intentions, procedures, and parameters for future actions and matters of coordination. A "memorandum of understanding" may express mutual understanding of an issue without implying commitments by parties to the understanding.

method of procurement

The process used for soliciting offers, evaluating offers, and awarding a contract.

modifications

Any written alterations in the specification, delivery point, rate of delivery, contract period, price, quantity, or other provision of an existing contract, accomplished in accordance with a contract clause; may be unilateral or bilateral.

monopoly

A market structure in which the entire market for a good or service is supplied by a single seller or firm.

monopsony

A market structure in which a single buyer purchases a good or service.

NCMA CMBOK

Definitive descriptions of the elements making up the body of professional knowledge that applies to contract management.

negotiation

A process between buyers and sellers seeking to reach mutual agreement on a matter of common concern through fact-finding, bargaining, and persuasion.

net marketplace

Two-sided exchange where buyers and sellers negotiate prices, usually with a bid-and-ask system, and where prices move both up and down.

net present value (NPV)

The lifetime customer revenue stream discounted by the investment costs and operations costs.

net sales

Gross sales minus discounts, allowances, and returns.

North American Free Trade Agreement (NAFTA)

A trilateral trade and investment agreement between Canada, Mexico, and the United States ratified on January 1, 1994.

novation agreement

A legal instrument executed by (a) the contractor (transferor), (b) the successor in interest (transferee), and (c) the buyer by which, among other things, the transferor guarantees performance of the contract, the transferee assumes all obligations under the contract, and the buyer recognizes the transfer of the contract and related assets.

offer

(1) The manifestation of willingness to enter into a bargain, so made as to justify another person in understanding that his or her assent to that bargain is invited and will conclude it. (2) An unequivocal and intentionally communicated statement of proposed terms made to another party. An offer is presumed revocable unless it specifically states that it is irrevocable. An offer once made will be open for a reasonable period of time and is binding on the offeror unless revoked by the offeror before the other party's acceptance.

oligopoly

A market dominated by a few sellers.

operating expenses

Selling, general, and administrative (SG&A) expenses plus depreciation and amortization.

opportunity

A potential or actual favorable event

opportunity engagement

The degree to which your company or your competitors are involved in establishing the customer's requirements.

opportunity profile

A stage of the capture management life cycle, during which a seller evaluates and describes the opportunity in terms of what it means to your customer, what it means to your company, and what will be required to succeed.

option

A unilateral right in a contract by which, for a specified time, the buyer may elect to purchase additional quantities of the supplies or services called for in the contract or may elect to extend the period of performance of the contract.

order of precedence

A solicitation provision that establishes priorities so that contradictions within the solicitation can be resolved.

organizational breakdown structure (OBS)

An organized structure that represents how individual team members are grouped to complete assigned work tasks.

outsourcing

A contractual process of obtaining another party to provide goods and/or services that were previously done within an organization.

overhead

An accounting cost category that typically includes general indirect expenses that are necessary to operate a business but are not directly assignable to a specific good or service produced. Examples include building rent, utilities, salaries of corporate officers, janitorial services, office supplies, and furniture.

overtime

The time worked by a seller's employee in excess of the employee's normal workweek.

parol evidence
Oral or verbal evidence; in contract law, the evidence drawn from sources exterior to the written instrument.

parol evidence rule
A rule that seeks to preserve the integrity of written agreements by refusing to permit contracting parties to attempt to alter a written contract with evidence of any contradictory prior or contemporaneous oral agreement *(parol* to the contract).

payment
The amount payable under the contract supporting data required to be submitted with invoices, and other payment terms such as time for payment and retention.

payment bond
A bond that secures the appropriate payment of subcontracts for their completed and acceptable goods and/or services.

performance-based contract (PBC)
A documented business arrangement in which the buyer and seller agree to use a performance work statement, performance-based metrics, and a quality assurance plan to ensure that contract requirements are met or exceeded.

performance bond
A bond that secures the performance and fulfillment of all the undertakings, covenants, terms, conditions, and agreements contained in the contract.

performance specification
A purchase description that describes the deliverable in terms of desired operational characteristics. Performance specifications tend to be more restrictive than functional specifications, in that they limit alternatives that the buyer will consider and define separate performance standards for each such alternative.

performance work statement (PWS)
A statement of work expressed in terms of desired performance results, often including specific measurable objectives.

post-bid phase

The period of time after a seller submits a bid/proposal to a buyer through source selection, negotiations, contract formation, contract fulfillment, contract closeout, and follow-on opportunity management.

pre-bid phase

The period of time a seller of goods and/or services uses to identify business opportunities prior to the release of a customer solicitation.

pricing arrangement

An agreed-to basis between contractual parties for the payment of amounts for specified performance; usually expressed in terms of a specific cost-reimbursement or fixed-price arrangement.

prime/prime contractor

The principal seller performing under the contract.

private exchange

A marketplace hosted by a single company inside a company's firewall and used for procurement from among a group of preauthorized sellers.

privity of contract

The legal relationship that exists between the parties to a contract that allows either party to (a) enforce contractual rights against the other party and (b) seek remedy directly from the other party.

procurement

The complete action or process of acquiring or obtaining goods or services using any of several authorized means.

procurement planning

The process of identifying which business needs can be best met by procuring products or services outside the organization.

profit

The net proceeds from selling a product or service when costs are subtracted from revenues. May be positive (profit) or negative (loss).

program management
Planning and execution of multiple projects that are related to one another.

progress payments
An interim payment for delivered work in accordance with contract terms; generally tied to meeting specified performance milestones.

project management
Planning and ensuring the quality, on-time delivery, and cost of a specific set of related activities with a definite beginning and end.

promotion
Publicizing the attributes of the product/service through media and personal contacts and presentations (e.g., technical articles/presentations, new releases, advertising, and sales calls).

proposal
Normally, a written offer by a seller describing its offering terms. Proposals may be issued in response to a specific request or may be made unilaterally when a seller feels there may be an interest in its offer (which is also known as an *unsolicited proposal*).

proposal evaluation
An assessment of both the proposal and the offeror's ability (as conveyed by the proposal) to successfully accomplish the prospective contract. An agency shall evaluate competitive proposals solely on the factors specified in the solicitation.

protest
A written objection by an interested party to (a) a solicitation or other request by an agency for offers for a contract for the procurement of property or services, (b) the cancellation of the solicitation or other request, (c) an award or proposed award of the contract, or (d) a termination or cancellation of an award of the contract, if the written objection contains an allegation that the termination or cancellation is based in whole or in part on improprieties concerning the award of the contract.

punitive damages

Those damages awarded to the plaintiff over and above what will barely compensate for his or her loss. Unlike compensatory damages, punitive damages are based on actively different public policy consideration, that of punishing the defendant or of setting an example for similar wrongdoers.

purchasing

The outright acquisition of items, mostly off-the-shelf or catalog, manufactured outside the buyer's premises.

quality assurance

The planned and systematic actions necessary to provide adequate confidence that the performed service or supplied goods will serve satisfactorily for the intended and specified purpose.

quotation

A statement of price, either written or oral, which may include, among other things, a description of the product or service; the terms of sale, delivery, or period of performance; and payment. Such statements are usually issued by sellers at the request of potential buyers.

reasonable cost

A cost is reasonable if, in its nature and amount, it does not exceed that which would be incurred by a prudent person in the conduct of competitive business.

request for information (RFI)

A formal invitation to submit general and/or specific information concerning the potential future purchase of goods and/or services.

request for proposals (RFP)

A formal invitation that contains a scope of work and seeks a formal response (proposal), describing both methodology and compensation, to form the basis of a contract.

request for quotations (RFQ)

A formal invitation to submit a price for goods and/or services as specified.

request for technical proposals (RFTP)
Solicitation document used in two-step sealed bidding. Normally in letter form, it asks only for technical information; price and cost breakdowns are forbidden.

revenue value
The monetary value of an opportunity.

risk
Exposure or potential of an injury or loss.

sealed-bid procedure
A method of procurement involving the unrestricted solicitation of bids, an opening, and award of a contract to the lowest responsible bidder.

selling, general, and administrative (SG&A) expenses
Administrative costs of running a business.

severable contract
A contract divisible into separate parts. A default of one section does not invalidate the whole contract.

several
A circumstance when more than two parties are involved with the contract.

single source
One source among others in a competitive marketplace that, for justifiable reason, is found to be most worthy to receive a contract award.

small business concerns
A small business is one that is independently owned and operated and is not dominant in its field; a business concern that meets government size standards for its particular industry type.

socioeconomic programs
Programs designed to benefit particular groups. They represent a multitude of program interests and objectives unrelated to procurement objectives. Some examples of these are preferences for small business and for American products,

required sources for specific items, and minimum labor pay levels mandated for contractors.

solicitation

A process through which a buyer requests, bids, quotes, tenders, or proposes orally, in writing, or electronically. Solicitations can take the following forms: request for proposals (RFP), request for quotations (RFQ), request for tenders, invitation to bid (ITB), invitation for bids, and invitation for negotiation.

solicitation planning

The preparation of the documents needed to support a solicitation.

source selection

The process by which the buyer evaluates offers, selects a seller, negotiates terms and conditions, and awards the contract.

Source Selection Advisory Council

A group of people who are appointed by the Source Selection Authority (SSA). The council is responsible for reviewing and approving the source selection plan (SSP) and the solicitation of competitive awards for major and certain less-than-major procurements. The council also determines what proposals are in the competitive range and provides recommendations to the SSA for final selection.

source selection plan (SSP)

The document that describes the selection criteria, the process, and the organization to be used in evaluating proposals for competitively awarded contracts.

specification

A description of the technical requirements for a material, product, or service that includes the criteria for determining that the requirements have been met. There are generally three types of specifications used in contracting: performance, functional, and design.

stakeholders

Individuals who control the resources in a company needed to pursue opportunities or deliver solutions to customers.

standard

A document that establishes engineering and technical limitations and applications of items, materials, processes, methods, designs, and engineering practices. It includes any related criteria deemed essential to achieve the highest practical degree of uniformity in materials or products, or interchangeability of parts used in those products.

standards of conduct

The ethical conduct of personnel involved in the acquisition of goods and services. Within the federal government, business shall be conducted in a manner above reproach and, except as authorized by law or regulation, with complete impartiality and without preferential treatment.

statement of work (SOW)

That portion of a contract describing the actual work to be done by means of specifications or other minimum requirements, quantities, performance date, and a statement of the requisite quality.

statute of limitations

The legislative enactment prescribing the periods within which legal actions may be brought upon certain claims or within which certain rights may be enforced.

stop work order

A request for interim stoppage of work due to nonconformance, funding, or technical considerations.

subcontract

A contract between a buyer and a seller in which a significant part of the supplies or services being obtained is for eventual use in a prime contract.

subcontractor

A seller who enters into a contract with a prime contractor or a subcontractor of the prime contractor.

supplementary agreement

A contract modification that is accomplished by the mutual action of parties.

technical factor

A factor other than price used in evaluating offers for award. Examples include technical excellence, management capability, personnel qualifications, prior experience, past performance, and schedule compliance.

technical leveling

The process of helping a seller bring its proposal up to the level of other proposals through successive rounds of discussion, such as by pointing out weaknesses resulting from the seller's lack of diligence, competence, or inventiveness in preparing the proposal.

technical/management proposal

That part of the offer that describes the seller's approach to meeting the buyer's requirement.

technical transfusion

The disclosure of technical information pertaining to a proposal that results in improvement of a competing proposal. This practice is not allowed in federal government contracting.

term

A part of a contract that addresses a specific subject.

termination

An action taken pursuant to a contract clause in which the buyer unilaterally ends all or part of the work.

terms and conditions (Ts and Cs)

All clauses in a contract, including time of delivery, packing and shipping, applicable standard clauses, and special provisions.

unallowable cost

Any cost that, under the provisions of any pertinent law, regulation, or contract, cannot be included in prices, cost reimbursements, or settlements under a government contract to which it is allocable.

uncompensated overtime

The work that exempt employees perform above and beyond 40 hours per week. Also known as *competitive time, deflated hourly rates, direct allocation of salary costs, discounted hourly rates, extended workweek, full-time accounting,* and *green time.*

Uniform Commercial Code (UCC)

A U.S. model law developed to standardize commercial contracting law among the states. It has been adopted by 49 states (and in significant portions by Louisiana). The UCC comprises articles that deal with specific commercial subject matters, including sales and letters of credit.

unilateral

See *bilateral contract.*

unsolicited proposal

A research or development proposal that is made by a prospective contractor without prior formal or informal solicitation from a purchasing activity.

variable costs

Costs associated with production that change directly with the amount of production (e.g., the direct material or labor required to complete the building or manufacturing of a product).

variance

The difference between projected and actual performance, especially relating to costs.

vertical exchange

A marketplace that is specific to a single industry.

waiver

The voluntary and unilateral relinquishment by a person of a right that he or she has. See also *forbearance.*

warranty

A promise or affirmation given by a seller to a buyer regarding the nature, usefulness, or condition of the goods or services furnished under a contract. Generally, a warranty's purpose is to delineate the rights and obligations for defective goods and services and to foster quality performance.

warranty, express

A written statement arising out of a sale to the consumer of a consumer good, pursuant to which the manufacturer, distributor, or retailer undertakes to preserve or maintain the utility or performance of the consumer good or provide compensation if there is a failure in utility or performance. It is not necessary to the creation of an express warranty that formal words such as "warrant" or "guarantee" be used, or that a specific intention to make a warranty be present.

warranty, implied

A promise arising by operation of law that something that is sold shall be fit for the purpose for which the seller has reason to know that it is required. Types of implied warranties include implied warranty of merchantability, of title, and of wholesomeness.

warranty of fitness

A warranty by the seller that goods sold are suitable for the special purpose of the buyer.

warranty of merchantability

A warranty that goods are fit for the ordinary purposes for which such goods are used and conform to the promises or affirmations of fact made on the container or label.

warranty of title

An express or implied (arising by operation of law) promise that the seller owns the item offered for sale and, therefore, is able to transfer a good title and that the goods, as delivered, are free from any security interest of which the buyer at the time of contracting has no knowledge.

Web portals

A public exchange in which a company or group of companies list products or services for sale or provide other transmission of business information.

win strategy

A collection of messages or points designed to guide the customer's perception of you, your solution, and your competitors.

work breakdown structure (WBS)

A logical, organized decomposition of the work tasks within a given project, typically using a hierarchical numeric coding scheme.

World Trade Organization (WTO)

A multinational legal entity that serves as the champion of fair trade globally, established April 15, 1995.

INDEX

C

Confronting risk, 17
Contract incentives
  Objective incentives, 132
  Problems with objective
    incentives, 136
  Special incentives, 139
  Subjective incentives, 138
Contract pricing
  Cost overruns and growth,
    124
  Effect of risk on
    performance, 125
  Uncertainty and risk, 123
Contract types
  Buyer's and seller's risk,
    146
  Choosing, 146
Contracts, incentive-type
  Cost-plus-award-fee, 140
  Cost-plus-incentive-fee, 140
  Fixed-price-incentive, 140
Cost accounting standards
  Generally, 44
  Requirements, 48
Cost allocability
  Factors, 60

Cost analysis, tools and
  techniques
  Activity-based costing
    technique, 70
  Cost breakdown analysis,
    64
  Economic order quantity
    method, 68
  Generally, 64
  Learning curve technique,
    67
  Life-cycle costing method,
    71
Cost determination, 122
Cost estimates
  Accuracy, 40
  Basic characteristics, 2
  Challenges, 26
  Government auditor's
    criteria, 37
  Key acquisition-related
    plans, 33
  Key elements, 23
  Methods, comparison, 41
  Types, 21
Cost estimating and cost
  analysis, difference, 20

Costing methods, primary
  Analogy, 4
  Engineering build-up, 8
  Parametric analysis, 5
  Technical consensus, 8
  Weighted average, 7
Costs
  Breakdown, 31
  Material and services, 26
  Tracking, 31

D

Data sources, 38
Design-to-cost allocations, 32

E

Earned value management
  systems
  Analysis, 230
  Application thresholds, 214
  Authorizing work, 216
  Budgeting work, 221
  Changes, 229
  Contract funds status report,
   237
  Contract implementation,
   215
  Contract management
   performance reporting,
   235
  Contract performance
   report, 235
  Contractor cost data
   reporting, 237
  Cost accumulation, 223
  Department of Defense
   reviews and reports, 230
  Generally, 214
  Integrated baseline reviews,
   234

Integrated master schedule,
  236
Internal audit, 230
Performance formulae, 230
Performance measurement,
  224
Scheduling work, 217
Software resources data
  report, 238
Statistical examples, 232
Understanding, 215
Verification, 230
Expenses, contract-related
  Examples, 25

H

High quality cost estimating
  process, 10

K

Key support plans
  Responsibility for preparing,
   36
Kickoff meetings
  Value of, 36

L

Labor-hour contracts
  Approval requirement, 160
  Commercial services, 170
  Contract line items, 163
  Dollar threshold, 160
  Generally, 154
  Handling costs, 165
  Hourly rates, 161
  Indirect costs, 165
  Justification requirement,
   159
  Materials, defined, 164

Noncommercial services, 178
Payment for materials, 165
Performance obligations, 159
Price ceiling, increase, 165
Pricing of, 161
Primary requirements, 158
Profit or fee on materials,
165
Records, government right
to inspect, 166
Time limitation, 159

O

Outsourcing
Make-or-buy plans, key
items, 33

P

Price analysis
Adjusting prices selected for
comparison, 196
Catalog prices, 187
Comparing adjusted prices,
196
Competitive proposal prices,
186
Effect of identified factors,
195
Estimates based on
parametric analysis, 187
Extent of competition, 189
Factors that affect
comparability, 188
Geographic location, 189
Historical prices, 187
Independent company
estimates, 188
Market conditions, 188
Quantity or size, 189
Selecting prices for

comparison, 186
Technology, 189
Terms and conditions, 189
Price determination, methods
Activity-based, 118
Cost-based, 109
Value-based, 117
Pricing arrangements
Cost-plus-fixed-fee, 130
Cost-sharing, 130
Cost-type, 129
Firm-fixed-price, 126
Fixed-price with economic
price adjustment, 128
Pricing methods, other
Letters of intent, 151
Memorandums of
understanding, 151
Purchase agreements, 150
Pricing strategies
Best-value pricing, 105
LPTA pricing, 104
Trade-offs, 106
Profit analysis
Generally, 80
Tools and techniques
Profitability, measures of, 83
Days of sales outstanding, 91
Earnings before interest,
taxes, depreciation and
amortization, 95
Generally, 81
Internal rate of return, 88
Measured operating income,
90
Return on assets, 85
Return on investment, 84
Weighted guidelines method,
92

R

Risk, sources of
Behavior of parties, 15
Deception, 16
Differing interpretations, 15
Haste, 15
Misunderstanding of
requirements, 14
Poor practices, 16

S

Small business
Subcontracting plans, 35
Software risks
Cost and schedule, common
sources, 39
Subcontract source selection
plans, 34

T

Team members, roles, 27
Time-and-materials contracts
Approval requirement, 160
Commercial services, 170
Contract line items, 163
Dollar threshold, 160
Generally, 154
Handling costs, 165

Hourly rates, 161
Indirect costs, 165
Justification requirement,
159
Materials, defined, 164
Noncommercial services, 178
Payment for materials, 165
Performance obligations, 159
Price ceiling, increase, 165
Pricing of, 161
Primary requirements, 158
Profit or fee on materials,
165
Records, government right
to inspect, 166
Time limitation, 159
Time phasing, 26
Total ownership cost
Efficient solutions, 206
Generally, 200
Integrated product teams,
207
Key performance
parameters, 203
Truth in Negotiations Act, 117

W

Work breakdown structure
Value of, 30